W9-AXF-378

Great Britain and the Taipings

GREAT BRITAIN
AND THE TAIPINGS

by

J. S. Gregory

FREDERICK A. PRAEGER, *Publishers*

NEW YORK · WASHINGTON

BOOKS THAT MATTER

Published in the United States of America in 1969
by Frederick A. Praeger, Inc., Publishers
111 Fourth Avenue, New York, N.Y. 10003

© 1969, in London, England, by J. S. Gregory

Library of Congress Catalog Card Number: 69-12306

Printed in Great Britain

Contents

To Mary

Acknowledgments

So many people have helped me in some way with this study since it first took shape as a doctoral thesis in the University of London that I hope I may be excused for not attempting to list them all here. My gratitude to them remains undiminished. I am, however, particularly indebted to Mr. J. Gerson of Toronto University for constant stimulation of ideas, to Mr. J. Gray of Glasgow University and Professor W. Beasley of London University for encouragement and sound advice when most needed, and to Mrs. Hung-ying Bryan for assistance with translations from Chinese documents. I am also grateful to the various missionary societies in London which so readily gave me access to their records, and to Lord Bruce and the Earl of Clarendon for permission to use their family papers. Finally, I am indebted to the University of Melbourne both for the study leave in 1966 which enabled me to complete my research on the subject and for a grant in aid which has facilitated its publication.

Introduction

ALTHOUGH DEFEATED by the government it challenged, the Taiping rebellion was undoubtedly one of the most formidable and remarkable movements of mass protest in Chinese history. The term 'rebellion' indeed does it something less than justice, for it was a revolutionary protest against many of the basic features of traditional Chinese society and government which, if successful, would have wrought far more than just another turn in the old dynastic cycle. It is not surprising that many contemporary historians prefer to speak of the Taiping 'revolution' and look back to this movement as marking, if not the definitive emergence of modern China, at least 'the beginning of the end of Confucian China'.[1]

The rebellion began in Kwangsi, one of the southernmost provinces of China, in the middle of 1850, and continued to pose a serious threat to the ruling Manchu dynasty until 1864. It was the explosive product of a combination of personal ambition and inspiring leadership with long-standing social and political discontents which had been aggravated in the years immediately preceding its outbreak by the effects of the defeat sustained by the Manchu government at the hands of the British in the first opium war of 1840–42. Its initiator was a frustrated intellectual named Hung Hsiu-ch'üan, who had suffered a severe nervous breakdown in 1837 at the age of 23 after repeated failures in the civil service examinations at Canton. He was then delirious for several days, had visions and underwent a kind of personality change in the direction of megalomania and *folie de grandeur*. For some years, however, he remained merely another obscure victim of the leviathan of the Chinese imperial examination system, failing yet again in 1843. This time, however, there was no breakdown but rather a breakthrough, for he now read a Christian tract called *Good Words to Admonish the Age*, which seemed to him to provide the key to his visions of 1837. He began to see himself as the younger brother of Jesus Christ, who had been called up to heaven to receive new revelation and a new divine commission to drive out the Manchu 'imps' and 'demons', and to bring men back to the worship of the true God. The basis for a new and revolutionary ideology in China was laid.

This ideology became the fusing agent in the creation of a new organization called the Shang-ti Hui or God Worshippers' Society. The assembling of the members of this society at the village of Chin T'ien in Kwangsi in the middle of 1850 may be taken as the real beginning of the rebellion, although it was not until January 1851 that Hung proclaimed his new dynasty, the T'ai-p'ing T'ien-Kuo or Heavenly Kingdom of Great Peace, and himself assumed the title of T'ien Wang or Heavenly King. Hung, however, remained a religious rather than a political or military leader, and soon had to share control of the new movement with other more practical-minded leaders. A kind of collective leadership emerged which was formalized in December 1851 with the creation of five other Wangs or Kings, one for each point of the compass and another called the I Wang or Assistant King. Of these the Tung Wang or Eastern King, Yang Hsiu-ch'ing, was the most forceful and was to emerge as the strongest challenger to Hung's position, even as a source of divine revelation. By the end of 1851 the movement had thus acquired strong leadership, the rudiments of an administrative system, substantial armed forces and an ideology which instilled a strong sense of mission and discipline into its followers.

The Taiping ideology always retained a religious core from which stemmed political, social and economic programmes of a revolutionary kind. Hung claimed to be the 'Son of Heaven' in a literal and not just a symbolic or moral sense, as did orthodox emperors, so that his dynasty was to be an altogether new kind of dynasty, one which ruled not simply by a mandate from Heaven but which was itself heavenly, above and beyond the laws of the Confucian dynastic cycle.[2] Until this new dynasty was firmly established, the family, the basis of the traditional social order, was to be broken up and men and women were to live separately and in chastity, as brothers and sisters all. This principle was meant to apply only to the close adherents of the movement, the new *élite*, though it was certainly not very stringently applied by the leaders to themselves. Among the population at large the family was to remain the basis of social organization, but was no longer to function as an independent economic unit. The land was to be re-divided among families according to the number of individuals in each, and was to be held not as private property but in trust for the community at large. Each family was to surrender production, beyond what it needed to feed itself and to plant the next year's crops, to the common treasury, from whence it would be re-distributed according to communal rather than family or individual need. The traditional Chinese state system and social order were to be transformed into a kind of agrarian-communist theocracy in which the old faiths—Confucian, Buddhist and Taoist—would be proscribed in favour of the new Taiping creed, which was a compound of some of the more superficial elements of Western Christianity with the personal visions and revelations of Hung and certain of the other rebel leaders, notably Yang. Taiping China was to make a revolutionary break with both the faith and institutions of the old order.

As originally conceived, Taiping China would have been no more able than Confucian China to cope with the modern Western world, which was then aggressively thrusting itself forward in East Asia. Yet there would appear to have been in this movement some potential for change and reform of the kind China was to need but not achieve for many years to come. This was revealed most strikingly in the proposals put forward by Hung Jen-kan, a cousin of the Heavenly King, who had rejoined the movement in 1859 after spending some years with British missionaries in Hong Kong. He was given the title of Kan Wang or Shield King, and made the chief administrator in the movement. His programme was one of technical modernization of a much more far-reaching kind than had ever been proposed in China before. It envisaged the development of railways, highways, postal services, banks and other services necessary for the encouragement of trade, and the extensive re-organization of government administration. There were many naïve features to this programme, but it was certainly such as to justify regarding Hung Jen-kan as one of the first and most far-sighted of China's modernizers.

Coming on the scene late as he did, when the movement had already lost much of its earlier fervour and was tending to break up into more or less autonomous military groupings, Hung Jen-kan probably never had much prospect of putting such a programme into any kind of effective operation. Yet its existence, and the fact that the movement had already accepted, albeit in distorted form, a creed of Western origin, at least leaves the question whether the Taiping potential for progressive reform was not significantly greater than that of the government which was to survive its defeat by another half-century. The question is not one which admits of any very certain answer, but it is not surprising that many modern Chinese historians, looking back upon the rebellion across those last fifty unprofitable years of Manchu rule and Chinese humiliation, answer it in the affirmative.

The military and political fortunes of the movement, upon which its ability to carry through its revolutionary programme ultimately depended, fluctuated considerably during its fifteen years of activity. In the first years Taiping armies had a fervour and discipline unmatched by their opponents. When hard pressed by the provincial forces of Kwangsi in 1852 they broke away northward and marched triumphantly towards the Yangtze valley, gathering strength and numbers as they went. They captured Wuchang in January 1853 and from there moved rapidly and irresistibly down the river, advancing as far as Chinkiang at the junction of the Grand Canal and the Yangtze and proclaiming Nanking, the second city of the empire, their capital after its capture in March. Manchu garrisons in captured cities were generally slaughtered or put to rout. The movement both fed upon and stimulated the tradition of resistance to Manchu rule which had been strong in south China since the foundation of the Ch'ing dynasty in the mid-seventeenth century. The expulsion of the Manchu 'demons' from China was naturally a feature of the rebel programme which led later leaders of the Chinese nationalist movement, especially Sun Yat-sen, to look back upon the Taipings as a source of great encouragement and inspiration, and has given them a secure place in the pantheon of modern Chinese nationalism.

From Nanking the rebels launched a drive northward to capture Peking, capital of the ruling dynasty. The north, however, was more resistant to their advance, and the forces sent were inadequate for the task. They reached Tientsin, not far from the capital, but were there turned back, mainly by Mongol auxiliaries, then dispersed and finally destroyed by the early months of 1855. A drive to the west was also checked by the end of 1854, this time by provincial Chinese armies raised by Tseng Kuo-fan, who was to become the main architect of the final defeat of the rebellion ten years later. By 1855 the early momentum of the rebellion had been lost and it was forced back upon the defence and consolidation of its new base around Nanking.

Several years of stalemate followed. The Taipings held the rich area of the lower Yangtze valley, but for some reason they had not advanced right to the coast as they almost certainly could easily have done in 1853, and they had lost control of many other areas through which their armies had passed. They defeated all efforts by Imperial armies to dislodge them from Nanking between 1853 and 1858, but were riven by bitter internal feuds at the end of 1856. These removed some of their most able leaders, including Yang, the Eastern King, by assassination and Shih Ta-k'ai, the Assistant King, by defection. New military leaders emerged in the following years, but they tended to create their own bases of power and to make their own decisions, so that there was a breakdown of effective central political control and of overall military strategy. Hung remained the movement's prophet and became again its sole source of divine revelation, but among the rank and file, and indeed among many of its new leaders, religious fervour and military discipline had greatly declined.

A partial revival began in 1859, with Hung Jen-kan's plans for reorganization and with the launching of successful new campaigns which at last carried Taiping armies to the coast and brought them into direct contact with Western bases in China. By that time, however, the organization of resistance to the movement by the Chinese officials and gentry of central China had progressed to the point where Tseng Kuo-fan's armies began to close in steadily upon Nanking. Despite many tactical successes and new captures, the rebels were unable to make a great strategic breakthrough as they had done in 1852 and 1853. With aid from the West, their enemies forced them slowly back upon Nanking, which was recaptured with great slaughter in June 1864. Remnant forces survived a few months longer in various places, but the Taiping rebellion as a serious threat to the Ch'ing dynasty and to the structure of traditional Chinese society was over.

It was a confused and complex movement, half backward, half forward looking, which fits neatly into no single category of description, whether Confucian, Christian or Marxist. It was much more than a traditional-type peasant uprising, and perhaps should not even be regarded as a peasant rebellion at all.[3] The religious aspect, although greatly dimmed in its last years, remained central to it, yet to describe the Taiping creed as an 'heretical' form of Western Christianity appears to be an almost irrelevant judgment. It is a movement which can be understood and judged only in terms of its own principles and objectives. Much of the praise and blame that has been heaped upon it tells more about its admirers and critics than about the movement itself. Its very magnitude and strangeness, a complex mixture of old and modern, Western and Chinese, rational and absurd, makes any attempt at final judgment upon it hazardous at best.

This book, however, is not about the Taiping rebellion itself but simply about the British reaction to it. It is a case-study of how mid-Victorian Britain reacted to a particular kind of problem—whether to intervene or not in a domestic military struggle in an area of potential rather than immediately vital economic interest. The contemporary reader will almost certainly be aware at many points of parallels with the American predicament in Asia today.

Many of the problems and some of the decisions taken in this particular instance anticipated, on a far less agonizing scale, those that have been in debate in our own time. Intervention once undertaken, how far and in what manner to pursue it—as 'advisers' merely or as active combatants; how to combine military aid with political reform and ensure the emergence of a viable, moderately progressive government from the struggle; how to avoid any permanent commitment to the area; how to answer charges of condoning, if not actually committing, atrocities and of preserving in power unpopular and reactionary rulers—all these questions, familiar enough in our own day, faced the administrators of British policy in China a century ago. In the study which follows I have not tried to point up such parallels, but it is difficult to resist the observation that Britain in the eighteen-sixties was luckier, perhaps wiser, than America in the nineteen-sixties. By the time she came to intervene in the struggle in China the forces she opposed were facing almost certain defeat at the hands of a government which, for all its inadequacies and conservatism, was never without widespread and powerful support within the country. From the point of view of her own short-term interest at least, Britain intervened in the right war at the right time.

The main objective of the study that follows is to describe the development of official British policy towards the Taiping rebellion over the whole course of its history. There are, in addition, two chapters discussing the reactions of interested groups outside the circle of official policy-makers, especially of the missionaries and the merchants. Certain aspects of British policy towards the rebellion have already been much commented upon in works concerned primarily either with the rebellion itself or with Western relations with China generally, but these have concentrated only upon the years 1853–54, when the rebellion first emerged as a serious threat to the existing government, and the years 1860–64 after the British had made new treaties with governments and, many have argued, were therefore anxious to preserve it in power even to the point of intervening against the rebellion. These were certainly the key years and provide the inevitable focal points in any study of this question. But merely to fill in the gaps, to examine the actual working of the policy of neutrality between 1853 and 1860, has seemed worth doing, while there are many current judgments about the development and motivation of British policy which should be tested against the detailed evidence of the official record.

The main kinds of question which I have sought to answer concern, first, the mechanics of British policy-making on this question. How did it actually take shape? To what extent was it the product of rational and controlled planning from the centre, as many writers infer that it was, and to what extent the chance product of local and short-term pressures? Was it in any significant way influenced by pressure groups from outside, and what was the attitude of these groups to that policy? What in fact do we mean by 'British policy'?

The second main group of questions, pursued especially in the last chapter, concerns the motivation of British policy, in particular the reasons for the change from neutrality to intervention that occurred in the last years of the rebellion. Were the Taipings attacked, as many modern Chinese historians argue, as proto-nationalists whom the British feared would establish a strong and popularly based government which would deprive the Western imperialists of the rich pickings they could expect to make in China after the second opium war? Was the continuing Taiping prohibition of opium-smoking, after the Manchu government had agreed to legalize the trade in 1858, a major reason for the British intervention? Were the rebels attacked as religious blasphemers or as dangerous socialists? What, in short, were the British afraid of?

Certain other questions are also pursued. One concerns the kind of neutrality laid down in 1853 and the manner of its application in the years that followed. Another concerns the actual extent of British intervention in the struggle. Just how many British troops were involved, in what ways and for how long? The answer to this last question bears upon a further question which is strictly beyond the scope of this study—that is, just how significant was the British intervention in bringing about the final defeat of the rebellion? To answer that question adequately it would be necessary to examine more closely the condition of the rebel movement in its last years and the progress of the Chinese-led campaigns against it than the material used for this study allows. In general, however, that material does seem to reinforce the view that the British intervention, very useful to the Manchu cause though it was, was too limited to be counted as in any way decisive, the exploits of 'Chinese' Gordon and his so-called Ever Victorious Army notwithstanding.

In fact, it is doubtful if the British response to the rebellion, still less the response of any other Western power in Asia at that time, exerted a decisive influence on its fortunes at any point, though the Marxist-Maoist historians of present-day China naturally put great emphasis upon the hostile machinations of the imperialists throughout the course of the movement. Basically, however, the struggle was decided in terms of the balances of power, ability and support within China itself. A study of British attitudes and policy toward the Taipings is of interest nevertheless, partly because it draws attention to a large body of reports and opinion about this strange rebellion by contemporary Western observers, and partly because it serves to illustrate the complex workings of the imperialist process in mid-Victorian Britain.

1

The Early Years
(1850-52)

THE REBELLION began in the middle of the year 1850, but nothing that can properly be called a British policy towards it can be defined before the early months of 1853, when the rebels began to approach the main area of British economic interest in China, the lower Yangtze valley. Certain views about the character and prospects of the movement were, however, formed by leading British officials in south China during its first years, while nearly ten years' experience of the working of the Treaty of Nanking, imposed on China by Great Britain after the first opium war of 1839–42, had considerably sharpened their views about the character of the government being challenged. The first question which poses itself, therefore, is how far British officials were predisposed to look favourably upon the rebellion when it emerged as a force of major importance in China at the beginning of 1853.

In that year of crisis the British government in fact quickly settled upon a policy of neutrality. The Marxist historians of modern China argue that this neutrality was from the beginning false in character and biased in favour of the ruling Ch'ing dynasty, an interpretation which will be discussed in the following chapters. Some other historians, however, have suggested that, in 1853 at least, the British tendency was to favour the rebels in principle although not in any practical way. The major reasons advanced for this latter view are that

British sympathy was aroused partly by the rebels' profession of a seemingly Christian ideology and partly by an acute sense of exasperation with the persistently obstructionist attitude of the Manchu government towards the Treaty of 1842. In these circumstances, it is implied, the idea of the overthrow of the ruling dynasty was by no means unacceptable to the British.[1]

Relations with the Manchu government under the terms of the Treaty of Nanking had certainly proved very unsatisfactory from the British point of view. Apart from the failure of trade to grow as expected, hopes of a brighter pattern in relations with China quickly withered in face of the long diplomatic wrangle over the right of British subjects to enter the city of Canton, and in face of the refusal of the Governor of that city after 1848, Yeh Ming-ch'en, to accord even minimal courtesy recognition of the consul at the port, Dr. John Bowring.

With the death of the Tao Kuang emperor and the accession of Hsien Feng in March 1850 a more aggressively anti-foreign party triumphed in court circles over such temporizing (though not fundamentally less anti-foreign) officials as Ch'i-ying, who had negotiated the 1842 treaty, while in that same year an attempt by Palmerston, then the British Foreign Secretary, to by-pass the unco-operative Canton officials by communicating directly with the non-existent 'Minister of Foreign Affairs' in Peking was rebuffed. After this Palmerston began to rumble of war in his best John Bull manner, telling the British Superintendent of Trade and Governor at Hong Kong, Sir George Bonham, that the time was fast coming 'when we shall be obliged to strike another blow in China. . . . These half-civilized Governments, such as those of China, Portugal, Spanish America, all require a Dressing every eight or ten years to keep them in order.'[2] Clearly the Treaty of Nanking had wrought no great change in the attitude of the Manchu government towards Britain, and apart from access to four new ports, of which only Shanghai gave much promise of becoming a major centre for foreign trade, the British position in China seemed to have advanced little from what it was before 1842. Official as well as non-official dissatisfaction with this state of affairs was certainly considerable by 1850.

Nevertheless, the limits to which Great Britain was prepared to go in its exasperation with the Manchu government need to

2

be recognized. In 1840, Captain Elliott, chief British representative in China at the time of the outbreak of the first opium war, had warned against a too vigorous attack upon the Chinese empire for fear that this might bring about the collapse of the dynasty. 'I can't conceive a more unfortunate consequence to ourselves than extensive political convulsion in China', he observed.[3] With that sentiment he expressed one of the great principles underlying British policy in China for the next hundred years and more, namely to regard with apprehension any internal movement for radical political change lest it result in the break-up of the country and the creation of a situation in which Britain would have either to cut her losses or be drawn more deeply and directly into regulating Chinese affairs. Fear that 'another India' was an all too probable result of the Taiping rebellion tended to inhibit official British sympathy towards it from the beginning.

Thus in December 1851, in a letter discussing general prospects in China, Bonham wrote to Hammond, a Foreign Office official who was to become the Permanent Under-Secretary of State for Foreign Affairs in 1854, to the effect that he would be sorry to see any coercion resorted to at Canton at that time, despite the continued intransigence of the Manchu government, 'inasmuch as such a measure *might* throw the whole of the Two Kwangs [Kwangsi and Kwangtung] into a confusion from which it might be very difficult to extract them; and it is clear that such a state of things could not be conducive to our interests'.[4] British officials in China had real grounds of complaint against the ruling government, but it was always to be preferred to a state of political chaos or uncertainty. Any sympathy they might feel for the Taipings on religious or other grounds was conditional upon the speed and thoroughness with which the rebels seized and held the Dragon throne.

This natural bias in British policy away from the idea of radical political change in China was accentuated in the years immediately preceding 1853 by a change in the general direction of that policy. When Palmerston left the Foreign Office at the end of 1851 he was replaced by men much less inclined to favour vigorous policies abroad, in China or elsewhere. Preoccupation with the newly created Second Empire in France and with the growing crisis with Russia in the Middle East meant that, in so far as affairs in China received any attention at all from the British government at this time, the emphasis was very much upon keeping things quiet. An improvement in the British position was still hoped for, but it was to be sought by negotiation for treaty revision, not by striking 'another blow'.

This change in the temper of the British government towards China is reflected in the instructions sent to Bowring when he was appointed Acting Superintendent of Trade at Hong Kong during Bonham's absence on leave between April 1852 and February 1853. Bowring, after his experience as consul at Canton since 1848, felt he had more cause for exasperation with the existing government than any other British official in China. Being, moreover, a proud, energetic and ambitious man, he was anxious to make his mark upon policy. However, during his temporary direction of British affairs in 1852 he was more than once instructed to avoid any kind of forceful policy and to keep everything 'as quiet as possible'.[5] Obliged to put aside his plans for transforming British relations with China, Bowring was thoroughly irked. He complained in a letter written in November 1852 to a former Foreign Secretary, Lord Granville, of the 'precious opportunities' lost because of the 'peremptory' orders sent him 'to do nothing and not to quit Hong Kong'. His hopes of doing any good in China had 'vanished', and he asked that on Bonham's return some other field be found for him, or at least that he be granted twelve months' leave of absence.[6]

Bowring got his leave of absence but, perhaps unfortunately for future Sino-British relations, was not transferred elsewhere. He returned in April 1854 as Sir John, to succeed Bonham this time with full powers and with renewed hopes of being able at last to pursue a more independent policy. Yet the instructions issued to him in 1852 represented more than a temporary *détente* brought on by his caretaker status at that time. This is indicated by the instructions he received at the beginning of 1854. In forwarding Bowring his full commission, Clarendon, who was Foreign Secretary by then, admonished him to 'endeavour to maintain the most friendly intercourse with the Chinese Authorities, and as far as possible avoid occasions of angry discussion calculated to lead to an interruption of friendly relations between this country and China'. In detailed instructions Clarendon went on to express himself far from dissatisfied with the progress made under the existing treaty system and, although he authorized Bowring to raise the question of treaty revision, his emphasis was very much upon continuing to work as harmoniously as possible with the existing government. He was even ready to accept the necessity of 'a moderate delay' in the revision of the treaties, since 'the Imperial Government, harassed by the insurrection which convulses so many of the provinces, cannot be expected to give its immediate attention to the subject'. There was no hint here that the rebels might be looked to sympathetically as offering a more favourable alternative. 'Justice and good policy equally prescribe to us the observance of the strictest neutrality between the contending parties', Clarendon insisted.[7]

It would be foolish to attempt to argue away altogether the existence of official British impatience and exasperation with the Ch'ing government about 1853, but it is important not to assume that this exasperation was strong enough to dispose British policy strongly towards the idea of political revolution in China. After Palmerston's departure at the end of 1851 the tone of instructions and observations on China from the Foreign Office itself, which was ultimately the final arbiter of British policy, was decidedly moderate. The difficulties which had been experienced in applying the 1842 treaty did, it is true, prompt the question whether things would not be better from the British point of view under a Taiping government, but the answer British officials gave to this question was always much less decidedly affirmative, much less ready to assume ultimate rebel success, than that given by many non-official observers. They were at least as much disposed to ask whether it would not be possible to improve the British situation in China as the price of aid to the Manchu government, and were certainly not *a priori* in favour of the idea of rebellion in China, not even Christian rebellion.

During these first Kwangsi years a rather shadowy but decidedly hostile view of the rebellion was formed by the chief spokesmen of British policy in China on the basis of such information about it as the consulate at Canton could glean from local rumours, 'the common newsman' and published official Chinese reports. The consulate at Canton sent fairly regular reports to the Superintendency at Hong Kong, and

5

copies of these were generally sent on to London, although in doing so Bonham emphasized 'how imperfectly we are informed of important, events occurring in our immediate vicinity'.[8] From these reports and from the comments of Bonham and later Bowring upon them three main questions about the rebellion emerge as occupying the minds of the chief British authorities at this stage. Given the lack of accurate sources of information, none was easy to answer with certainty, but this did not prevent fairly decided opinions being formed.

The first and basic question was whether the rising should be regarded as a serious political revolt or simply as a big-scale bandit movement. The first reports from the Canton consulate, written in August 1850 by Interpreter T. T. Meadows, referred to 'rebels or robbers' defying the authorities in Kwangsi for some months past. Bonham, in forwarding copies to the Foreign Office, gave his own opinion that 'plunder and not the overthrow of this Dynasty seems to me to be the real motive of the Rebellion'.[9] A few months later, in noting reports of the capture and dispersion of many 'banditti' near Canton, he expressed himself strengthened in his belief that 'there never has been adequate ground for investing their incursions with the title of insurrection', and dismissed rebel pretensions to any kind of effective political organization. 'No person of respectability has joined them, and it is the habit of such marauders, as from Chinese history it would appear always to have been, to endeavour to lure the disaffected to their side by the assumption of rank, display of badges and banners, and similar artifices.'[10] Bowring also, when relieving Bonham during 1852, referred to these 'rather predatory than political movements' and argued that, politically, the Manchu government was far less weak than it might appear.[11]

On the other hand, as early as June 1851 Meadows reported his conviction that the rebellion was a serious and organized political movement. He described the Taiping rebels, in terms very reminiscent of descriptions of later, more successful Communist rebels in China, as levying contributions according to established rules and paying for their own supplies; as being 'at some care not to make themselves obnoxious to the lower classes', even sharing with the poor what they took from the rich; as for the present not seeking to fight the Imperialists but never hesitating to engage 'and almost always signally defeat' any forces sent against them; and finally, as being 'far from sanguinary in their treatment of regulars who fall into their hands while merely obeying orders', but ruthless towards mandarins or volunteers going beyond the strict line of their duty in acting against them. 'I conceive', Meadows concluded, 'that men who seem to have on the whole consistently kept in view these object and rules for a whole year, and whose aggregate numbers are never given at *less* than 20,000 cannot, without plain perversion of language, be termed "robbers". . . . That the Imperial Government considers the affairs nothing less than what we would call a rebellion, and a very serious rebellion, is made sufficiently plain by the measures it is taking.'[12] Meadows' sympathetic view of the rebellion was not shared by his superiors in 1851, however, any more than it was to be shared ten years later, when he was still writing vigorously in its defence, although for a time during 1853 his views did have some influence upon Bonham.

A second question which was asked at this time concerned the religious nature of the movement. In 1853, when authentic information was obtained on this point, there was naturally great astonishment, and among some, delight, at the sudden emergence of a native movement of rebellion proclaiming a Christian faith. Yet something of this was suspected, although not fully realized before 1853. In September 1851 Meadows reported that an Imperial Edict had been issued which attributed the disturbances to 'Strange Doctrines'. No mention was made of Christianity, he noted, 'but it is evidently included in the term "Strange Doctrines" '.[13] Bowring, however, was convinced that the movement was no more genuinely religious than it was political. In May 1852 he told the Foreign Office that there had been for some time past reports of Christian inscriptions upon the banners of the insurgents, but quoted Protestant missionary opinion that rebel use of the term 'Shang-ti', by which the Protestants translated the Western concept of God into Chinese, referred not to the Christian God but to a Chinese god of war. In fact at this stage, according to Bowring, the Protestant missionaries claimed that native Catholic converts had fomented the uprising, while the Catholics put it all down to the activities of the Protestant Dr. Gutzlaff. Bowring concluded, very inaccurately but perhaps not unreasonably in face of such confusing and conflicting views, that it was doubtful that the movement had 'anything whatever of a religious character'.[14]

Nor did it represent a serious political threat to the dynasty, he continued in this singularly unprescient despatch, and altogether it had 'far more of a local than a national character'. As such it had not affected and was not likely to affect British interests directly 'except by interfering with the regular course of trade, and the probability is, even were any of the five ports menaced, of which at present there are no symptoms whatever, that there would be no meddling with the persons or property of Foreign residents'.

The conclusion of this despatch indicates the third major point of interest to British officials in the early reports on the rebellion, namely, how it might affect British interests in China. In 1850–51 Bonham had expressed occasional fears for the security of Canton and the fate of trade there, but by 1852, as Bowring's despatch just quoted shows, no great alarm seems to have been felt for the treaty ports. On the contrary, there was a tendency to see the outbreak of rebellion as a possible advantage, since as an embarrassment to the Manchu government it might perhaps be used as a lever with which to extract full observance of the Nanking treaty, and even favourable revision of that treaty. So Bonham, despite his warning at the end of 1851 against throwing the Two Kwangs into confusion, was writing only a couple of months later that 'the present time is as favourable for coercing the Chinese Government as the reign of Taukwang, because although the reigning Emperor is less friendly than his father, his hands are full of the Kwangse Rebellion, and his Exchequer emptied by the same cause'. Bowring also thought the rebellion provided a good opportunity to press the question of entry into Canton.[15]

However, between the reluctance of the Foreign Office after Palmerston's departure to encourage forward moves in China and the sudden change in the course of the rebellion itself, these early speculations about how best to take advantage of it came to nothing. In any case, the danger always remained that if the British attempted to use the rebellion as a lever to prise open a wider door into China they might in fact help to bring the whole structure down. As an instrument of British policy the rebellion was always to prove decidedly difficult to handle and was never to be turned to much advantage, whether as a means of forcing treaty revision in its early years or, in its last years, as a stimulus for reform within the Manchu government.

The views formed by Bonham and Bowring of the rebellion during its Kwangsi period cannot be said to have had any very significant influence upon the trend of British policy during 1853. They may perhaps have helped incline Bonham for a short time towards intervention in the early months of that year, but it was soon apparent that it was necessary to re-think the official view. Bonham, who was the least imaginative but the most open-minded of the three officials quoted, was prepared to do this, though with due caution, and some qualified hopes in the movement were expressed by him during 1853. By mid-1854, however, the earlier view reasserted itself, and the rebellion was once again written off in most official reports as of very doubtful political or religious capabilities, even though it remained militarily formidable. This was to remain the prevailing official British view of the movement until its final defeat in 1864, a view clearly anticipated in the first, poorly based reports of 1850–52.

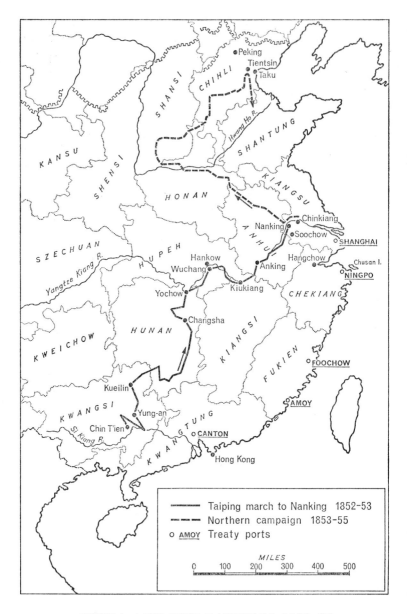

CHINA AND THE TAIPINGS 1853–55

2

Neutrality
(1853)

WHILE THE REBELLION was confined to the hinterland of Kwangsi, British representatives in China were in the position of interested spectators who were not seeing much of the game. The Foreign Office itself displayed no particular interest and made no comments. But once the rebels began to move down the Yangtze valley towards Nanking and the tea and silk districts around Shanghai the case was very different. The need to discover more about the rebellion and to define the official British attitude towards it became urgent, especially when Chinese officials at Shanghai began requesting the aid of foreign vessels to check its advance.

The major objectives of British policy in China at this time were to secure full implementation of the terms of the 1842 treaty, as interpreted from the British side, and to extend these terms to include direct diplomatic representation at Peking and the right to trade in the interior as well as on the coast. Policy towards the now serious rebellion had to be fitted into this general framework of policy, but in the absence of any very certain knowledge about its character and about the attitude of its leaders towards foreigners, and in the prevailing atmosphere of military and political insecurity, this was not easy to do with any confidence. Would the larger ends of British policy best be served by helping the Manchu government to suppress the rebellion, by treating with the rebels as a new *de facto* power, or by holding strictly aloof and awaiting the outcome of the struggle? The answer was far from obvious in the first months of 1853.

Since it then took from three to four months for despatches from China to reach London and instructions in reply to be received, while events in China itself were moving very swiftly, the responsibility for the early definition of British policy necessarily rested squarely upon Bonham as Chief Superintendent of Trade at Hong Kong. He soon decided upon the last course as the best from the British point of view, but certainly did not ignore other alternatives altogether. In particular, intervention on behalf of the Manchu government was for a short time seriously considered.

The chief advocate of an interventionist line of policy in the early months of 1853 was the consul at Shanghai, Rutherford Alcock. As early as November 1852 he had begun to anticipate that he might soon have to treat with what he called 'authorities *de facto* in the absence of those representing the Emperor Hienfung'.[1] By January he was busy trying to define the possible dangers and advantages to be found in such a situation. If the rebels brought in their train obstinate civil war it could be fatal to British interests, he suggested to Bonham, but if they continued the efforts hitherto attributed to them to establish law and order in conquered areas 'it may be a mere change of rulers in which, at first at least, we may not be very directly concerned'.[2]

A month later, by February 26, Alcock was more alarmed. He then felt the fall of the dynasty was nearly certain, but recent reports of erratic and destructive behaviour by the rebels made him question whether they could effectively replace the Manchus, and he expressed serious fears for the future of foreign trade in China. By now the Chinese authorities at Shanghai were asking for the assistance of foreign vessels to resist the rebel advance, and Alcock was quick to ask Bonham whether the occasion was not opportune for 'rescuing the Empire from a threatened disintegration', securing as the condition of aid 'unrestricted access to the furthest confines'. It was not for him to say, he admitted, but he hoped he could be allowed to urge upon his superiors 'how critical were the circumstances, how easily and certainly England with threat from

12

steamers and men of war might fling a sheathed sword into the balance with decisive effect, and dictate her own terms'.[3]

A few days later, on March 3, he was urging the point even more strongly, insisting that the time had come, 'and no one may safely predict how soon the opportunity may pass away', for the foreign powers together or for Britain alone to secure from the Emperor, 'while he is yet in a position to make treaties', such long-desired advantages as unlimited access to the interior and to all ports on the coast, direct representation at Peking and the legalization of the opium trade—all to be had, by Alcock's calculation, within two months. He dismissed any scruples as to the ungenerosity of taking advantage of the distress of a friendly power as irrelevant in dealing with the Emperor of China, who had never been disposed to carry out the existing treaties in their true spirit.[4]

As he several times admitted in these despatches, Alcock was making suggestions on issues of policy 'which do not strictly fall within the province of a Consul to discuss', and they should certainly not be taken as authoritative statements of British policy towards the rebellion in the first months of 1853. They are of some significance, however, for they clearly influenced the cautious but impressionable Bonham, only just returned to Hong Kong from leave, and set him thinking for a time in terms of a policy of aid to the Manchus in return for trading and diplomatic concessions. Thus on March 10, in forwarding a copy of Alcock's report of February 26 to the Foreign Office, Bonham commented that the views it contained were 'on the whole entitled to weighty consideration', and asked for the advice of the home government, 'particularly *to what extent* if assistance were given, it should be granted'.[5] Next day, having received Alcock's despatch of March 3, Bonham reported his intention to go north to Shanghai himself so as to be able, in the event of matters coming to a crisis, to take more decisive steps than a consul could be expected to authorize. Alcock was clearly sympathetic to the requests for aid he had received from the Shanghai authorities, but had not taken it upon himself to do more than pass these requests on promptly to his superior. Bonham assured the Foreign Secretary, actually by this time Clarendon, although Bonham was still addressing himself to Malmesbury, that he would exercise the greatest prudence, and not proffer aid too readily nor accede to any application for assistance 'unless that application is made directly by a High and properly accredited Functionary, and not even then without making that assistance the condition of advantages to our commerce in China'.[6] Probably Bonham was still thinking of the rebellion in much the same kind of terms as he had thought of it before he went on leave in 1852. In any case, in the first weeks of March 1853, intervention against it appeared to be a quite possible line of British policy, provided the price was right.

Bonham left Hong Kong on March 12 in the gunboat *Hermes* and reached Shanghai on March 21. Once arrived he quickly dropped all idea of intervention on any terms at all. In the same despatch in which, a week after the event, he reported his arrival he reported also his determination 'not to interfere in any shape in favour of the Chinese Government, as I feel confident that any such interference on my part could only prolong the struggle, though in the first place it might appear to have a totally different result'.[7]

The capture of Nanking by the rebels on March 19, although rumoured rather than certainly known among British residents in Shanghai when Bonham was writing this despatch, was certainly an important reason for his change of direction, for it clearly revealed the strength of the movement and the probable costs and difficulties inherent in any policy of intervention. Nevertheless, to argue as does Lo Erh-kang that the rebel success constituted a major setback to Bonham's plans for making a 'counter-revolutionary agreement' with the Manchus would seem to exaggerate the extent to which the Chief Superintendent had actually moved in that direction before his despatch of March 28.[8]

That this was the drift of his early search for a policy is beyond dispute; that he was ever likely to arrive at the point of actually implementing such a policy on his own initiative is much more doubtful. Bonham was not an official who relished making the big decisions himself, and in this crisis he frequently expressed his anxiety to receive precise instructions from the home government. He was prepared to talk with suitable Chinese officials about aid, but was certainly less eager than Alcock to commit British forces to the struggle. He was also more realistic than Alcock as to the prospects of actually negotiating successfully on a *quid pro quo* basis, recognizing that no provincial Chinese authority was likely to be very willing, even in such a crisis as that of March 1853, to memorialize the emperor in favour of making very large concessions to the barbarian in return for aid against the rebel. To use the outer barbarian to suppress the domestic rebel was certainly in the best traditions of Chinese policy, but not to pay a stiff price first, though it sometimes happened that the barbarian exacted a stiff price afterwards, as the Manchus themselves had done in 1644. When, some weeks before the fall of Nanking, Alcock urged sending a British war vessel there to back proposals for legalizing the opium trade, Bonham dismissed this as 'somewhat premature'.[9] He also discounted the danger to Shanghai, finding the probable line of rebel advance 'an interesting subject for speculation' rather than one for alarm.[10] Bonham, by nature more cautious and less imaginative than Alcock, took a calmer view of the situation, both as to its possibilities and its dangers.

The argument is difficult to clinch satisfactorily because Bonham wrote no despatches himself between March 11, when he was certainly thinking about intervention, and March 28, when he adopted a firmly neutral stand. Also, unlike Alcock or Bowring, he was not given to lengthy exposition or analysis in his despatches, so that the official record gives no very clear picture of the development of his thought on this question during these crucial weeks. He seems clearly to have been influenced by a report dated March 26 written by Meadows, transferred as Interpreter from Canton to Shanghai in January 1852, in which Meadows argued that 'the insurrectionary movement is a national one of the Chinese against the continued rule, or rather misrule, of the Manchoos', and that foreign interference would only have the effect of prolonging hostilities and anarchy for an indefinite period.[11] In his own despatch of March 28 Bonham echoed Meadows on the probable effect of intervention, but not on the national character of the movement. In such a crisis as this, a neutral, bystander role was far more consistent with Bonham's whole temperament and career in China than a policy of active intervention launched without prior approval from London. There seems little reason to doubt that he turned away from this line of policy without any feelings of frustration or regret.[12]

15

In London also, tentative probings in the direction of intervention were made but soon dropped. Telegraph news of the fall of Nanking reached the capital at the end of April. On May 7 Clarendon prepared a despatch to Bonham in which, after noting that events in China were moving so rapidly as to make it useless for him to lay down any precise rules for guidance, he went on to state that the British government was of the opinion that 'the most just and prudent course under existing circumstances is that they should observe a strict neutrality between the two contending parties, should abstain from taking any part whatever in the dissensions now prevailing and should not interfere for the settlement of the question in dispute'.[13] This was drawn up three weeks before Bonham's despatch of March 28 reached London. However, since he did not anticipate that his own despatch could reach China in time to influence Bonham's conduct decisively, Clarendon held it back for a few weeks while he tested the reactions of the other treaty powers to a proposal that they instruct their representatives in China 'to take such a course in conjunction with Her Majesty's Plenipotentiary as may be calculated to turn to best account the opportunity afforded by the present crisis for opening the Chinese Empire generally to the commercial enterprise of all the civilized nations of the world'.[14]

This rather vague formula elicited no very positive responses save from the French, who indicated a general readiness to co-operate, though hardly in a manner which suggested that they felt a major issue of policy was involved. The Americans felt unable to instruct their representative to do so because, as the British minister in Washington reported to Clarendon, 'the exact nature of those measures was not specified in Your Lordship's despatch with sufficient distinctness'. Without presuming that interference in the civil war was intended, the Americans made it plain that they would not authorize their Commissioner in China to take part in any such proceeding. The Russians welcomed the British initiative and approved the general objective, but emphasized the practical difficulties in the way of any direct intervention on their part.[15]

It is not very clear from this abortive correspondence exactly what course of action Clarendon had in mind. Probably he had no very clear idea himself. To call it a 'plan for joint intervention' would seem to be giving it more precision than it ever acquired.[16] Clarendon never really got beyond testing the possibility of working out a joint plan to put pressure upon the Manchus, but just how this pressure was to be applied and in what form was never spelled out. It was a trial balloon which never got very far off the ground.

The neutral line adopted by Bonham at the end of March thus became the settled British policy towards the rebellion for almost ten years. Bonham adopted it in the first instance 'pending the instructions of Her Majesty's Government', but in the following months it was confirmed both by Clarendon's despatch of May 7 and by his own further actions and instructions to his subordinates in the treaty ports. Even before Clarendon's instructions could reach him Bonham was at some pains to make this policy of neutrality plain to both sides, as well as to British subjects in China. His most important step in this direction was his visit to the rebels at Nanking in the *Hermes* at the end of April.

The rebels, as Bonham had anticipated, had made no attempt to advance as far as Shanghai after their capture of Nanking. At the end of March they had captured Chinkiang, on the junction of the Grand Canal and the Yangtze but still over a hundred miles from the coast. At the beginning of April Imperialist forces under Hsiang Jung established the 'Great Camp of Kiangnan' from which a siege of Nanking itself was conducted, with one major interruption, for over seven years, and for the present the rebels were content simply to hold their gains in the lower Yangtze basin short of the actual coastline, while conducting major campaigns to the north and west.

Politically, their northern campaign was of vital importance, for it represented their most direct thrust at Peking, the capture of which was essential if they were to overthrow the Manchus entirely. Although the forces sent north reached the neighbourhood of Tientsin, within striking distance of the Imperial capital, their eventual destruction was perhaps the real turning-point in the fortunes of the rebellion. The rebels were still to win great victories, especially during 1860–2, but their threat to the Ch'ing dynasty was never again so immediate nor their chances of complete political and military success so great as in the early stages of their northern campaign. In the west opposition to the Taiping advance centred around the Chinese official Tseng Kuo-fan who, despite defeats which sometimes reduced him to despair, slowly built up the provincial armies which were to become the main agents in the final defeat of the rebellion. The failure of the rebels to establish themselves on the coast by taking Shanghai, which they could probably have done without difficulty in the middle of 1853, was doubtless a major strategic error, for it denied them easy access to the Western arms and supplies which were to become an increasingly important element in the struggle, as well as to a valuable source of revenue from the customs duties of the port. But none of this was apparent when Bonham made his journey up the river to Nanking at the end of April 1853. For the Western powers the important thing was that the rebel advance had stopped short of Shanghai.

This meant, however, that the rebels remained very much an unknown quantity still. Efforts made early in April to get accurate first-hand information about them, first by sending Chinese messengers and then by Meadows attempting a journey in secret through the Imperialist lines at Chinkiang, did not yield much, although Bonham noted after them that there was 'a somewhat strange peculiarity distinguishing these insurgents. The accounts received from Mr. Meadows describe them as Puritanical and even fanatic. The whole army pray regularly before meals. They punish rape, adultery and opium-smoking with death, and tobacco-smoking with the bamboo . . .'. But, he added, he was by no means satisfied in regard to their intentions towards foreigners, and as they appeared to be a more formidable body than had hitherto been supposed, he was unwilling to rest until he had obtained a declaration of those intentions. Further, although he had refused the repeated requests of the Shanghai authorities for aid, giving an 'invariable reply . . . that we were determined to remain perfectly neutral', this had not prevented the Taotai (prefect) of the city, Wu Chien-chang, putting out reports that such aid was in fact being given. The two main objectives of the trip, therefore, were 'to undeceive the insurgents in regard to the false statements made by the Shanghae Taoutae', and to find out what the rebellion was really like.[17]

Bonham was certainly less favourably impressed by what he saw of the rebels at Nanking than was Meadows, who went as chief interpreter, or than Captain Fishbourne, who commanded the *Hermes*, but the tone of his reports to Clarendon on this trip was sceptical rather than hostile.[18] He was at some pains to show that the firing from rebel batteries to which the *Hermes* was subjected as it approached both Chinkiang and Nanking was understandably due to the false reports put out by Wu and that it ceased when the *Hermes* made no reply. Once arrived at Nanking, he assured the rebel leaders of British neutrality, but also reminded them in no uncertain terms of British rights under the treaty of 1842, threatening that, if they injured in any manner the persons or property of British subjects, immediate steps would be taken 'to resent the injury in the same manner as similar injuries were resented ten years ago'.

This threat was provoked by evidence that the rebels, although they spoke of Westerners as their 'brethren' and not as 'barbarians', were still far from abandoning the old Chinese assumptions of superiority towards 'tribute-bearing' nations. 'The sooner the minds of these men are disabused in regard to their universal supremacy the better for all parties', Bonham commented to Clarendon. But in 1853 there seemed no reason to regard the Taipings as likely to prove more difficult to deal with on this account than the Manchus had already proved. On the contrary, it seemed reasonable to argue, as did Meadows, that their greater readiness to assimilate Western ideas in religion meant that such prejudices were likely to disappear more quickly among them than among the Manchus. Thus, thought Meadows, 'with their success a totally unhoped-for prospect would open to us of obtaining, by purely amicable means, complete freedom of commercial action throughout the whole of the Chinese empire'.[19] Bonham himself did not express such high hopes immediately after his trip to Nanking, but a few months later he was saying something similar in a report to Clarendon.

Bonham's innate caution and scepticism were most apparent in his comments on the religious ideology of the movement and on its prospects for complete success. Of the former, he wrote they had established a new religion 'which may be called a kind of spurious revelation', supposedly founded upon the Old

Testament and religious tracts but to which they had added 'a tissue of superstition and nonsense which makes an unprejudiced party almost doubt whether there is any real sincerity in their faith, or whether it is not used merely as a political engine of power by the Chiefs to sway the minds of those whom they are anxious to attach to their cause'. As to their military prospects and chances of ultimate success, Bonham did not commit himself, but warned against speculation, 'as so much depends upon circumstances with which we are not at all familiar'. He anticipated that the next rebel advance would be towards Peking, not Shanghai, but noted the existence of still powerful Imperial forces around Nanking. There was no thought of offering aid to the rebels, nor did the Taipings seriously ask for it, being flushed with victory and confident that 'Our Heavenly Father helps us, and no one can fight with Him'. It would, indeed, have been contrary to all English ideas of international law to have aided any rebels against a power with whom treaty relations existed, even such unsatisfactory relations as those with the Manchu government at that time. Some observers, in fact, thought Bonham went too far in even visiting Nanking, at least in person, since this might be taken to imply a sort of *de facto* recognition, but Clarendon fully approved his proceedings. His journey had served to provide much valuable and remarkable information about the rebellion. It also served to confirm in his own mind the wisdom of a policy of strict and watchful neutrality, for it was still not plain which side would triumph nor which was really the more likely to serve British interests in China.

This policy was given more general application by Bonham after he left Shanghai in the middle of May, convinced by then that the crisis at that port was safely past. On his way back to Hong Kong he called at Amoy, which had recently been captured by rebels belonging to a secret society independent of the Taiping movement. Having satisfied himself that they offered no serious threat to British lives or property in that port, he instructed the British vice-consul there to maintain strict neutrality, although he anticipated an early recapture by the Imperialists.[20] Once back in Hong Kong, reports were received from Canton expressing fears of renewed rebel outbreaks, and there were indirect enquiries from the Chinese authorities there about the possibility of British aid. These, Bonham assured Clarendon, he would certainly reject, adding that he looked with some anxiety for the views of the Government 'not only on this particular question, but on the whole subject relative to the state of affairs in this country'.[21]

Thus the policy of neutrality determined on at Shanghai was extended by Bonham during the latter part of May to cover the whole revolutionary situation that was developing in southern China under the stimulus of Taiping successes. It was also explicitly applied to all British subjects in China by a proclamation on July 7 warning them that any direct engagement in the conflict was contrary both to statutory and to common law.[22] The whole object of Bonham's policy at this stage was to avoid becoming involved in the struggle in any way, whether officially or by the irresponsible actions of British nationals on the China coast so that, whichever side ultimately triumphed, British treaty rights might not suffer.

Certain features of this policy of neutrality are worth noting before examining its working in practice. As Bonham's warning to the rebel chiefs indicated, and as Clarendon's instruction of May 7 confirmed, the neutrality adopted was distinctly an armed neutrality ready to 'resent' any injury to British interests in China. The difficulty was to determine how far British forces should be used to defend those interests. In response to a query from Bonham on this point Clarendon thought it impossible to lay down any general rule. At Amoy, where Clarendon believed there was no distinct area within which British interests were concentrated, protection could not be provided indefinitely, and the consul there should advise British merchants that they must either withdraw or stay at their own risk. But at Shanghai, which proved to be the chief case in point, the situation was different. 'There the factory is distinct from the Town and I believe, more easily defensible', Clarendon wrote. 'There also British Residents are more numerous, and the amount of property much larger; and at Shanghai, therefore, Her Majesty's Government would wish a concentration of Naval Force and the immediate chastisement of the party in power from whom any injury is received.'[23] At Canton, roughly the same situation obtained. Where possible it was the foreign settlement areas or 'factories' which, as the focal points of British persons and property, were to be defended against both sides. These were to be placed outside the field of conflict between the rebels and the Manchu government.

But these areas were legally still Chinese territory. At Shanghai the British concession, later to become part of the International Settlement, was leased in the first instance by the British consul from the local Chinese authorities on payment of an annual ground rent. An area of 23 acres set apart for a consulate in 1843 was extended to 120 acres in 1846 and to 460 acres in November 1848.[24] This lease of a distinct area of land outside the city but close to the river front on which British subjects might build their residences and warehouses provided a convenient arrangement both for the British community and for the local Chinese authorities, who had no desire to see the foreigners established within the Chinese city. But the land was not leased in the way that, for example, part of the Kowloon area opposite Hong Kong was leased in 1898, that is by an agreement between governments transferring sovereignty for the period of the lease from one to the other. In the latter case the British government acquired a clear right in international law to defend the leased territory against any attack, but no such right can be said to have existed in the case of the foreign settlement areas at the treaty ports. Britain's 'right' to defend them was based simply on her actual occupation of them and on her capacity to do so as a power militarily stronger than either of the two combatants in the civil war. Under the terms of the 1842 Treaty of Nanking British subjects had acquired a right to reside at the treaty ports but no clear right to reside within areas specially set apart for them, even though it suited the Chinese authorities to allow them to do so. The British government itself cannot be said to have acquired any clear right by that treaty to use its forces to maintain virtually independent control over such areas, or to forbid Chinese forces and authorities access to them.[25]

Yet, however presumptuous and however questionable its basis in law, this policy was recognizably a policy of neutrality of some sort. The essence of neutrality in international law is impartiality in action. It does not preclude sympathy with one side as against the other, nor even the right to intervene if a belligerent violates a principle of international law.[26] Putting aside the complication that neither the Manchu government nor the Taiping rebels would have admitted themselves to be bound by any Western-derived principles of international law, both sides in the civil war, and certainly the Manchu government itself, can be said to have had a belligerent right to occupy the foreign settlement areas if necessary for the success of their campaigns. So long as British subjects were not molested such action would not, strictly speaking, have constituted a violation of British treaty rights. But so long as the British government refused to allow either side to make use of the settlement area then its stand, although perhaps not strictly legal, was not inconsistent in practice with a declaration of neutrality. It was very much a mid-nineteenth-century, strong-power type of neutrality, able and determined to defend what it alone decided were the proper limits of its 'rights' in China.

It was not, in the beginning, a neutrality which masked a decided preference for one side or the other. Such a preference, in favour of the Imperialists, later revealed itself but cannot be said to have been present during 1853. It is true that at the end of May Bonham instructed Alcock to avoid all unnecessary communication with the Taipings and to 'rigidly abstain from any act by which the Chinese Government could be led to believe that the British Government gives any countenance to the Insurgents, or indeed feel any interest in their success'.[27] But this concern to avoid becoming associated with the rebels too closely is an illustration of Bonham's caution rather than of any hostility towards them. In fact, in conversations he had with the French and United States representatives in China at the beginning of August he expressed qualified hopes in the Taipings, in contrast to both de Bourboulon and Colonel Marshall, who made no secret of their preference for the Imperialists. Bonham, however, was of the opinion that 'more Political and Commercial advantages are likely to be obtained from the Insurrectionists than we should ever obtain from the Imperialists, supposing a favourable opportunity presented itself for opening negotiations with them. With the former we should have to deal with a new set of men by no means disinclined to serve us, or indisposed towards us, as far as we have hitherto been able to discern. Whereas with the Imperialists we should find them what they have ever proved themselves to be, proud, overbearing and inimical to an extension of Foreign Intercourse.'[28] At this stage Bonham seemed to have higher hopes in the rebels than he had had upon his return from Nanking early in May.

His report on these August conversations also reveals how far he had moved away from the idea of intervention, for he strongly opposed a suggestion from Clarendon that this was a good time to reopen the question of treaty revision. There never was a more unpropitious time he insisted, asking with whom such a revised treaty was to be made. 'If with the Emperor, supposing, for the sake of argument, that all approaches to His Majesty were smoothed down and made easy, and His Majesty's wish was as strong as our own to enter into close bonds (all of which suppositions, I need not say, are not within the limits of probability), the first condition of such a treaty would be that assistance should be given to him to put down the Rebellion—an application, I presume, not to be entertained for one moment and entirely at variance with the course of policy prescribed by Her Majesty's Government.' In any case, Bonham went on, Britain might miss her aim by treating with the Emperor and then finding the rebels triumph. 'The wisest if not the only policy is to wait some time longer the issue of Events in the North', be concluded. Clarendon agreed.[29]

The core of Bonham's policy of neutrality was simply to watch and to wait because there was nothing much else that could be done. He had no firm and consistent preference for either side, nor was he merely biding his time until he felt the conditions for intervention against the rebellion were favourable. British neutrality, as formulated by Bonham and approved by Clarendon, was not benevolently inclined towards anything but the preservation and possible extension of British interests in China. Whichever side showed itself to be the more able and ready to protect and further those interests would, in the end, win British support. But which side this would be was still quite uncertain in the middle of 1853. Bonham advised, therefore, that all that could be done was to keep well clear of the struggle and await the outcome. Naturally, as the situation changed policy might change also. But what the course of events would be, and how British policy might change, neither Bonham nor anyone else had any clear conception, still less any clear plans, in the middle and later months of 1853.

3

Neutrality in Practice
(1853-55)

EVENTS SOON SHOWED that it would be difficult to await the outcome of the struggle without becoming in some measure involved in it. Difficulties arose at first not so much over the main rebellion at Nanking, since this did not attempt to advance any nearer to the coast until 1860, but rather over other anti-dynastic risings at Amoy, Shanghai and near Canton. British interests were for the time being more directly affected by these risings than by the Taiping rebellion itself. But since they were stimulated by the success of the Taipings, and since the British experience of them, especially at Shanghai, helped influence the development of British policy towards the larger movement, they must receive some consideration here. Further, the argument that British neutrality 'existed in name only' and was from the beginning pro-Manchu in inclination is based partly on an examination of British policy towards these risings, which are also seen by many modern Chinese historians as part of a great national revolution of the Chinese people against Manchu rule. As such, it is argued, the success of the rebels who seized Amoy and Shanghai was feared by the British government no less than was the success of the Taipings themselves.[1]

Much the most important of these risings was that which occurred at Shanghai in September 1853, when the city was suddenly seized by members of the Hsiao Tao Hui (Small Sword Society), an offshoot of a larger secret society known as

25

the San Ho Hui (Triad Society). The Shanghai rebels are consequently generally referred to as Triads. Following the capture
of the city, the Taotai Wu, whose requests for aid against the
Taipings had been rejected by Bonham in March and April,
fled in disguise into the foreign settlement and was sheltered by
American friends. After a few weeks in hiding, Wu set about
gathering forces to recapture the city and requested aid from
Alcock, who refused it in accordance with Bonham's instructions. When informed of these happenings at Shanghai, Bonham
even went so far as to instruct Alcock not to allow Wu to take
refuge again in the foreign settlement, on the grounds that if
this were done 'it cannot be affirmed that the British Authorities
are observing the strict neutrality which it is desirable that they
should maintain'.[2] The cautious Bonham thus began by being
very strictly neutral indeed towards the Triad rising.

A more complex issue than the sheltering of refugee Imperial
officials was the fate of the customs duties at Shanghai. Much
the most important result of the Triad rising was the emergence
of the foreign-administered Inspectorate of Customs, first established at Shanghai in the middle of 1854 and later extended to
other treaty ports. The creation of this efficient and honest
administration of the Imperial Customs was to prove one of the
main pillars of continued Manchu rule in China, for it ensured
to the Imperial government a dependable and growing revenue
and it helped provide the finances for the campaigns that
eventually defeated the Taiping rebellion. In addition, the
indemnity payments exacted from China after the second opium
war of 1856–60 were met from it. It was a system highly unpopular with most British merchants in China, who preferred a
customs service more easily evaded and bribed, but it was
criticized by one of those merchants, John Scarth, as providing
clear evidence of the readiness of what he called 'mandarin-
worshipping' British officials in China to co-operate with an
unpopular Manchu government at the expense of the national
rebellion.[3] Taking account of the very complex origins of this
system, however, it seems clear that it was in no sense designed
by the British officials who helped establish it to further the
Imperialist cause against the rebellion at large. It began as a
local solution to a local problem, not as a first step in a secret
campaign against the Chinese revolution.[4]

When the Triad rebels captured Shanghai the Chinese customs house, although situated in the foreign settlement area, was completely looted and destroyed, with the result that Wu had no headquarters from which to collect this important revenue. Alcock and the American consul were quick to institute a provisional system of collection, not in order to protect the revenues of an Imperial government no longer able to administer foreign trade at Shanghai, but to maintain the treaty basis upon which legal foreign trade with China depended. Under the tariff regulations attached to the Treaty of Nanking the British consul was required to act as security for the payment of customs duties by British merchants and to see that no British vessel left port without a customs clearance from the Chinese authorities. Alcock feared that failure on his part to observe these provisions, even during a rebellion against the government with which the treaty had been concluded, might impair the legality of British trade at the port. The payments due from the British vessels were therefore collected by him in the form of promissory notes which were to be honoured by the merchants if the British government approved Alcock's action and agreed with him that it was legally necessary for the duties to be paid, whatever the political situation at Shanghai.

Needless to say, the merchants protested most strongly and argued that if the Manchu government could not maintain its authority at Shanghai it had no right to a revenue from a foreign trade which it was no longer administering or protecting. However, while instructions from Whitehall were awaited, Alcock continued to collect the promissory notes, at the same time refusing to recognize Wu's authority to collect the duties himself and denying him any facilities for re-establishing a customs house in the foreign settlement. The American Commissioner, Colonel Marshall, was much more sympathetic to Wu's attempts to re-establish control over the customs, but in face of opposition from American merchants, who were no more inclined than the British to pay duties to a discredited Imperial authority, his endeavours during October 1853 to end the provisional system came to nothing. Bonham, although rather sympathetic to the merchant point of view, did not himself oppose Alcock's measures but left it to the Foreign Office to decide. Alcock's stand was between that of the majority of the merchants and that of Colonel Marshall. He believed that customs duties should continue to be collected by some authority or other, but in the circumstances existing at the end of 1853 was not prepared to recognize the Imperial Taotai at the port as a satisfactory authority for the purpose. There was no question of recognizing the Triads, besieged as they were by Imperialist forces and in control only of the walled city, not the port.

In January 1854 the views of the Foreign Office on the question were received. Clarendon held that the obligation placed on British consuls by the tariff regulations of 1843 was not binding if the Imperial authority was subverted, and although he commended Alcock's attempt to deal with the situation, he agreed with Bonham that the consul should not be expected to act as if the Imperial authority would return. He therefore ordered that Alcock's measures 'should only be enforced so long as it is reasonable to suppose that the suspension of Imperial authority is of a temporary and accidental character'.[5] The Triads still controlled the city, so that, lacking Foreign Office approval and in face of merchant opposition, Alcock abandoned the provisional system of collection. By this time Wu had established a new customs house outside the foreign settlement area, and this was now recognized by the British and American consuls. But it was generally and easily evaded by the foreign merchants, who were less inclined than ever to pay duties in cash and who argued that in the confused political circumstances Shanghai should be made a free port. The ending of the provisional system of promissory notes and the inability of Wu to get the authority of his customs house acknowledged by the merchants meant that foreign trade at Shanghai, during the first half of 1854, was conducted on a highly irregular basis.

Such a situation was regarded by both Alcock and Bowring, who had replaced Bonham at Hong Kong in April, as being against the long-term interests of foreign trade on the China coast. They feared the spread of disorder and smuggling and also possible Imperial retaliation for the loss of the customs duties in the form of an interruption to the tea trade, which could mean a serious loss of revenue to the British exchequer. They therefore urged upon the Manchu authorities at Shanghai the need to reorganize the customs service there entirely and this, they argued, could best be done by the introduction of European officers who would be in the employ of the Chinese government but above the peculation and connivance at smuggling which characterized Imperial officials.

In order to persuade the Shanghai authorities to accept a measure of foreign participation in the customs administration of the port, Bowring, together with the American authorities, promised to try to secure collection of the back duties for which promissory notes were still held, subject once again to the approval of the home government. But although Bowring felt that the Imperial government had a just claim to these duties, this was a secondary consideration with him. His primary concern was for the preservation of regular and orderly conditions of trade at Shanghai.[6] For the British government the moral claim of the Imperial authorities to the lost customs revenue was not even a secondary consideration, however, and Bowring was sharply reprimanded for making the agreement to secure payment of the back duties. British merchants were not required to honour their promissory notes, which amounted to about one-quarter of a million pounds, although a part of the American duties were paid.

Nevertheless, the principle of a foreign element in the administration of the customs service at Shanghai did become established in the later months of 1854. But in so far as it can be regarded as an example of co-operation, it was co-operation only between local British and Chinese authorities, not between governments, and it was in no sense a co-operation against rebellion, Triad or Taiping. By 1861, the use of foreign officers in the Chinese customs service did become an important element in a British policy designed to strengthen and uphold the Manchu government. But in origin it was intended to serve a much more limited and local aim, and its first introduction in 1854 at Shanghai cannot be regarded as evidence of a particularly pro-Imperialist policy on the part of the British government at that time.[7]

Shanghai was eventually recaptured by the Imperialists, with substantial assistance from French forces, in February 1855. Not surprisingly, some Chinese historians have taken the French action on this occasion as proof of the falsity of treaty-power neutrality towards the rebellion generally, and identify the British and the Americans more or less explicitly with the French action.[8] In point of fact, however, the British government at home was most adamant in its refusal to allow British forces to be used in any way to assist the Imperial assault, although it is true that some British officials on the spot would have liked to co-operate with the French. But both in a formal sense and in actual practice British policy during the period of the Triad occupation Shanghai remained effectively neutral.

The best proof of this is provided by the controversies which developed over the building of a wall or stockade to prevent supplies reaching the rebels from the foreign settlement area, and over the right of Imperial forces to have access to this area in order to complete their siege of the city. Because of the possible risk to foreign life and property involved in any fighting on the north side, where the foreign settlement lay, the foreign representatives at Shanghai refused to admit any Imperial right of access, although, as already suggested, their stand could hardly have been sustained in an international court of law. It meant, however, that Western neutrality at first worked decidedly in the interests of the Shanghai rebels, who could certainly never have held out for so long had this neutrality been more legally correct in application.

Further, in April 1854, this insistence on keeping the foreign settlement area outside the field of conflict resulted in quite a serious armed clash between an Anglo-American force, composed largely of volunteers, and Imperial forces, accused of encroaching upon the settlement area. During this 'Battle of Muddy Flat', as it came to be called in Shanghai annals, an Imperial encampment close to the settlement bounds was destroyed at the cost of several lives on both sides.[9] In his memorial to the Emperor on the incident, Hsü Nai-chao, the governor of Kiangsu province, presented the British as the most troublesome and the most pro-rebel of the barbarians, and reported that the Taotai Wu had upbraided their consul after the event by reminding him of the Imperial benevolence in allowing foreign trade at the port over the past ten years, and by suggesting that if they could not help in exterminating the rebels the British should at least not obstruct government forces in doing so, or they would come to be regarded as rebels themselves.[10]

According to the Chinese report, Alcock was properly contrite, but his own reports hardly suggest this. When, shortly after the Muddy Flat clash, the rebels took advantage of the situation to attack the weakened Imperial position he grimly observed that 'both parties in the course of skirmishing occasionally crossed within our limits, but were speedily warned off by a few shots from parties of British and American marines, conveniently posted for that purpose'.[11] This whole episode, which is ignored by those who maintain the 'false neutrality' argument, illustrates not so much the falsity as the forcefulness of the British application of the policy of neutrality laid down in 1853.

At the same time, although they had no regard for the calibre or discipline of the Imperial troops besieging the city and made their task more difficult by refusing to allow them to attack from the north side, the British authorities at Shanghai did recognize an obligation to try to prevent supplies and arms reaching the rebels. Consular notifications forbidding trafficking in arms with either side were accordingly issued, although in the absence of any kind of a police force it was difficult to enforce these upon a population in which there was a large adventurer element, drawn mainly from deserting seamen, and many traders who habitually engaged in the smuggling of opium, if nothing else. The China coast generally, and Shanghai in particular, was already a focal point for the riff-raff of East and West, a fact which did not make the strict enforcement of a policy of neutrality any easier.[12] There were frequent complaints from the Manchu authorities conducting the siege at the continuance of a trade which, even if not condoned by foreign officials at the port, certainly constituted a large breach of neutrality on the part of the foreign community as a whole and without which the rebels could never have held the city so long.[13]

Alcock admitted that in this respect British neutrality in the Triad struggle at Shanghai was indeed simply verbal, but he meant this in exactly the opposite sense to those later historians who have characterized it thus. For Alcock it was the Manchu not the rebel cause which suffered from British inconsistency. On one occasion he demanded: 'How shall we maintain that to be neutrality in any sense of the word that is not meant to deceive which allows a beleaguered city to draw succour daily under the protection of our Flag, our guns, and the prestige of our power without which they could not have held the City in insurrection against the Government of China, and the withdrawal of which is certain destruction to them. If we really desire neutrality and to give it effect, this can only be done by isolating the Foreign Settlement from both camps and denying succour or supplies to either.'[14] With the support of Bowring, Alcock therefore agreed to co-operate with the Imperial and French authorities in the construction of a wall between the foreign settlement and the besieged rebels.

Unexpected difficulties in the way of a British contribution to this project were soon met with. Captain Callaghan, the Senior Naval Officer at Shanghai, to whom Alcock addressed the complaint just quoted and upon whom he called for forces to assist in the construction and protection of the wall, refused to co-operate, on the ground that his instructions forbade him to use his forces for any other purpose than the actual protection of the lives and property of British residents in the port. Against the protests and arguments of both Alcock and Bowring, his stand was approved by the then Commander of British naval forces on the China station, Sir James Stirling, and eventually by the Foreign Office and Admiralty also. Clarendon, on receipt of reports on this issue, insisted that Imperialist troops were not to be permitted to enter the foreign settlement at all, even if only to build a wall, and that any action taken by British forces 'must not assume the character of active intervention in favour of either parties'.[15] By the time these instructions reached the scene the whole affair was actually over. The wall had been built with French assistance, supplies to the rebels were cut off, and the city recaptured in the middle of February 1855. But the British contribution to this result cannot be put in the same category as that of the French. When the latter, provoked by rebel fire across their settlement, attacked the city on January 6 and made a breach in the wall, at the cost of some fifty casualties to themselves, the British forces merely looked uncomfortably on. Alcock complained bitterly that 'the impossibility, under existing circumstances, of our taking part in these operations has necessarily placed the British authorities, civil and naval, in a very painful position'.[16]

In all this it is apparent that both Alcock and Bowring had a strong preference for the Imperial authorities over the Triad rebels and wanted actively to help restore them to power in Shanghai. But their wishes and preferences did not constitute British policy. Hammond made this plain in a memo attached to the draft of a despatch from Clarendon to Bowring. 'The only safe course appears to be perfect neutrality as far as the Government is concerned', Hammond observed, 'although Bowring clearly wants to take an active part in favour of the Imperialists, and Alcock shares his opinion.'[17] Clarendon approved of some attempts at mediation made by Bowring in the middle months of 1854, but firmly instructed him 'to adhere to the policy of not interfering by force between the Belligerents'.[18]

Thus, although Shanghai was eventually recaptured with foreign assistance this was French assistance only, not British. However inclined the British officials on the spot were to stretch the policy of neutrality in a pro-Imperial direction, they were not successful in actually doing so, because of the insistence of the Foreign Office upon not helping either side and because of the stand taken by the commanders of British naval forces in the area on the question of the barrier wall. The one occasion on which British forces were seriously engaged in this struggle was at the expense of the Imperialists, not to their benefit.

The rising at Amoy occurred some months before that at Shanghai and anticipated many of its features. In particular, the question of the payment of customs duties arose, as at the larger port, and Clarendon gave a similar ruling that the British consul was to accept no responsibility for the actual collection of the Imperial customs revenue.[19] In some ways the problem of avoiding involvement in the struggle was even more difficult at Amoy than at Shanghai, for the Imperial campaign to recapture the city was mainly a naval one, so that foreign vessels in the harbour had to be always ready to move from their anchorages if they were to avoid being used as stalking horses by the Imperial war-junks. Requests from Imperial officials for the direct assistance of British war vessels were refused, as they were elsewhere, but foreign merchants carried on a highly profitable trade in arms and gunpowder with both sides. When the city was finally recaptured in November 1853 the British consul intervened to put a stop to the indiscriminate slaughter of the unfortunate inhabitants of the city, all of whom were treated as rebels by the Imperial forces, and British vessels rescued many from death by drowning. It is difficult to see that British action at Amoy in any way compromised the declared policy of neutrality. Six months after the capture of the city Bowring reminded the vice-consul there of 'the necessity of every precaution in order that Her Majesty's functionaries may not be supposed to be partisans in the unfortunate commotions which agitate so many parts of the Chinese Empire'.[20]

In the case of the disturbances around Canton during 1854-55 the issue is less clear cut, but the main conclusion seems broadly the same. Lo Erh-kang says that England, France and America smuggled supplies of arms and gunpowder to such an extent that, on the admission of the Manchu officials themselves, the fact that Canton did not fall to the rebels was because of the help received from Hong Kong.[21] This argument seems to confuse the actions of Western nationals with the policies of Western governments, and to assume that when the former helped the Imperialists, as some of them certainly did at Canton, it was with the active encouragement of their governments. The smuggling of supplies of 'Chinese snuff' (gunpowder) and Enfield 'umbrellas' became a considerable business on the China coast in these years, but it was essentially a private enterprise which was not selective about its customers. Moreover, Governor Yeh at Canton later complained in a memorial that at this time (December 1854 to January 1855), 'the barbarians secretly furnished the insurgents cannon and powder, and sold their loot for them'.[22] It cannot be claimed that one side only benefited from the smuggling of arms.

The colonial government at Hong Kong attempted to check this trade, as well as other breaches of neutrality, by an Ordinance passed by the Legislative Council of the colony on January 17, 1855. This strengthened earlier proclamations prohibiting British subjects from taking service with either side in the conflict. The January Ordinance fixed penalties of imprisonment of up to two years and a fine of up to five thousand dollars for any British subject in any part of China who assisted either side, whether by personal enlistment, by furnishing supplies, by fitting out vessels 'or by knowingly and purposely doing any other act to assist either party by which neutrality may be violated'.[23] To enforce such regulations over a wide area of the China coast upon a British population which, although small in number, was not remarkable for its amenability to legal restraints was no simple matter, but they cannot be dismissed as mere window-dressing. In December 1854, when reports were received that an American named Drinker was recruiting a force of foreign mercenaries, mainly British, to attack the rebels near Canton, both the American and the British authorities took quick action to prevent any such development, just as seven years later they were at first to discourage the famous 'Ever Victorious Army' at Shanghai.[24]

Bowring himself went to Canton in mid-December, partly in response to a back-handed sort of request for assistance from his old adversary, Governor Yeh. Bowring's primary objective was to check the defence of the foreign factory area, but despite his reply to Yeh that he could not interfere in the conflict beyond securing the persons and property of British subjects he seems to have envisaged some kind of co-operation with the Imperialists. He sought to use the crisis to advance the long-standing British claim of the right of entry to Canton itself, and when Yeh proved as adamant as ever on this Bowring left at the end of the month sorely displeased. He wrote to Yeh complaining that 'the state of our intercourse is most unsatisfactory and intolerable, that many great grievances remain wholly un-redressed', while to his son Edgar he expostulated that he was 'exhausting patience with these stubborn Mandarins. Pressed and perplexed as they are they had rather let the city be devastated and destroyed by their own savage people than meet the friendly hand which I have stretched out to them, that being the hand of a "foreign barbarian".'[25] Clearly, whatever was in Bowring's 'friendly hand', and it does not seem to have con-tained anything beyond co-operation in defence of an extensive neutral area around the factories, it did not lead to any kind of effective joint action. British neutrality remained in fact, if not altogether in intent, unimpaired.

One difficulty in the way of following a policy of perfect neutrality which was especially apparent in the south of China was how to distinguish between rebels who had some sort of a genuine political character, into which category the Taipings certainly came, and bandits or pirates who simply called them-selves rebels as a convenient cover for their normal activities.

Bowring more than once pointed to the difficulty of following any simple policy towards the 'interblending of patriotism and piracy, robbery and rebellion' which he found prevailing on the south China coast.[26] The rebels seemed to him to have no means of support save in plunder, and 'the small amount of patriotism' involved in their activities which entitled them to any respect from a neutral power was, in his view, of minimal significance compared to their hopes of sacking the opulent city of Canton. The rebel chiefs near Canton were therefore told that the British would recognize no right of blockade by them of the city,[27] and this is one point at which British neutrality may reasonably be described as effectively biased in favour of the Imperialists. It is unlikely, however, that this denial of belligerent rights was a major reason for the failure of the very diverse and poorly integrated rebel forces attacking Canton to take the city. No direct or substantial British aid was given to the Imperialists there any more than at Shanghai or Amoy.

Thus it seems reasonable to argue that the policy of armed and limited neutrality laid down in 1853 was applied as consistently as was possible in the exceedingly difficult circumstances created by the epidemic of rebellions on the south China coast during these years. The legal basis of that policy may certainly be questioned, but so far as the strictly historical question of its actual application is concerned, there seems little real evidence to support the argument that it was at this stage either a seriously biased or a merely temporary policy. The 'Battle of Muddy Flat'; the failure of British forces to help build the barrier wall at Shanghai or to assist the French in their attack upon the city; the consistent refusal of the requests of Imperial officials for the direct assistance of British forces; the Foreign Office attitude to the fate of the Imperial customs revenue at both Amoy and Shanghai—all these show that British policy during these years cannot accurately be described as especially inclined to favour the Manchus, despite the anti-rebel attitude of certain British officials in China.

The question now arises how far British officials in China and in the Foreign Office itself identified the rebellion at Nanking with these risings on the coast, which they certainly came to regard as undesirable movements, more piratical than rebellious. As we have already seen, this was at first the view taken of the

Taiping rebellion also, but after 1853 it could not be regarded as other than a major political and military challenge to the reigning dynasty. During the years now under consideration, the shift in official British opinion about it was, broadly, that although it was still regarded as a genuine rebellion, and in that respect in a superior category to most of the other risings, its chances of ultimate success were increasingly discounted, and it came to be seen as a probably worse rather than as a possibly better alternative to the continuance of Manchu rule.

That it was put in a quite different category to the risings at Shanghai and elsewhere is shown clearly by a memo of Clarendon's attached to the draft of a despatch he sent Bowring on the wall question at Shanghai. Clarendon there observed that the case of Shanghai differed somewhat from the Nanking rebellion, for at Shanghai 'a band of thieves having no political objects and who are wholly repudiated by the Nanking rebels have got possession of a wealthy commercial city and inflict serious injury upon the foreign trade that by returns (?) is shown to be carried on there'. Their expulsion would on every account be desirable, he continued, 'but as there would be great risk in making the Factory ground a battlefield we had better adhere to the neutral position that has hitherto been maintained'.[28] Clearly, Clarendon made a distinction between the Taiping rebels and the 'robbers' at Shanghai. If he insisted, whatever the grounds, on remaining neutral between the latter and the Imperialists, it is hardly necessary to point out how much more disposed he was to maintain that policy between the Imperialists and the Nanking rebels.

Further evidence of the existence of this distinction in the minds of British officials is provided by a *Note on the Rebellion in China*, 1852–55, published in September 1855 by Thomas Wade, then Chinese Secretary at Hong Kong. Bowring commended this to Clarendon's attention as the best summary of the rebellion to that date. In it Wade wrote that the seizure of Amoy and Shanghai in 1853 and the attempt on Canton in 1854 were episodes in the rebellion's history, but there was no ground for believing that these coastal movements were recognized by the Taipings 'and the wide differences between the character credibly attributed to the occupants of Nan-King and that of the other rebels in question, of which we have had evidence more direct and convincing, would of itself incline us to dispute that assumption'.[29] The argument that Britain opposed the lesser risings of 1853–55 as part of a policy of 'false' neutrality towards the Taiping rebellion is thus weak at two points. Although they were certainly looked on with great disfavour, British policy did not set out, secretly or openly, to help destroy them, and they were in any case clearly distinguished as inferior in character and importance to the larger rising at Nanking.

Nevertheless, during these years the hardening of official British opinion about the Taipings was unmistakable. The early view that the movement was worthless both from a political and religious standpoint began to reassert itself, though many doubts remained. One reason for this hardening of attitude was the failure of the rebels' northern campaign. As early as November 1853 even so sympathetic an observer as Meadows admitted that the difficulties this campaign was meeting went far to destroy all hopes and anticipations based upon the superiority of Taiping forces over Imperial.[30] In June 1854, when forwarding a report on further rebel defeats in the north, Bowring commented that 'the insurrectionary tide is not so irresistible as it has been generally considered among foreigners', and he expressed the conviction that the Taipings could not resolve the internal divisions of China.[31] 'Even if the Nanking party should obtain the mastery at Peking, there is great reason to apprehend that a very large portion of the vast empire would not recognize nor obey its authority, and that it would not be competent to subdue the elements of sedition and disorder so universally scattered', he argued.[32] The hopes, never more than half entertained by British officials during 1853, of a quick settlement of the rebellion one way or the other were soon entirely abandoned by 1854.

Apart from this loss of momentum in the rebellion itself, doubts were increased as a result of the few contacts made with the Taiping rebels by Westerners after Bonham's initial visit to Nanking. No other Western visitor actually reached the rebel capital until the French minister, Bourboulon, arrived in the *Cassini* in December 1853. Before then Bonham had instructed Alcock to avoid unnecessary communication with the rebels, and the rebels themselves had shown no disposition to make contacts. A few missionaries attempted to reach them by independent means but without success, so that for many months Western knowledge about the organization and character of the movement, as distinct from its military fortunes, did not advance much upon what it was immediately after Bonham's visit. Official Western opinion varied from the frankly hostile, as in the case of the American Commissioner, Colonel Marshall, to dubious but moderate approval, as with Bonham. Non-official Western opinion, which will be discussed in the following chapter, was more favourable and hopeful, though less unanimously and certainly so than is sometimes suggested. There were many who were sceptical or hostile from the beginning, especially the French missionaries who mistrusted the Protestant origins of Taiping Christianity. The visit of the *Cassini* does not seem to have changed things greatly. Those who were hopeful about the rebellion found confirmation of their ideas in the rebel treatment of the French visitors, as did those who were sceptical. On the whole, so far as British views on the rebellion were concerned, things remained as they were immediately after Bonham's visit.[33]

The journey of the newly appointed American Commissioner, Robert McLane, in the *Susquehannah* at the end of May 1854 had a more disturbing effect. McLane reported very unfavourably on the Taiping attitude towards 'tributary' nations and on their religious and political organization.[34] According to Bowring's report of this visit to Clarendon, although McLane thought the rebels might still succeed in overthrowing the reigning dynasty he saw 'nothing among them out of which a future Imperial dynasty can be permanently constructed'. Bowring himself still expressed the hope that 'this most extraordinary movement' would somehow still facilitate 'the opening of China, the development of commerce and the altimate reception of gospel truth', but the prospects of all this actually happening as a consequence of the rebellion were clearly receding.[35]

They receded still further, virtually to vanishing-point, after the visit of two British vessels *Rattler* and *Styx* to Nanking a few weeks after the return of the American vessel. The *Rattler* and *Styx* were sent up by Bowring with the object of obtaining information both about the rebels and about trade and coaling prospects on the Yangtze. Bowring at this time was attempting to negotiate a revision of the 1842 treaty with the Manchu authorities, and hoped that this would include the right to trade on the Yangtze, hence the double object of the visit. It was led by W. H. Medhurst, son of the missionary and at that time Chinese Secretary at Hong Kong, and by Bowring's own son, Lewin, who had accompanied him to China for a short time to act as his private secretary. Bowring himself did not make the visit, as some writers on the subject mistakenly suggest.

No official report of this visit was ever published,[36] but it was of hardly less significance than Bonham's in determining the official British attitude towards the rebellion. It greatly strengthened the already perceptible swing of foreign opinion against the movement and, although it did not immediately alter official British policy it made any future movement of that policy in a pro-rebel direction very unlikely.

The first summary report was such, as Bowring commented to Clarendon, 'as not to leave a shadow of doubt as to the political or religious nature of the movement'. Medhurst and Lewin Bowring were baffled in their attempts to reach higher Taiping authorities and by what they called 'the misguided and absurd pretensions, religious and political, put forward by the promoters of this remarkable movement'. Though no actual insults were offered, 'beyond styling us as "Barbarians" and issuing letters to us in the form of mandates', yet it was evident that there was little disposition on the rebel side for friendly communication, they reported. They saw 'no indication whatever of any popular demonstration of sympathy with the views of the Insurgents, no commerce or traffic of any kind going on' and no evidence that any 'properly organized form of government' existed among them, though they added, not very consistently, that implicit obedience was shown to the commands of the higher rebel authorities. They noticed 'a total absence of men of age, of education or of respectability', and concluded that the rebels appeared to have 'no money or resources adequate to maintain a long protracted struggle, and their ultimate success appears from what we saw to be very problematical'.[37]

The full report submitted by Medhurst and Lewin Bowring a few days later simply expanded this catalogue of condemnation, significantly adding anticipations of ultimate collision between the rebels and the Western powers. Scepticism as to the real effectiveness of the Taiping prohibition of tobacco- and opium-smoking was expressed with the comment that 'it is doubtful whether the leaders of the movement implicitly follow these tenets'. On the religious question, the claims of Yang, the Eastern King, to such titles as 'Holy Ghost' were presented as by no means the result of simple ignorance but rather of blasphemous arrogance. There was, therefore, little hope that missionary labours among them would meet with any success.[38]

The justice and accuracy of these reports from Medhurst and Lewin Bowring are perhaps open to some question. The prevailing tone in them is less one of open-minded scepticism, as in the case of Bonham's report of 1853, as of marked hostility and impatience. Like nearly all other official British visitors to rebel-held territory, Medhurst's and Bowring's view was limited, and no doubt to some extent distorted, by the fact that they saw only the river face of the rebellion at centres which were more or less constantly under threat of attack from Imperial forces. There were never to be many first-hand reports from the interior, where conditions were, at least at certain periods, more settled and normal. But although they certainly cannot be accepted as completely objective or completely accurate in their delineation of the rebellion, these reports, coming as they did soon after similar reports by French and American observers, naturally seemed to provide irrefutable proof of the decline and hopelessness of the movement. The remarkable replies of Yang to the queries put to him, and the no less remarkable questions he asked in turn, did nothing to lighten the picture.

The 1854 visit thus marked the virtually complete abandonment of the qualified hopes in the rebellion occasionally expressed during 1853. The policy of armed and watchful neutrality was far from being abandoned, and the Taipings continued to be thought of as serious rebels with genuine political objectives, though with little promise of being capable of achieving them. But whereas in August 1853 Bonham had expressed the view that more political and commercial advantages were likely to be obtained from the rebels than from the imperialists, by July 1854 Bowring, in sending the full report of the *Rattler-Styx* visit to Clarendon, observed that future

British commercial relations with China 'are certainly not likely to be served by the progress of the rebellion, but rather endangered thereby'. Clarendon, acknowledging Bowring's despatch and the reports enclosed in it, noted with regret that 'the Mission appears to have only been successful in establishing the fact that the person styled as the Eastern King is an impudent impostor, and that the Imperial Authorities are more friendly to Great Britain than the Rebels'.[39]

One other aspect of British policy in China in the years 1853–55 which is relevant to any assessment of its bearing towards the rebellion remains to be noted. This is the attempt at treaty revision made by Bowring, with the co-operation of the American Commissioner, McLane, during 1854. These negotiations have been seen as an ill-advised attempt to revive the policy advocated by Alcock at the beginning of 1853, namely, to persuade the Manchu government to make further trading and diplomatic concessions in return for aid against the rebellion, and their failure has been explained as stemming from 'the fallacious assumption originating with Bonham that the desperate Manchu court would meet whatever demands the foreign powers might make in order to obtain their assistance in suppressing the rebellion'.[40] Apart from attributing to Bonham views which he did not really hold, at any rate after March 1853, this argument is open to objection on other counts. In the first place neither Bowring nor McLane were under the delusion that the Manchu court was 'desperate' for help against the Taipings, and in the second place there seems to be no firm evidence to support the idea that they actually tried to negotiate on this basis.

On the contrary, even when Bowring made his opening move in April 1854 by sending Medhurst with a despatch to Governor Yeh at Canton requesting a meeting on the question of treaty revision, the idea of offering aid to the Imperialists against the rebels was explicitly rejected. Bowring told Medhurst that he might 'have an opportunity of referring to the disorganized state of China, and of stating that the Authorities both at Shanghai and Amoy, have applied to the British Consuls for intervention and assistance', but Medhurst was also to state that 'it is not the purpose of our Government to interfere in the contentions which unhappily prevail in China unless the duty of providing for the safety of British subjects, or British property, should require interference'.[41] Bowring certainly thought of the possibility of negotiating on the basis of aid in return for trading concessions, and asked Clarendon in a private letter, 'What if a condition *could* be obtained from the Tartar dynasty that they would *open China* if the Western powers would give them support?'[42] But this was presented as only one possibility among several, and Bowring was never authorized to test it. He used the rebellion as a talking-point during these negotiations, but only as a useful means of putting pressure on the Imperial government by threatening to come to terms with the rebels, not by offering to help suppress them, though no doubt he would have liked to have been able to do so.

When, after fruitless negotiations at Canton and Shanghai, Bowring and McLane eventually went north to the Peiho in October their interpreters, Medhurst and Parker, had a series of conversations with lesser Chinese officials before they themselves met an Imperial envoy, Ch'ung-lun, in front of the Taku forts on November 3, 1854. Medhurst submitted a long report to Bowring on these preliminary conversations. On October 18, after discussing the duty question at Shanghai, Medhurst went on to speak of his visit to Nanking a few months earlier, and told the Imperial officials of 'the progress of the rebellion in the Yangtseekeang valley, the power and resources of the insurgents, their willingness to trade with us, the entire absence of Imperial authority and the consequent removal of all actual obligation on our part to apply the Treaty in these regions'. The picture he drew of the Taipings for the benefit of the Imperial authorities in the north was thus strikingly different from that he had drawn for Bowring in July. At Shanghai they had been presented as backward, disorganized and declining, but at Taku it was more expedient to present them as flourishing, powerful and co-operative, in short as a group to whom the British might credibly turn if they failed to get what they wanted from the Manchu government.

This threat, unreal though it was given the true state of official British opinion about the rebellion by this stage, was made quite explicitly in further conversations held a week later. Medhurst then told the Imperial officials that the Western powers 'were aware that the Chinese Empire was in a disorganized condition, that the Dynasty itself was in peril . . . they desired nothing more than to see the Dynasty upheld and order restored throughout the Empire. But if their friendly and reasonable advances were rejected, nothing remained for them but to take such steps as they might deem fit to revive their trade and protect their interests independently of the Imperial government—and they might possibly find it necessary to enter into negotiations with the Insurgents.'[43] All this might perhaps be interpreted as an oblique invitation, Chinese fashion, to take up the question of aid against the rebels, but if this was really what Bowring and McLane wanted they would hardly have failed to press the point more directly at some stage. In fact there was nothing in their own conversations with Ch'ung-lun on November 3 about aid against the rebels, and they returned to the south empty-handed.[44]

This is what, on the whole, they had expected to happen. In pursuing these protracted negotiations up and down the coast of China their immediate aim was to exhaust the diplomatic means at their disposal for persuading the Manchu government to accept the principle of treaty revision. 'The move upon the Peiho is a grave measure', Bowring admitted to Clarendon privately, 'very doubtful in its results, except that it will enable us to say "we have exhausted every peaceful effort to obtain the changes which the state of things in China necessitates".'[45] Except in rare moments of optimism Bowring did not expect immediate results, as he surely would had he gone to the north ready to make a firm offer of aid in return for concessions. With Britain at war with Russia and his instructions from the Foreign Office frequently enjoining strict neutrality upon him he was simply not in a position to bargain in this way. In reporting the failure of the negotiations he emphasized that at least now there could be no doubt that British grievances about the treaty were well known to the court, despite Yeh's obstructionism at Canton. 'But I doubt much if peace will be maintained without the demonstration of war', he added.[46] To his son Edgar he wrote philosophically, after it was all over, 'I am by no means dissatisfied with the progress I have made. For at all events I have cleared much rubbish away and have enabled "my masters" to see pretty clearly the state of things.'[47] The way was cleared, when events and his 'masters' would permit, for a more forward policy.

The British situation in China was clearly approaching a crisis. Nothing had been achieved by efforts to persuade the Manchu government to make further diplomatic and commercial concessions, and practically all faith in the Taipings as a possible alternative government had been abandoned. China seemed both intractable and chaotic, and unless Britain was prepared to be content with the gains made in 1842, gains which might become nearly worthless if the prevailing state of rebellion continued and spread, then a change in British policy towards either the Manchu government or the rebellion, or both, was bound to come. During 1854–55, however, no one saw very clearly just what the change ought to be, or how best to bring it about. In the Foreign Office, indeed, there was no disposition to try to bring it about. Bowring's suggestion that a demonstration of force was needed was squashed. Clarendon told him very firmly that 'Such a course would be doubtful as a matter of right and very questionable as matter of policy . . . it is therefore the positive injunction of Her Majesty's government that you abstain from raising unnecessarily questions with the Chinese government calculated to make a recourse to force incumbent on this country . . . . You will take no part, directly or indirectly, in the Civil contests now raging in China. Your duty is to remain a quiet observer of events which may be passing around you, keeping Her Majesty's Government fully informed of what is passing, but holding yourself aloof from all participation in the intestine troubles of the Country.'[48] So far as the British government was concerned there were more important issues at stake at the beginning of 1855 than the fate of British trade in China.

British officials in China, however, although obliged to remain 'quiet observers', could not help but search for some way out of what seemed to them a frustrating and dangerous situation. The assumptions upon which British policy had been based since the emergence of the rebellion as a major force in China began to be questioned. Neither of the contingencies upon which his instructions were grounded were likely to result from the civil struggle in China, Bowring claimed in the middle of 1854. 'I do not expect the present Manchu dynasty will be able to maintain its authority over a large part of the Chinese territory; nor do I believe that the Nanking rebels are by any means likely to establish a Government which will be generally recognized or obeyed in China.' In these circumstances the demands for protection of British interests in China were likely to increase, and thereby the danger of involvement in China's internal struggles also. Bowring was clearly apprehensive of the possible results. 'It is impossible to turn away our attention from consequences contingent upon such interference. The history of British India is full of instruction . . . it is no unusual characteristic of the Anglo-Saxon race, when settling in foreign regions, that they begin by trading and end by governing. It is only by anticipating the great tendencies of events that our policy can be safely guided. I do not hesitate to state to your lordship that I have often my misgivings lest the future should re-tell the tale of British India, over a vaster field, on a grander scale and with larger interests involved.'[49]

A radical Whig and Free Trader, Bowring was no spokesman for extending the political bounds of Empire. Indeed, there were few such in England in the mid-nineteenth century, and the lesson of the Mutiny in India in 1857 was to serve to reinforce the sort of fear expressed by Bowring in 1854, for that event made the expense and danger of formal empire in Asia seem all too plain. One of the objects behind the later British policy of giving direct aid to the Manchus was, in fact, to prevent the crisis in China developing to the point where Britain had either to govern the country herself in order to trade or not trade at all. As early as 1854–55 British officials in China were beginning to feel that a situation was developing in which such a choice might have to be made. But for the time they could only continue to wait upon the development of events in China and in Europe. It seemed a frustrating and unrewarding position, remaining neutral between two sides, one of which was unlikely to be able and the other had proved quite unwilling to widen the openings for British trade with the most populous empire in the world.

4

The Public Response
(1853-56)

THE DISAPPOINTMENT by 1855 of such official hopes as there had been that the rebellion would somehow improve the British position in China was paralleled among interested groups outside the circle of official policy-makers also. It is not apparent that official policy was in any significant way influenced by these outside views. Nevertheless, they deserve some attention as part of the total British response to the rebellion, although the uneven and scattered nature of the record, involving as it does missionaries, merchants and press, both on the China coast and at home, makes the task of description and definition a considerably less tidy one than for the official view.

More than any other group, the missionaries had a vital interest in the rebellion. Some writers, indeed, have seen in the failure of the missionaries to support the Taipings vigorously and consistently the passing of their one great opportunity to bring about the widespread conversion of China to Christianity.[1] Although it may be doubted whether the rebellion really offered them so great an opportunity as this, it certainly posed a great problem and a great challenge for the missionaries.

Their reaction to the rebellion has generally been presented as moving from enthusiastic and largely uncritical support for it in its early years to total and intolerant rejection of it in its last years.[2] This is broadly the spectrum as it appears in the records of British missionary societies, but the sharpness of contrast can easily be exaggerated. The reaction of British missionaries to the startling and confusing phenomenon of a seemingly Christian movement of native revolt was itself confused, and although often enthusiastic and unguarded was never without its hesitations and its qualifications. Their eventual rejection of the Taipings as too heretical and authoritarian to be acceptable as allies in the task of Christian conversion before them was clearly implicit in many of their earliest comments upon the rebellion.

The situation of the Protestant missionaries in China during the years preceding the rebellion was certainly such as to predispose them towards welcoming it enthusiastically. Converts were few, difficulties many and the immediate prospects poor. 'That the Lord will choose to bless this numerous people in His own good time I doubt not,' wrote one Anglican missionary in 1848, 'but that there is yet a stirring among the "dry bones" I do not think, at least to any extent.'³ In 1853 the Presbyterian William Burns observed that he had laboured for seven years in China, but 'I do not know of a single soul brought to Christ by me',⁴ and the London Missionary Society's representatives at Shanghai felt 'not a little gratified' that after nine years of labour by several missionaries there they could speak of a native church of twenty-one members.⁵ The home society philosophically concluded that, 'in a country where the prevailing systems of belief and the social usages of the entire population have been stereotyped for ages . . . it can be no matter for surprise that the indefatigable labours of our Missionaries in China, though followed by many tokens of encouragement, have hitherto made little or no impression upon the masses of the people'.⁶

Having faith, the missionaries did not despair, but being human they looked for a sign. It is not surprising, therefore, that they greeted news of a Chinese movement of reform which proclaimed some kind of a Christian ideology with great joy and enthusiasm. Yet it was a joy and enthusiasm tempered from the very beginning with a considerable element of caution, and even of doubt. This is apparent in the report of the first missionary to make direct contact with the rebels, the Rev. W. H. Medhurst, the senior London Missionary Society representative at Shanghai and father of the consular official of the same name and initials. Medhurst accompanied Bonham on his visit

48

to Nanking in April 1853, and there collected and translated a number of rebel religious publications, on the Christian worth of which he reported cautiously that he found it 'exceedingly difficult to arrive at a definite conclusion. There are some things good, very good, in the productions before us. . . . There are, however, some things of which we most highly disapprove.'[7]

On the day following Medhurst's return from Nanking his colleagues at Shanghai requested the home society that, should it publish any account of his visit, it gives the whole, 'coupled with a caution not to look at the fair side of the picture only, nor be carried away by those semblances of *good* that perhaps are after all hollow and false, while they are mixed up with much that is undoubtedly presumptuous and criminal'.[8] The Rev. J. Hobson, in forwarding Medhurst's translations of the Taiping pamphlets to the Church Missionary Society, observed that 'while on the one hand they will grieve you by showing marks of rampant pride and ambition in the leaders of the rebellion, and worse than these a systematic attempt to wrest Christian truth to serve mere political purposes, on the other hand you will rejoice to see these men in possession of so much Christian truth . . .'.[9] The emphasis varied, but the early reports of British missionaries on the rebellion did emphasize both the hopeful and the less hopeful features of the movement, as seen from the missionary viewpoint.

On the basis of such reports the home societies in England warned their supporters against excessive optimism. The Committee of the Church Missionary Society, while noting the enthusiasm of many Christians for the movement, did not itself go beyond the expression of 'hopeful but anxious expectations'. It saw many tokens of the good hand of the Lord in this new development in China, but was anxious 'lest the evils which now hover above the movement should settle upon it—of religious fanaticism, or of reactionary vengeance, or of destructive socialism . . .'.[10] The London Missionary Society, in publishing its first reports on the movement in September 1853, warned that 'the better element that characterizes the movement is evidently mixed up with much that is heterogeneous and immoral'. At the end of the year the warning was repeated that Taiping religious development was 'very partial and imperfect', and it was 'doubted whether the chiefs and teachers of the

Chinese Insurgents can even be regarded as *almost* Christians'.[11] Both in China and in Britain early missionary reaction to the rebellion was far from unguarded in its optimism.[12]

This is not to deny that hope in fact mounted far higher in missionary circles than did doubt, nor that an immense improvement in the missionary's position and prospects in China was looked for as a result of the rebellion. 'As a missionary, when I came to China, I felt all around the gloom of midnight darkness', wrote the Wesleyan, Josiah Cox, from Canton. 'Now the clouds are breaking and [though] I know not what the day may bring I hail the glimmering dawn.'[13] Especially encouraging to the missionaries was the prospect of China being thrown open by a government friendly to them and their teachings, for little doubt was entertained that the fall of the Manchus was imminent. The Rev. W. Muirhead of the London Mission felt that, 'the prospect thus presented to our view is indeed too glowing to be pressed. Should the country be thrown open, should we be permitted to penetrate into the regions beyond and unfold to their myriad, myriad inhabitants the tidings of a Saviour's love, it were a privilege too great to be realized in thought.'[14] The Bishop of Victoria even speculated on the possibility of a native Christian ministry being drawn from the ranks of the rebels, while Medhurst looked forward to the day when the Christian scriptures would replace the Confucian classics as the examination texts of China.[15] The Bishop, who was one of the most enthusiastic in his support of the rebellion, reported to the Church Missionary Society that it appeared to be 'a wonderful moral revolution. We behold a hundred-thousand Chinese living separated from their wives, abstaining from wine, opium, tobacco, quarrelling, lying and bad words, and engaging in daily worship, a common table, a common treasury—and no pay.'[16] There could hardly be a more far-reaching change.

At home also the same enthusiasm was to be found. William Gillespie, a former London Missionary Society agent in China, called the rebellion a 'mighty moral miracle', while the *Chinese Missionary Gleaner*, the organ of the Chinese Evangelization Society, which was the forerunner of the later China Inland Mission, was persuaded that 'these men will ultimately prove the pioneers of the greatest work that has been accomplished since the days of the apostles. The axe is laid at the root of idolatry, and the decayed trunk will soon fall'.[17] Strongest proof of popular faith in the movement was provided by the Million New Testament Scheme, launched by the British and Foreign Bible Society.[18] The subscription target, calculated at fourpence a copy, was quickly passed and the two-million mark reached by June 1854. Mid-nineteenth-century Britain wanted very much to hasten the conversion, which would also be the opening, of China.

There were some, however, who even in 1853 viewed the movement with suspicion, if not with actual hostility. The *Christian Times*, although approving a policy of neutrality, was convinced that it was all a Jesuit plot, and that Taiping Christianity was 'a palpable and offensive imposture'. Premature hopes and hasty sympathies could not be too carefully discouraged, it insisted.[19] A Rev. W. H. Rule also argued that the teaching of the insurgents was 'but a continuation or reproduction of the elementary teaching of the Jesuits in China', and saw nothing to further the cause of evangelical Christianity in the movement.[20] But for many others the rebellion was not only Christian but Protestant, and its supposed Protestantism was for them its great virtue. The influence on Hung of the tracts he received from a Protestant missionary at Canton in 1836; his later brief association with the American Baptist, I. J. Roberts; the printing and circulation of portions of scripture in Protestant translations by the rebels; their destruction of Chinese temples and idols; the hostility shown towards them by Catholic missionaries in China—all these things were taken as evidence of the essentially Protestant nature of the movement. The committee of the Church Missionary Society reported in October 1853 that 'It is with Protestant Christianity these people sympathize, not with Romanism. The idolatry of Rome is utterly repugnant to them. But to Protestant Christianity they look as a kindred element, and in their ignorance of its real character, believe it to be identical with their own religious views.'[21]

This concern to fit the Taiping movement into Western religious categories was the great limitation in the attitude of the Protestant missionaries towards it. Their failure to consider the possibility of a Christian movement which was neither Protestant nor Catholic but simply Chinese made their ultimate disappointment in it certain. But given their intellectual background, compounded of a rigorous set of religious beliefs and of the assumption (by no means peculiar to the missionary) that all things Western were superior to anything Chinese; and given also the claims made by Hung and other Taiping leaders to new and authoritative Divine revelation, it would have been surprising had the missionaries adjusted themselves easily to so Chinese a form of Christianity as this. The thought of Hung Hsiu-ch'uan, like the thought of Mao Tse-t'ung, added too many new strands to the received doctrine to be readily acceptable to the old believers.

What is surprising, however, is that the missionaries made so little positive effort in the first years of the rebellion to influence the Taiping rebellion in the direction of greater Protestant orthodoxy. They talked of this and saw the danger of still greater heresy if they did not. Yet apart from the attempts of a few missionaries, mainly American, to reach Nanking, no serious effort seems to have been made during 1853–54 to establish a permanent mission among the rebels. The difficult and changing military situation and probably also discouragement of such an enterprise from the consular authorities help to explain this, but in view of their mixed fears and hopes about the nature of the movement it seems hardly to have been consistent with their own large objectives in China.[22] There was not even any significant increase in the number of missionaries in the China field in the years after 1853, and at the end of that year Medhurst was writing that the rebels were 'a class of men that can with difficulty be controlled. They must for a time be allowed to go their own way. It may not be in every respect the way which we could approve, but it does not appear to run directly counter to our objects. In the meantime we can go on in ours.'[23] Such a policy invited the growth of heresy, but until the end of 1858 there were no further direct contacts between British missionaries and the rebels.

During these years, the decline in the fortunes of the rebellion on the one hand and the improved prospects created for the missionaries as a result of the second opium war on the other meant that less and less consideration was given to the possible place of the Taipings in missionary plans for the conversion of China. The element of doubt became more marked in their observations on the rebellion and its prospects, now made only occasionally. Alexander Wylie reported to the London Missionary Society in June 1854 on the 'evident reaction in the popular mind' in China following the visit of the American Commissioner, McLane, to Nanking and observed that 'The arrogance of their assumptions, one chief calling himself the Son of God, and another entitling himself the Holy Spirit, has given rise to a feeling of disappointment in the minds of many of their friends. . . . That Tae-ping-wang will succeed in subverting the present dynasty there seems little room for doubt. Whether he will realize the high anticipations that have been formed respecting his religious character is more open to doubt.'[24] On receiving this report the secretary of the London Missionary Society confessed himself 'greatly perplexed and dismayed by the extravagant and blasphemous doctrines recently preached by [Hung]', adding that while it was 'difficult at first to disengage the mind from the pleasant illusions which so fair a beginning had inspired' it was clear that much missionary labour would have to be expended yet before China was converted.[25] The Taipings no longer seemed likely allies in this work. By September 1855 Medhurst was admitting that 'we cannot but withhold our assent to their being denominated Christian brethren until we know more of them, and are enabled to separate the precious from the vile'.[26]

The death of Yang, the Eastern King, in 1856, encouraged some to hope that 'the most mischievous and dangerous element in the revolution has thus been taken away', but the *Church Missionary Record* warned that 'with such internal elements among the Taiping leaders, it will be wise for the friends of Christian missions to form very moderate expectations of the immediate results to the cause of true Christianity'.[27] The Chinese Evangelization Society clung more persistently than any other missionary body in Britain to its early high hopes in the rebellion, and in January 1857 was still hoping for 'the best from this remarkable movement. The good even at present far outweighs the evil.'[28] But by that time missionary opinion generally, both at home and in China, had moved very far from the hopes of 1853.

The same is true for merchant and other public opinion, both in England and on the China coast. On the coast, indeed, the English-language press was deeply divided over the merits of the rebellion even in the year of its greatest success, and although the decidedly anarchical tone and highly personal nature of the journalism of this press makes one doubt at times whether its strongly worded editorials represent anything more than the personal prejudices of individual editors and proprietors, it is reasonable to assume that it gives some kind of a reflection of the range of British opinion on the China coast. In so far as this coastal press is a guide, it shows that there was always much scepticism, not to say hostility, towards the rebellion among British residents in China, and that by mid-1854 even its keenest supporters among them had tempered their earlier hopes considerably.

The two most consistently hostile papers at this time were the *China Mail* and the *Register*, both published at Hong Kong. As early as February 1851 the *Mail* had attacked the rebels as 'nothing more than freebooters who attempt to conceal their real character under a pretence of patriotism', and throughout 1853 it maintained a critical stand, discounting both the religious fervour of the movement and its chances of ultimate success. 'The restoration of tranquillity under a purely Chinese dynasty is an event which we fear few of our age are likely to witness', it insisted in October 1853. It was also critical of Bonham's policy as unduly tender of rebel interests, and condemned his neutrality proclamation of July 7 as 'negatively supporting the Rebels'.[29] For the *Register* the rebellion was 'a dark and ominous affair' which time alone would unravel. It doubted whether anything would be gained by substituting a Taiping for a Manchu dynasty, and attacked the 'stupid irreflecting wonder' of those who took the religious aspect of the movement seriously.[30]

A particular object of attack for both the *Mail* and the *Register* was the Shanghai-published *North China Herald*, which, after some early uncertainty, came down enthusiastically and even rhapsodically in support of the rebellion by April 1853. It was, the *Herald* claimed, 'an intellectual, yea a moral, nay more a religious movement such as the world has never witnessed'.[31] This paper looked forward to early and complete success for the rebels, and was confident that under Hung's more enlightened rule 'our merchants will speedily exchange present difficulties and impediments for all the advantages of a free, reciprocal and unblemished traffick'.[32] By the middle of 1854, however, after reports of the visits to Nanking by McLane, Medhurst and Lewin Bowring, the *Herald* felt obliged to modify its views, to the great satisfaction of its Hong Kong rivals, and to admit that 'crazy and deluded fanatics' were in possession of Nanking.[33] For some time it still refused to take an actively anti-rebel stand and continued to argue strongly against any kind of intervention in the struggle, but it now felt it useless to speculate upon the 'obscure workings' of the movement. The Canton-published *Friend of China* was more consistent in its support of the rebels, whom it referred to always as 'patriots', but even it admitted in August 1854 that it was 'disappointed and shocked at their recent proceedings'.[34]

As already suggested, how far all this may be taken as reflecting any specific viewpoint among British residents on the China coast about the rebellion is uncertain, but it should be noted that a recent study of this China coast press says of the pro-Taiping *Friend of China* that it 'may be considered as writing in the interests of the mercantile community, from which it received considerable financial and personal support', whereas the anti-rebel *China Mail* is described as not automatically supporting merchant opinion, with which it had no personal ties.[35] From this it might be inferred that the merchants' hopes in the rebellion, like the missionaries', were very high during 1853, and not much dampened until the latter half of 1854. The evidence provided by the detailed business correspondence of Jardine, Matheson & Co., the largest of the British trading firms on the China coast at this time, suggests, however, that the merchant reaction was always rather guarded and less concerned about possible improvement in long-term prospects than about immediate profits.

For the years 1853 to 1855 the Jardine, Matheson correspondence reveals no very decided views either for or against the rebels, but it does reveal doubts as to their real attitude towards foreigners and much concern for their immediate effect upon trade. At the end of April 1853 David Jardine reported the 'disheartening intelligence' of the fall of Nanking to some of his correspondents in India, adding: 'It is said that the rebels of late have expressed no friendly feelings towards Foreigners in consequence of a number of American vessels purchased by the Chinese authorities having proceeded up the river towards Nankin.'[36] To others he expressed the conviction that, 'it is now pretty evident that whichever of the Contending parties prevails, the disorganized state of the country will continue to exercise an injurious influence on all commerce for some time to come'.[37] Dallas, the firm's agent in Shanghai, also reported in April that 'Nothing certain is known as to the intentions of the rebels towards foreigners, but as they have a large army and are likely to be joined by all the vagabonds in the country, it is thought only prudent to be prepared for any contingency'.[38]

Later reports on the rebels do not appear to have caused any marked swing in their favour. In June 1853 Jardine reported that 'the opinion is beginning to force itself upon people's minds that the days of Tartar rule in China are numbered', but gave no sign of himself regarding this prospect with any particular approval.[39] At the end of July, Dallas still felt considerable doubt about the ultimate designs of the rebels towards foreigners, and showed no confidence that commercial prospects would be better under Taiping than under Manchu rule.[40] During 1854 and 1855 the suppression of the risings on the coast was greeted with relief and approval.[41] As a source of evidence on the views of British merchants on the China coast about the rebellion in its early years, the Jardine, Matheson correspondence suggests that they never felt sure enough about the attitude of the rebel leaders towards foreigners and foreign trade to accord it any very positive support.[42]

In Britain itself merchant views seem to have been, in keeping with public opinion generally, more decidedly sympathetic to the rebels. It is true that early in 1853 one firm, Moffatt & Co., issued a circular expressing concern for tea supplies and suggesting the desirability of foreign intervention against the rebellion, but its views were firmly rejected by the *Economist* and by Lawson's *Merchant Magazine*.[43] The latter journal was sharply critical of 'the laxity of morals with respect to the rights of independent nations' reflected in such a proposal, but it also went on to attack those who indulged in exaggerated anticipations of the results likely to flow from the rebellion. The disposition of the rebels towards foreigners and foreign trade was still a matter for conjecture, it insisted in June, and any increase in trade which might result from their victory would at best be gradual.[44] This journal also expressed scepticism as to the real chances of rebel success and argued that little commercial benefit was likely to be found in China. 'If we want new markets we must seek them elsewhere; in this quarter the "opening" for extension is narrow indeed.'[45]

In the middle months of 1853 such sober ideas as to the probable effect of the rebellion would appear to have been exceptional among those concerned with the extension of trade with China, and most preferred to believe that Christian rebellion in China must bring considerable commercial advantages with it. As one editorial expressed it, 'Hitherto Christianity and Commerce have gone together. As Christianity spreads, civilization will grow, with all its corresponding wants. It is impossible to anticipate the effect of Christianization upon China. No country in the world is better adapted from situation, climate and products for extensive commerce.'[46] The two ideas went naturally together in mid-nineteenth-century Britain, so that the fact that the rebels were believed to be well disposed to Christianity made them also appear to be well disposed towards trade.[47]

News of the success of the Taipings in 1853 was, indeed, welcomed above all for the promise it seemed to contain that the traditional isolation and exclusivism of China was at last about to be broken down from within. The author of one of several popular accounts of the rebellion which appeared during 1853 and the early months of 1854 wrote enthusiastically that 'The issue of the contest now going on will be the opening of China to the European world. It is impossible to overrate the wonderful significance of these words—the opening of China. The greatest, the most compact, the most intelligent, the most enterprising, the most industrious and the most populous nation of the East . . . will then form part of the vast union of civilization which has metamorphosed the West, and must produce still greater revolution in the East.'[48] The *Daily News* anticipated that the insurrection would 'end in bringing the immense Empire of the East into communion with Western civilization', and *The Times* that it would help to 'complete that circle of civilization and unrestricted intercourse which will one day encompass the globe'.[49] Unlike British observers in China itself, there were few at home in 1853 who doubted that success for the rebellion would mean a vast extension of and improvement in British relations with China.

It is some measure of the confidence and optimism of mid-Victorian Britain that there was no sense of alarm at the prospects of a great nation with ten times the population of Britain itself setting out along the path of 'progress' and entering the world community. Change had to come to the 'obscure nations of the earth', such as China, India and Japan, the *Morning Post* observed. These were now being sought out by the nations of the West. 'They see their betters, mingle with them, imitate them, learn their arts and share their improvements. To this "genius" of our "epoch" China, like the rest of the world, must yield and is yielding. . . . By the force of circumstances, China must be revolutionized.' It would indeed be less a revolution than 'a fearful awakening', the *Post* added. But fearful for China, not for the West. 'Four hundred millions coming suddenly upon the knowledge that all their philosophy is a lie will be an unprecedented spectable. A trying crisis will that be when the Celestial Empire opens its eyes to read that all along it has treasured up a false history, a false geography, a false chronology, a false morality, a false religion. . . . '[50] The popular *Chambers's Edinburgh Journal* felt more simply that, now that 'the spell which has hitherto made this singular people move in circles' was about to be broken, a great and interesting future lay ahead for China.[51] Although at least one voice was raised to protest against the 'common but preposterous notion that this most ancient of empires had undergone no changes since its first establishment', and to suggest that the rebellion would inaugurate 'a stirring and revival of the national intellect . . . which will astonish the self-complacent critics of the West',[52] for the most part it was a confidently patronizing interest which was displayed towards the prospect of a new China regenerated under Taiping leadership.

The reported Christian character of the rebellion naturally evoked much enthusiasm. The author of a *History of the Christian Missions and of the Present Insurrection*, another of the popular accounts published about this time, was confident that the genius of Christianity had 'at length penetrated the very heart of the oldest empire in the world' and gave a highly romantic account of how 'a small band of Protestant Missionaries, with the Bible in hand and clothed in the armour of Truth, succeeded in penetrating into the very heart of the country, and laying prostrate the superstition and idolatry of five thousand years'.[53] The *Standard* also rejoiced especially in the Protestantism of the rebels, and with a nice sense of discrimination dismissed charges of polygamy against them. 'This we do not believe of any *Protestant*, though we can easily understand how difficult it may be to prevail upon the newly converted polygamists to put away all their supernumary wives.' Some deviations in doctrine and teaching were to be expected, but it was enough that 'the Holy work of bringing three hundred millions of human beings to [Christian] light has been auspiciously commenced'.[54] The *British Journal* also thought that Taiping religious publications breathed 'the purest Christian philanthropy', excepting only the punishment of death imposed for looking on Hung's harem.[55] The *Eastern Star* described the rebellion as 'a Christian, liberal, progressive movement against the savage, cruel, lop-sided despotism of the Mantchus'.[56]

Such views were certainly very widely held, especially among the numerous readers of religious journals, but against them must be set more critical assessments of the religious character of the movement. *The Times*, for example, felt that 'although the foundation of their faith may be Christian, there is nothing to show that the superstructure is not as extravagant a superstition as Mormonism itself and, as we have seen, they proselytize by massacre as much as by faith'.[57] John Oxenford, the translator of Callery and Yvan's *History of the Insurrection of China*, the book which was the basis for most early accounts of the movement, reversed the emphasis of *The Times* and judged that the rebels were 'orthodox Confucians with a superstructure of spurious Christianity',[58] but in neither case were the rebels seen as propagators of anything like a 'pure' form of Christianity. The *Spectator* wrote of 'Christianity à la Chinoise' and the *Daily News*, while welcoming the rebellion as the commencement of great moral and intellectual changes for China, emphasized that Taiping Christianity was 'defiled by the admixture of much that is degrading and superstitious'.[59]

59

In one of the most judicious of the articles on the rebellion which appeared during 1853 the *Quarterly Review* argued that it was far from impossible that the rebels would yet receive a check, and warned that nothing was really known of the disposition of the people at large towards the new creed. 'All ordinary experience is against their throwing up their ancient superstitions at the mere bidding of any army who are but a handful of the vast population, and if the rebels win the prize it is no unlikely alternative that they will compromise their creed to consolidate the throne.'[60] Critical and balanced comments on the religious aspect of the rebellion were by no means lacking in 1853, therefore, but since they mainly appeared in the more serious political and literary journals they certainly did not at once dispel more fervent and uncritical hopes.

The view suggested by the *Quarterly Review* and others that the rebellion was essentially a political rather than a religious movement, was argued most strongly in a work called *The Cross and the Dragon*. Basing his argument largely on the evident weakness of the Christian missions in China, its author maintained that the rebellion must be 'but feebly charged with the spiritual element'. Its real strength came from the secret societies, and in that sense it was a rebellion in traditional Chinese style, 'only a repetition of phenomena that have startled and annoyed the governments of the empire of China, at various periods, during the last two centuries'.[61] As a political movement the rebellion won no less general approval in Britain than as a religious movement, however, and the likelihood of its early success in overthrowing the Manchus was rarely questioned. *The Times* noted with approval in mid-August that the progress of the rebels 'or rather of the "patriot army", as it is now called by our Eastern informants, continues as wonderful as ever. To us, of course, nothing can be so intelligible as that a nation should suddenly throw off the authority of an alien and hated race. The wonder was', it added, confidently changing tense, 'how the Manchus had held China so long.'[62] For Charles Macfarlane, author of another popular account of the movement, the rebellion was in the best Whig tradition. 'The political principles put forth by the partisans seem to have been conceived in an English or Anglo-American spirit', he wrote, and the rebel government at Nanking was for him 'impressed and

permeated with European ideas, and is such a form of government as never yet originated in an Asiatic mind'.[63]

It seems clear that public reaction in Britian was more completely unanimous in its approval than was the case among
British residents in China, although some signs of a reaction at
home appeared even before the end of 1853. 'With the progress
of the Chinese rebellion a doubt also makes progress as to what
may be the effect of the movement on the ethics of the empire,
commercial as well as religious', observed the *Spectator* at the
end of October, noting possible difficulties over the religious
pretensions of the rebels, over the opium trade, and over the
general state of corruption and disruption in China which might
well end in the establishment of 'bandit adventurers' in the seat
of government. 'There appears, therefore, good reason in those
who look forward with some anxiety to the course hereafter',
the *Spectator* concluded.[64] In November *Fraser's Magazine*
expressed fears 'that the first impressions respecting the
character of the insurgents have been too favourable', while in
December the *Quarterly Review* concluded that 'with the very
limited information we possess, the conclusions that have been
formed of the ultimate issue of the rebellion appear over-
sanguine and hasty'.[65] For some time yet, however, the highly
favourable, optimistic first reaction remained the prevailing one
in Britain. At the beginning of 1854 *The Times* still felt that
'there can be no doubt that the total change of institutions
contingent upon the rebellion will communicate a new tone to
the foreign policy of the [Chinese] Government'.[66] Nevertheless,
the size of the question-mark over the rebellion was growing
rather than diminishing by the end of 1853.

During 1854 there was inevitably a considerable falling away
of public interest in the rebellion, as well as of optimism about
it. Whereas the *Athenaeum*, reviewing Oxenford's translation of
Callery and Yvan in September 1853, could say with confidence
that the book 'could hardly fail to find a curious and interested
public', by June 1854 its comment upon Gillespie's *Land of
Sinim* was that 'public attention has naturally been diverted
from the progress of the insurrection in China by the war with
Russia'.[67] By July the *Daily News* could scarcely believe that the
rebellion would 'produce any immediate great change in the
manners, the religion or the civil institutions of a people who for

five and twenty centuries have undergone little material alteration'.[68]

The reports of the McLane and the Medhurst-Bowring visits to Nanking in mid-1854 naturally tended to confirm such doubts, although *The Times* for the present maintained a charitable view of the movement, in contrast to its later extreme hostility. It was impossible to believe, it stated in September, that the Chinese had 'imbibed anything like the spirit of true Christianity', but added that there was 'no necessity for hastily despairing of Chinese Christianity, or concluding that the Divine doctrines of the Gospels have been deliberately depraved for any purpose of men. . . . It will, probably, be long before this extraordinary revolution is consummated, but we do not see that the hopes entertained of the eventual conversion of China need be despondingly abandoned.'[69] But save for occasional general reports on developments in China, papers and journals in Britain now carried but rare comments upon the Chinese rebellion. 'Intelligence from China is of the old kind', the *Spectator* observed in December 1854. 'The rebels have failed before Canton, and trade was reviving. At Shanghai they were becoming demoralized; from Nanking and Pekin there was no news.' It was not long before the wits were complaining that China, like Uranus, was slow to make a revolution.[70]

Hopes in the rebellion and its effect upon China did not completely disappear, however. An article in the *Edinburgh Review* for April 1855, prompted by the appearance of an English translation of Huc's *Travels in China*, stated that 'Revolution has occurred, and the ultimate auguries are assuredly bright, whether its immediate course be prosperous or adverse, whether it lead to the quiet establishment, at a comparatively early period, of a new and renovated empire in which Christian and European ideas shall be predominant, or whether an epoch of political anarchy and religious fanaticism be destined first to intervene'. One thing was tolerably certain, this article continued. The old exclusive empire was broken up and China was opened at last. 'Into it the elements of light, civilization and Christianity will continue to flow.'[71]

In 1855 also there appeared the book *Impressions of China* by Captain Fishbourne, who had commanded the *Hermes* on Bonham's visit to Nanking in 1853. An active supporter of the

Chinese Evangelization Society, Fishbourne expressed continued faith in the religious worth of the rebel movement, despite the baneful influence upon it of Yang, the Eastern King. For Fishbourne, as for many other sympathizers, it was the apparently un-Chinese features of the rebellion which seemed to him most remarkable and praiseworthy. He described the rebels as being 'most frank in their manner, quite unlike what we are accustomed to in Chinese. . . . It was obvious to the commonest observer that they were practically a different race. . . . The quiet self-possession of the leaders we came into contact with was quite un-Chinese.'[72] It required a conscious effort for even sympathetic British observers of that day to recognize the possibility, as *The Times* magnanimously did a few years later, that 'these Chinamen have their civilization, their affections, even their virtues'.

Fishbourne's book was variously received by the critics. A religious periodical such as the *British Quarterly Review* could praise it and echo his continuing hopes in the rebellion, but the *Athenaeum*, while still referring to 'that wonderful movement', believed that Fishbourne accepted 'too credulously the best interpretation of events', and the *Spectator* described the book as based on 'the groundless hopes and headlong reasonings of a sanguine man engaged in riding a hobby', observing of the rebels that it appeared that 'their arrogance and self-sufficiency are quite as great as those of the present Tartar rulers, with the notion of a religious superiority added'.[73] Rutherford Alcock, in an article in the *Bombay Quarterly Review* in October 1855, described Fishbourne as a 'shallow enthusiast', and took his book as the starting-point for questioning the value of the work of Protestant missions in China. As then being carried out, Alcock believed this to be 'a vast waste of money and time', and was strongly of the opinion that '*the whole work is yet to do*'. Certainly the Taipings had not advanced it, whatever Fishbourne said.[74]

By 1856 it was becoming necessary to remind people in England of the continuance of rebellion in China. 'We have almost forgotten China as a theatre of civil war', the *Manchester Examiner and Times* stated in October of that year, going on to insist that the Chinese rebellion was really of greater significance than 'movements of inferior importance nearer home', such as those of Kossuth, Garibaldi and Louis Napoleon.[75] These unusual reflections were the result of the publication of a letter from an American missionary, W. A. P. Martin, urging the American government not to give any active support to the Manchus, an object with which the *Examiner and Times* fully sympathized. This letter of Martin's also led the *Daily News* to reassert that 'the interests of the Western world are far more identified with the success of the revolution than with the perpetuation of the effete dynasty of the Mantchoos and the worn-out type of the old civilization'.[76]

The man who argued this view most thoroughly was T. T. Meadows, at home on extended leave during these middle years of the eighteen-fifties. At the end of 1856 his outstanding book, *The Chinese and Their Rebellions*, appeared. The extent to which public interest in the Taiping movement had receded by this time is reflected in the reviews which this work received at the time of publication. Apart from Meadows' involved style and poor organization of his ideas, what chiefly aroused the interest and comment of reviewers was his exposition of the principles underlying Chinese philosophy. This was a new theme, and certainly a major part of his book. But his sympathetic account of what he called 'the politico-religious rebellion' of the Taipings, which included some very perceptive observations on the economic and social content of the movement and was by far the most searching analysis of it that had until then appeared, was much less remarked upon. The reviewer in *The Times* was chiefly delighted and amused by the idea that here at last was a spokesman for the superior virtues of Chinese civilization. 'According to our loose barbarian notions the Chinese Empire is an overgrown anomaly', his review began, but now 'let the barbarians, meaning the British, henceforth perform the kotow with their faces towards the direction of Pekin, for their interpreter has come to the Flowery Land, and has been enlightened as to the inferiority of his countrymen.' Meadows' book, he suggested, corresponded with its subject in a variety of ways. 'It is studious and accurate, like the products of Chinese penmanship; it is quaintly luminous, like a Chinese lantern; it is as destitute of proportion as a Chinese picture; and it is quite as involved as a Chinese puzzle.' The idea that thought or civilization in China had much advanced over the past two

64

thousand years he completely rejected. 'The geological trans-formation of the earth's surface affords a fair parallel to Chinese advancement. Coal is made quicker than Chinese ethics, and continents grow while their philosophers sleep.' Certainly the Taipings were not now seen as being likely to hasten the process of change. They received but one brief mention at the end of the review, Meadows being described as their 'worthy historian'.[77]

In the *Eclectic Review* also it was Meadows' account of Chinese philosophy which was of chief interest, though it was observed that he 'elucidated' the revolt, and his arguments against foreign intervention were briefly commended.[78] The *Athenaeum* gave much the same emphasis, though with a little more weight on the arguments against interference. 'If the Taepings are worthy to be free they will doubtless achieve their own freedom', its reviewer commented, after a lengthy sum-mary of the 'metaphysical jargon' in which Meadows had presented his account of Chinese philosophy.[79]

The Chinese and their rebellions had indeed ceased to be a subject of much interest to the British public by the time Meadows' book appeared, and it was no best-seller.[80] Public interest in China was soon to be vigorously renewed, not by the rebellion, but by the events at Canton which led to the second opium war of 1856–60. *The Times*, which in 1853 had welcomed the Taipings as the probable means whereby 'that huge, strange-looking, amphibious hulk of antiquity—China' would be unmoored and brought into the main stream of world history, now looked to Englishmen to perform that task unaided.[81] The rebellion was becoming merely another obstacle in the way of this objective.

5

The War Years
(1856-60)

THE SOLUTION to the dilemma facing British policy in China by 1855 came not as a result of the success of the rebels, as Bonham had thought possible in 1853, nor by persuading the Manchu government to accept treaty revision, as Bowring had attempted in 1854, but by direct force of arms. The second opium war of 1856–60, fought by Britain in military alliance with France, forced the Manchu government to concede the wider openings for trade and the direct diplomatic access to Peking which had been the chief objectives of British policy in China since at least 1850. These were eventually secured by the Treaty of Tientsin (1858), supplemented by the Convention of Peking (1860). The primary concern of British policy in China thereafter became not so much the winning of further concessions as the full implementation and enjoyment of those now gained.

Certain difficulties remained in the way, however, chief among them the continuance of the Taiping rebellion in the area of greatest potential importance to the expansion of British trade, the Yangtze valley. The conditions for a change in British policy were, therefore, created by the end of 1860. A new and satisfactory treaty settlement was concluded with the existing government while the rebellion, from which no great advantage not already gained was now to be looked for, gave no sure sign of triumphing, of dying out, or of being suppressed by the unaided efforts of the Manchu government. Many historians have accordingly concluded that here was in fact the turning-point in British policy. 'Precisely in 1860' the British attitude changed; the attitude of foreigners 'suddenly took a pro-Manchu tendency'; after the Manchus had satisfied their demands the invaders 'at once turned to the Taiping revolution'—these are some of the phrases which have been used to describe the timing of the shift in British policy from neutrality to intervention.[1] In fact, however, this shift in policy did not follow immediately or inevitably upon the treaty settlement of 1860, and Great Britain moved towards a policy of intervention in a manner much less certain and abrupt than such statements as these suggest. The course of events between 1856 and 1860 was certainly such as to make a change in British policy thereafter very probable, but it was also such as to make for considerable doubt and hesitation in adopting that change.

The fortunes of the rebellion during these intermediate years were very mixed. By May 1855 the forces sent north in 1853 were finally destroyed, but in the west considerable fighting continued between the provincial armies of Tseng Kuo-fan and the rebel forces under Shih Ta-kai, the Assistant King. Tseng gradually established himself in the middle reaches of the Yangtze, creating a base from which he was later to advance to the siege and capture of Nanking itself. Generals under his command captured Wuchang in December 1856 and Kiukiang in May 1858. The greatest rebel success before 1860 was their defeat of the Imperial armies besieging Nanking and Chinkiang in the middle of 1856. Hsiang Jung's 'Great Camp of Kiangnan' was destroyed and the siege of Nanking was temporarily lifted, only to be reimposed at the beginning of 1858 by reorganized Imperial forces under Chang Kuo-liang, who also captured Chinkiang in December 1857. Thus the rebels failed to win any decisive advantage from their victory over Hsiang Jung.

The chief reason for this failure was the outbreak of savage internal feuds among them at the end of 1856. A struggle for power had been implicit within the leadership of the movement for some years before this but had been held in check by the exigencies of the military situation. The lifting of the siege of the rebel capital opened the way for an attack upon the dominant figure within the movement by that stage, Yang Hsiu-ch'ing, the Eastern King. In September 1856 he was murdered, together with some twenty thousand of his adherents, by Wei Ch'ang-hui, the Northern King, who himself soon fell a victim in the struggle. Two of the other Wangs, Feng Yun-shan, the Southern King, and Hsiao Ch'ao-kuei, the Western King, had already been killed in the advance northward from Kwangsi, so that by the end of 1856 the early collective leadership of the movement had virtually disintegrated. Only Shih Ta-k'ai, the Assistant King, remained to share power with the Heavenly King, who withdrew more and more from the real world and left near relatives to speak in his name.

Shih Ta-k'ai, apparently in fear of further purges, himself abandoned Nanking in May 1857, taking with him many of the best commanders and troops. He eventually made his way to Szechuan, where he attempted to establish an independent kingdom, but was finally defeated there in 1863. New leaders soon began to emerge at Nanking and many new Wangs were created, but the rebellion had lost much of the fervour and force of its early years. The energies not dissipated in faction fighting were, until the middle of 1860, mainly directed towards the central Yangtze valley, away from the existing centres of Western trade. Neutrality in these circumstances was not so difficult an attitude to maintain as it had been, or was to become.

For the time being the rebellion, which had once seemed to offer the prospect of rapid and radical change, became just another complication in the great Chinese puzzle, though no longer a very distracting one. Even in the middle of 1855 Bowring had been able to report that his apprehensions were 'much diminished', and that the tendencies were 'rather towards tranquillity and the restoration of commerce than in a contrary direction'. He had to admit that 'the usual uncertainty' existed as to the position of the contending parties in China, but regarding British interests he saw 'nothing at present seriously to compromise them'.[2] From Shanghai also, D. B. Robertson, who had replaced Alcock there as consul in April 1855, reported at the end of the year that there were no disturbing movements by the Taiping forces, their headquarters at Chinkiang and Nanking being then still watched by the Imperialists 'from a convenient distance'. The state of affairs was at 'deadlock', Robertson concluded.[3]

There was no change during the early part of 1856, and the few official reports made on the subject during that year emphasized the hopelessness of both sides from the British point of view. 'The rebel cause cannot be pronounced to be prospering anywhere on a grand scale', Wade reported in January, adding that around Canton he could find 'no sympathy with the Rebels in any class, labourers, shopkeepers or, so far as I had access to them, literary men'.[4] But the Imperial government also appeared to have no reserves of popular support. In forwarding another of Wade's reports, Bowring commented that he himself found 'nowhere any growing confidence or affection for the Imperial Government. It is utterly unable to grapple with the difficulties of its position. On the other hand, the various rebel bands appear only to represent a wild disorder, quite sufficient to disorganize society but helpless for the establishment of authority. The successful inroads of these revolutionary bands shake all confidence in the Peking Government, whose blindness, pride and obstinacy seem impervious to all lessons of experience.'[5]

In the report to which Bowring added these comments Wade concluded that the rebel movement was more indebted to the 'imbecility' of the Imperial Government for its continued existence than to any vigour of its own. Wade could see 'no incident in this wretched history that may enable one to name a term of years within which the struggle shall be concluded. The Emperor recovers ground lost in one province, only, as it were, to see the rebellion condense in another; and the rebels, though stubborn and formidable, are still, considered as a whole, on the defensive, and have now to recommence, geographically speaking, from a point little in advance of where they were at the beginning of 1854.'[6] British officials in China naturally became increasingly impatient with the general state of affairs in China, but their efforts to prod the Foreign Office into thinking about a future policy received no encouragement. Clarendon preferred to leave relations with China 'to their own operation, and a better state of things may thus be prepared without being precipitated'.[7]

The situation changed temporarily in May 1856 when the Taipings suddenly routed the forces besieging Chinkiang, preparatory to their attack on Hsiang Jung's forces at Nanking.

For a time they threatened the important city of Soochow, and it seemed possible that they would at last advance to the coast and attempt to occupy Shanghai. The unwelcome prospect of a second rebel occupation of that city and a second Imperialist siege, so soon after the expulsion of the Triads, prompted a significant shift in British policy. Rather than allow a re-enactment of the scenes of the last few years, Consul Robertson argued that 'the city should be taken possession of by the three treaty powers and held intact', although with one man-o'-war in port at uncertain intervals he was in no position to initiate such a move himself.[8] But at least, he suggested in another despatch a fortnight later, 'it would not be inappropriate to let the [Rebel] Chiefs know that we should view with dissatisfaction any movement on their part calculated to disturb us in a place we reside in by Treaty Right'.[9]

The Chamber of Commerce at Shanghai even suggested that Soochow should also be brought under foreign protection, since as the main entrepôt for trade with the interior its fall alone would have a serious effect upon Shanghai.[10] For a time trade did suffer badly at the treaty port, although neither it nor Soochow was actually taken by the rebels. Robertson reported at the end of June that 'even Opium finds no purchasers' and that tea supplies from the interior were very uncertain. But even the total cessation of trade was, he recognized, 'merely one of those chances that all must run whose interests are placed in a country where civil war was raging'. What chiefly concerned him was the physical security of British residents. To secure this adequately, he suggested, the existing policy towards the rebellion needed revision. 'Your Excellency's instructions for my guidance have hitherto been to observe a perfect neutrality', he wrote to Bowring, 'and so long as matters go well there can be no question of the wisdom of such a course; but I would respectfully submit, and I hope you will not deem it presumption on my part, that times and circumstances may occur when that policy can be carried a little too far.'[11]

Bowring did not deem it presumption, for such a view fitted in with his own attitude to the struggle going on in China. But in forwarding a copy of Robertson's despatch to the Foreign Office, Bowring inverted the consul's argument and told Clarendon that it was not the molestation of British subjects

71

that was to be feared so much as the stagnation of British trade. To secure this he suggested that '*all parties* should be interdicted from making the Five Ports the seat of hostilities', and further, that 'in case of absolute need' the city of Shanghai should be put under the direct protection of the Treaty powers.[12] With the war in the Crimea settled Clarendon was more sympathetic to complaints from China and his reply, sent early in September 1856, promised more naval forces at Shanghai in future. Moreover, he instructed Bowring to inform the rebel chiefs that, 'any attack upon the City of Shanghai, which is full of British subjects and property, will be repelled by force of arms; but that the British Government will in no way interfere in the Civil War if the Ports in which British Commerce is carried on and to which British subjects are admitted are respected by the Insurrectionary Forces'.[13] Clarendon agreed, in effect, that neutrality could be carried too far. The limits of British neutrality were accordingly extended to include not just the foreign settlement areas at the treaty ports, but the Chinese cities as well.

To exclude both sides from the settlement areas was, as I have already argued, if not strictly legal at least not inconsistent with a stand of neutrality in the civil war. But to forbid one side from attacking 'the Ports in which British Commerce is carried on', and from Shanghai in particular, which is what Clarendon's instructions amounted to, was another matter. In actual fact, these instructions were never acted upon at all. By the time they arrived in China, at the end of 1856, the crisis at Shanghai was safely past and was not to be renewed until the middle of 1860, when a Taiping attack on the city was actually made. On that occasion Shanghai was defended by British forces, but not on the authority of Clarendon's instructions, which appear to have been quite forgotten. By then, Bowring had been replaced by Frederick Bruce as British Plenipotentiary in China, Clarendon by Russell at the Foreign Office, and Robertson by Meadows as consul at Shanghai. Thus none of the principals concerned in the redefinition of British policy at Shanghai in mid-1856 were on the scene four years later. Bruce apparently did not study the consular archives at Hong Kong closely on his arrival there in April 1859 and he soon moved on to Shanghai, which became his headquarters until the end of 1860. When the rebels did attack that port in August 1860 he ordered its defence by British forces quite consciously on his own authority. Russell later approved his action, but neither referred to the fact that such action had been authorized four years earlier as part of a revised British policy towards the rebellion, and it would seem clear that they were ignorant of this.[14]

Both the origin and fate of these instructions provide an instructive illustration of the decidedly *ad hoc* nature of British policy on this question. They were an immediate response to a sudden, local crisis, and when that crisis passed and was not repeated for several years, they were forgotten. Certainly they were not referred to in 1860. Such facts make it difficult to accept the idea of any systematic, astutely planned, British policy towards the rebellion. At times it is difficult to resist the conclusion that it was not made or planned at all; that it just happened.

Yet the objection remains that by their very existence on paper, even if never acted upon, these instructions of Clarendon in September 1856 compromised British neutrality in a decidedly pro-Manchu direction. They made it potentially, if not yet in actual practice, a neutrality which protected the Manchus. All the ports in which British commerce was carried on and to which British subjects were admitted were at that time in the hands of the Manchu government, and it was impossible to warn the rebels away from them without at the same time protecting the interest of that government, unless the ports and the revenues derived from them were taken over entirely by the treaty powers. One can, therefore, begin to accept in part the Marxist complaint against the nature of British neutrality towards the rebellion, while still rejecting such emotional and unhelpful adjectives as 'false' and 'empty'. It was not a case of British neutrality being consciously devised to deceive one side and to favour the other. But given a situation in which the British government was able and determined to protect the area (generously defined) within which the interest of its own subjects residing in China were to be regarded as inviolate, and given also that those interests were concentrated in ports exclusively in the hands of one side, then British policy could not help but work in favour of that side as against the other. By 1856, the natural bias in British policy away from the prospect of any change or disturbance in China which might upset the *status quo* there began to turn that policy into a course which ran actively counter to the success of the Taiping rebellion. But it was not for some years yet that any conscious direction and added impetus was given to this trend.

Clarendon's instructions of September 1856 were certainly not part of any general move towards abandoning the policy of neutrality altogether, however peculiar a character they may have given that policy. This is made plain by Bowring's correspondence with the newly appointed American Commissioner, Dr. Peter Parker, over the latter's renewal late in 1856 of the attempt to secure treaty revision. In August Parker sought Bowring's co-operation in this venture in a letter stating that he had evidence that the Imperial government contemplated seeking foreign aid against the rebellion, though by indirect means and 'in a manner peculiarly Chinese'. Parker urged therefore that, if the representatives of the Western treaty powers were now to present themselves at Peking, 'most important consequences *might* follow'.

Having no warships readily available for such a purpose, Bowring was in no position to co-operate, and thought the whole venture hopeless, not to say positively prejudicial to long-range Western interest in China. On the question of aid against the rebels he told Parker he was not authorized to make such an offer as that suggested. In his despatch to Clarendon on the question he went even further, stating that although he was convinced that British interests in China were seriously endangered by the present state of anarchy in the country, yet he was 'less willing than ever to see the British Government interfering with the internecine quarrel', and could not advise participation in 'that policy of intervention which is darkly indicated in Dr. Parker's despatches'.[15] Clarendon replied in November, fully approving Bowring's stand and rejecting also the idea of offering armed intervention in favour of the Imperial Government as the condition of political or commercial concessions.[16]

On the eve of the outbreak of the second opium war in China, therefore, British policy towards the Taiping rebellion was in a rather peculiar position which defies definition in simple and usual terms. Fundamentally it remained in intent and application what it had been since 1853, a policy of armed and limited neutrality, limited in the sense that it was not prepared to permit either side to bring the main treaty port areas into the field of conflict. Yet the limits of this neutrality had been extended in such a way as to make British policy one which might, in certain very possible circumstances, work in favour of the Manchu government, while on the other hand there was explicit rejection of the idea of offering direct aid to that government. In addition, hopes in the possibility of either side settling the conflict satisfactorily and establishing a firm government conducive to the interests of foreign trade had receded still further from what they had been in 1853–54. If the conditions for the expansion of that trade were to be created, it seemed that it could only be as a result of independent Western action.

Clarendon was in fact preparing for such action just at the time when the *Arrow* affair was precipitating the crisis at Canton which led to the outbreak of war. With the Crimean War settled, Clarendon began negotiations with the French government for combined action 'to avert the calamities and ruin' facing their interests in China. The object was to be treaty revision, and the means a joint expedition to the Peiho of far greater strength than any previously made. In this way, Clarendon argued, the Treaty Powers would either place their relations with China under the existing dynasty on a better footing than they had hitherto been, or would be 'set free by the obstinacy of the Chinese government from any obligation by which they may be morally restrained from adopting measures requisite for the security of their subjects and calculated to extend their commerce with the Chinese territories'. Great Britain was far from desiring to see the overthrow of the ruling dynasty in China or the success of the insurgents, Clarendon told the British Ambassador in Paris, 'but Her Majesty's Government consider that it would be imprudent in the Treaty Powers much longer to remain in a state of listless indifference'.[17]

Just what measures Clarendon had in mind if the Manchu government again refused to accept the idea of treaty revision does not emerge in the negotiations as far as they had gone up to the time when events at Canton led to action even more direct than a mere show of force at the Peiho. The threat of attempting to make terms with the rebels was perhaps among them, although equally intervention against the rebels might have proved the outcome. Clarendon was determined to get either concessions or what he considered moral freedom of action, which could have meant any one of a number of things. Whatever it meant, the French were very willing to co-operate, and were confident that the appearance of the banners of war off the coast of China would bring quick results.[18]

By the time Bowring received news of these preparations the banners of war were already flying at Canton. In October 1856 a crisis developed over the seizure by the Chinese authorities of the opium vessel *Arrow*, and England and France set about securing their objectives by the direct use of force against the Manchu government. The length of time taken to build up effective fighting forces in so distant a theatre of war as China, especially after some of the British troops sent out were diverted to help quell the Mutiny in India, meant that despite the vast superiority of the allies in weapons of war it was not until June 1858 that peace was concluded and the Treaty of Tientsin signed. Even this was to prove far from the end of the struggle. Ratification of the new treaty was required by June 1859, but before then officials favouring the continuance of the war regained control in the counsels of the Manchu government, and when Bruce, the newly appointed British Minister Plenipotentiary to China, attempted to make his way up the Peiho on his way to present his credentials and exchange treaties at Peking, his naval escort was repulsed with heavy losses at the Taku forts. The war was thereupon laboriously renewed, and Bruce's elder brother, the Earl of Elgin, who had negotiated the original treaty, was sent back to China a second time as Minister Extraordinary to exact full compliance from the Manchu government. This was eventually secured in October 1860, the Treaty of Tientsin being then finally ratified, together with the Convention of Peking, which imposed additional conditions upon China.

The task of forcing from the Manchu government the diplomatic and commercial concessions demanded thus proved a bitter and protracted one. Apart from the fact that the Manchu government renewed the war rather than ratify, at least in a manner acceptable to the British, a treaty already negotiated and signed, other incidents which occurred during the campaign of 1860 also exacerbated feelings. In September a number of British and French emissaries who had been sent out to negotiate a truce near Tientsin were seized and imprisoned, some of them dying as a result of their maltreatment, and in October Elgin ordered the burning of the Summer Palace outside Peking to punish what he regarded as a thoroughly perfidious court. At the approach of the allied armies the Hsien-Feng emperor himself had fled to Jehol in Manchuria, leaving his half-brother, Prince Kung, the task of soothing the fierce barbarian. Such a background of deceit and destruction naturally left no great legacy of faith or goodwill on either side. The Manchu government had been forced, very much against its will, to accept new terms on paper by the end of 1860, but its readiness to carry them out sincerely remained, for some time yet, highly suspect to the British representatives. Not surprisingly in such circumstances, there was no immediate rush towards helping such a government as this to suppress a rebellion which, by the end of 1860, had suddenly again become a formidable threat to its security.

On the other hand, the existence of a state of war with the Manchus did not dispose the British government to look much more favourably on the rebellion, or to give it any kind of encouragement. In October 1856 rebels near Canton who claimed to be connected with those at Nanking sought aid from Bowring, but he rejected their request, and Elgin ignored a similar request from a Taiping chief on the Yangtze at the end of 1858.[19] The reasons for this refusal to regard the rebels as possible allies are obvious. Apart from absolute confidence that, having once concentrated their forces in China, military victory would quickly be won, the view of the rebellion formed by British officials since 1854 made any active encouragement of it practically unthinkable. Doubts as to the real nature of Taiping feelings towards foreigners remained, and until 1860 the rebels seemed to have lost all their former military vigour. They were therefore neither desirable nor necessary allies.

In any case, in the war with the Manchus it was no part of the British objective, and still less of the French, to overthrow the Ch'ing dynasty entirely. The instructions issued to Elgin when he set out for the first time in April 1857 were largely devoted to defining the terms which it was hoped the Manchu govern-

ment could be 'induced' to accept,[20] and even when Elgin had
to be sent a second time, after the Manchus had shown their
intractability at the Taku forts, the Foreign Office urgently
instructed him not to go too far in undermining the authority of
the Emperor. If that were to happen, the Foreign Secretary
warned, 'the Rebels would take heart, the great officers of the
Empire might find it difficult to maintain the central authority,
the governors of provinces might hardly be able to quell
insurrection. In short, the whole Empire might run the risk of
dissolution. Her Majesty would see with great concern such a
state of things. It might portend a great catastrophe, and the
bonds of allegiance, once loosened, might never again be firmly
united.'[21] Elgin himself wondered at times whether the Manchu
government either could or should be upheld in this way, but
despite the suspicions of his French colleague, Baron Gros, his
instructions on the point were definite. Setting the rebels up in
place of the Manchus was never the policy of the British government, even when at war with the Manchus.

During these years of war between Britain and China reports
on the rebellion were much less regular than formerly, but they
provide unexpected variety. At the beginning of 1857 Robertson
wrote one of the few official British despatches not from the pen
of Meadows which praised the rebels. Under their rule no
oppression of the people was allowed, he reported, taxation
was moderate and the administration just and efficient. Taiping
discipline, he continued, 'stands out in such bold relief against
the fearful demoralization of the Imperial Armies as to instil a
feeling of respect into beholders and enthusiasm into its
followers'. Despite these great virtues, however, Robertson
doubted whether the rebels could achieve more than partial
national reform, and he questioned also whether they really
wished to co-operate with foreigners. 'The Manchoo Government may be effete and the people demoralized, but at all
events the first assures to us a security for life and property
in so far as it can, and the last a trade worth above nineteen and
a half millions sterling. Whether the Rebel Government will do
as much is a matter of doubt.' Bowring was not impressed by
Robertson's sudden burst of praise for the rebels, while
Clarendon merely expressed polite interest.[22]

In any case, Robertson's enthusiasm did not last long, and

twelve months later he was reporting, in a singularly ill-written despatch, that 'a deep feeling of discontent pervades the countryman, and had the Taiping-wang movement had in it any of the elements of progress, and guarantee for an ameliorated condition and peaceful enjoyment of property, the Tartar dynasty would have ceased to exist, but it did not; the people see in it only an exchange of masters, without any benefit to accrue therefrom, and extinction of their religious rites, to be replaced by a formula which threatens religious persecution and the uprooting of their religious systems and institutions'. These were the more usual views for a British consular official, and in harmony with the reports submitted by Wade during 1857.[23]

Through the greater part of the following year, the rebellion received virtually no attention at all in consular reports. The advance of Chang Kuo-liang's armies forced the rebels still further from the coastal areas, while Western energies and attention were mainly directed towards the campaign against the Manchus. It could hardly be entirely forgotten, however, for Article X of the Treaty of Tientsin, signed on June 26, 1858, read, 'British merchant ships shall have authority to trade upon the Great River (Yangtze). The upper and Lower Valley of the River being, however, disturbed by outlaws, no Port shall for the present be opened to trade, with the exception of Chinkiang, which shall be opened in a year. . . . So soon as Peace shall have been restored, British vessels shall also be admitted to trade at such ports as far as Hankow, not exceeding three in number . . .'.[24] Thus the continuance of the rebellion nullified the chief commercial benefit gained from the recent war—the right to trade upon the Yangtze. In October 1858, however, before leaving for England, Elgin persuaded the Imperial authorities, at the price of modifying the clause in the treaty relating to the residence of the British minister in Peking, to allow him to make an exploratory voyage up the river and to select suitable ports for foreign trade. Elgin stated that his main object was simply to confirm the principle that the river would eventually be opened, but part of his intention was to investigate afresh the state of the rebellion, about which little had been heard for some time. With a convoy of five vessels he left Shanghai on November 8 and returned on January 1, 1859, after reaching Hankow, six hundred miles inland.

His progress was watched with a good deal of apprehension by Chinese officials and especially by the emperor himself, who feared that the unfathomable barbarian would 'spy out the situation and establish contact with the rebels and create more trouble'.[25] Some modern Chinese historians, on the other hand, see Elgin's voyage as a kind of reconnaissance intended to prepare the way for expelling the rebels from Nanking.[26] Certainly on the way upriver shots were exchanged between the flotilla and Taiping shore batteries, but on the way back reasonably amicable relations were established with the rebels. There does not appear to be any sound reason to suppose that Elgin had any ulterior motive beyond finding out what the interior of China was like and whether the Yangtze was easily navigable for large vessels.

The reports brought back by Elgin and his companions on the rebels served to confirm the official view formed since 1854. The two main points which emerged from Elgin's own report were his conclusion that the Taiping movement now lacked real popular support, and the total absence of commercial activity observed in Taiping territory as compared with Imperial. Elgin stated that he was 'inclined to believe that there is little or nothing of popular sympathy with the rebel movement, in the sense which we give to that phrase in Europe. It is no doubt true that the general attitude of the population does not argue much enthusiasm on either side of the dynastic controversy, and it is also certain that we saw more of the districts in Imperialist than those in rebel occupation. But the tone of natives with whom I conversed certainly left on my mind the impression that they viewed the rebellion with feelings akin to those with which they would have regarded earthquake or pestilence, or any other providential scourge.' The towns in Taiping hands appeared to be merely desolate garrison centres, although Elgin recognized that in some cases at least this was the inevitable result of their being almost constantly in a state of siege. Yet the contrast with Imperialist-held territory was very marked indeed.[27] For Wade, who accompanied Elgin as an interpreter, it was simply a 'motley, planless insurrection . . . without a vestige of capability to reconstruct the edifice it has done something to undermine'. The only thing to be hoped for from it in Wade's view was its early collapse.[28]

A readiness to help towards its collapse certainly became apparent in official British considerations on the rebellion immediately after the conclusion of the Treaty of Tientsin. Before Elgin's report reached England the instructions to guide his brother as the first British minister to China were drawn up. These show that at the beginning of 1859 intervention against the rebellion was considered as a possible development in British policy in China, although not as a certain or immediate development. In February 1859 Bruce wrote to the then Foreign Secretary, Malmesbury, setting out the major questions in Anglo-Chinese relations he thought likely to arise after his arrival in Peking. One of the most important of these, he suggested, was 'the language I am to use to the Imperial Government with regard to the rebels'.[29] Malmesbury made a pencil note opposite this passage in Bruce's letter stating, 'I think we ought to help them and drive them out of Nankin—the promise of this would induce them to repay us by good faith &c. It is important that we should open the Nanking trade.' The actual instructions he issued to Bruce were, however, rather more guarded.

In these Malmesbury emphasized that any possible request for aid against the rebels by the Manchu government would involve a question of 'momentous importance'. On the one hand it was certainly desirable that peace should be restored to the interior of the empire and the Yangtze opened to foreign trade, but on the other hand 'in the present imperfect state of our information as to the nature, extent and prospects of the insurrection, it is impossible to judge whether any attempt to serve the purposes of the Central Government by contributing to suppress it might not do more harm than good'. If the insurrection were confined to a few places accessible to naval forces aid might be given, though 'even in this case I need scarcely say that Her Majesty's Government would not be disposed to enter upon such a course without previous concert with and without the assured co-operation of its allies'. But as far as present information went, Malmesbury warned, the insurrection was still widely spread throughout the interior with many adherents. Elgin's report might change the picture but, the Foreign Secretary concluded, 'in the present state of our knowledge it would not be proper for you to encourage any expectation of material assistance on our part'.[30]

Malmesbury clearly favoured the idea of intervention, but not at any price. He wanted proof that it was likely to be effective even if given on only a limited scale. Elgin's report indicated, though it certainly did not state, that effective aid might be possible without a large and expensive commitment of British forces, but Bruce's treatment at the Taku forts in June 1859 meant that any possibility of such British action was for the time being discarded. A large and expensive commitment of British forces to China had, in fact, to be made, but they carried war not aid to the Manchu government.

The events of 1859–60 served to complicate rather than resolve the immediate problems of British relations with China. The fact that the Manchu government had been prepared to renew hostilities rather than submit to the terms of 1858, and perhaps even more its seizure and maltreatment of the truce negotiators in September 1860, made many question whether it was not completely untrustworthy and better overthrown. Baron Gros certainly suspected Elgin of such thoughts, and by the end of 1860 Elgin was at least as well disposed towards the rebels as towards the Manchus.[31]

By then indeed it appeared that the dynasty might be overthrown in any case, if not by the Western barbarians invading its capital and burning its palaces then by the long-haired rebels. In the early part of 1860 the Taipings had suddenly reasserted themselves as a formidable military force under new military leaders of whom the most outstanding were Li Hsiuch'eng, the Chung Wang or Loyal King, and Chen Yu-ch'eng, the Ying Wang or Brave King. In May the Imperial armies besieging Nanking were routed for a second time and Li's forces advanced triumphantly towards the coast, capturing Soochow at the beginning of June. In the following months they overran the rich coastal province of Kiangsu, attacking Shanghai itself in August, and with other Taiping forces began a great drive along both sides of the Yangtze towards Hankow, in an attempt to relieve the vital centre of Anking. Despite some brilliant campaigning and many tactical victories, strategic errors by the rebels and the superior resources and organization of the opposing armies finally defeated this last great military challenge, and by the end of 1861 Tseng Kuo-fan's armies were able to advance to the third and final siege of Nanking. The military resurgence of the Taiping movement thus proved abortive.

But at the end of 1860 and the beginning of 1861 this was by no means apparent. With rebel armies ranging through wide tracts of Imperial territory on the coast and along both sides of the Yangtze, and with Western barbarians occupying its capital in the north, the fall of the Ch'ing dynasty seemed once again a distinct possibility. As in 1853, the political future of China seemed all uncertain, and this uncertainty affected the development of British policy towards the rebellion. It is not very surprising that Elgin, on the eve of his own entry into Peking, should write to his brother, then still at Shanghai, questioning whether it was wise for Bruce to consider moving north and taking up residence in the capital, thus identifying Britain diplomatically with a régime that appeared to Elgin to be 'tottering to its fall'.[32] There was no thought in Elgin's mind of rushing to the aid of this effete and untrustworthy dynasty. In some ways the prospect of British intervention on its behalf was more remote at the end of 1860 than at any time since the early months of 1853.

Against this must be set the fact that in August 1860 British forces were used to prevent the Taiping rebels capturing Shanghai. In May, just before the capture of Soochow, the Chinese authorities at Shanghai requested foreign aid against the advancing rebels and to this Bruce, in conjunction with the French minister, agreed, although refusing to go beyond the defence of Shanghai itself. There is some doubt whether the rebels were fully aware of the allied intention to defend the city, and Li Hsiu-ch'eng claimed that he was actually invited to advance upon it by foreigners visiting him at Soochow. Whatever the truth on these points, the rebels attacked Shanghai on August 18 over a period of three days, and were repulsed by British and French forces, the latter incidentally firing a suburb outside the walls to deprive the Taiping forces of cover. While some allied forces were thus defending an Imperial city in central China, their brothers in arms in the north were storming the troublesome Imperial forts of Taku preparatory to an advance on Tientsin and Peking. It is difficult to apply the normal criteria for neutrality and belligerence to so Gilbertian a situation.[33]

Yet although certainly a breach of neutrality in any normal and acceptable sense of the term, the British action at Shanghai in August 1860 did not mark a radical change in policy towards the rebellion.[34] In so far as it was intended merely to defend Western interests at Shanghai it was of a piece with the action taken in 1854 at Muddy Flat, with the difference that it was now the rebels who were attacked as threatening those interests while, in addition, what the British government now regarded as the legitimate limits within which it might use its forces to defend those interests had been extended to a point at which they could not help but include Manchu interests also. But unlike a similar action in January 1862, the action of August 1860 was not intended to be, nor did it become, the starting point of a sustained and deliberate policy of active intervention against the rebellion on behalf of the Manchu government. British policy towards the Taiping rebellion was entering a sort of shadowy no-man's-land, somewhere between neutrality and active hostility.

It seems, therefore, over-simple to say that 'precisely in 1860' British policy towards the rebellion changed, or that the Manchus had 'no sooner' been forced to accept the new treaty dispensation than the British government and its representatives in China began to supply them with aid. The best proof of this lies in an examination of British policy during 1861, but even looking at the situation as it was at the end of 1860 it cannot be said that abandonment of the admittedly peculiar, presumptuous and imperfect kind of neutrality followed since 1853 was a certain or immediate development. The repulse of the Taipings from Shanghai was an isolated response to an immediate crisis such as had threatened in 1856, not part of a general campaign against the rebellion such as a similar crisis provoked in 1862, while the evidence of renewed vigour in the rebellion itself on the one hand, and of the continued weakness and obstinacy of the Manchu government on the other, left many doubts and questions as to possible future developments in China, including the future of British policy towards the rebellion. Would the Manchu government really abide by the new treaty settlement? Was the resurgence of the rebel movement permanent and more than military? Was it possible to negotiate with them, and would they recognize British trading interests and treaty rights in

China? Was intervention, in fact, really necessary? Was it, in any case, possible to intervene effectively without a large and expensive commitment of British forces such as Malmesbury had hesitated over early in 1859?

These were the kinds of question which had to be answered before the British government was likely to be prepared to commit itself to a policy of active intervention, and there were certainly no easy, sure answers to them at the end of 1860. There can be no argument that the conclusion of a satisfactory treaty settlement with the Manchu government by that stage made a policy of aid and support to it far more likely, or that most British officials in China took a very hostile view of the rebellion. But it is misleading to argue back in the knowledge that aid was in fact eventually given to the conclusion that this was settled British policy at the end of 1860. The terms of the political equation in China had been radically altered by the war of 1856–60, but they still did not add up beyond all question to intervention against the Taiping rebellion by the British government.

6
Year of Indecision
(1861)

DURING 1861 British policy did not proceed on the assumption that it was absolutely necessary to assist the Manchu government in destroying the Taiping rebellion before the new treaties could be implemented satisfactorily. Its main concern was simply to get the treaties operating as fully as possible, with the co-operation of the rebels where necessary but without actively intervening in the dynastic struggle between them and the Manchus. The established policy of limited neutrality was re-affirmed, negotiations were carried on with the rebels to allow British vessels on the Yangtze to pass through the territory under their control and there were even suggestions, never very thoroughly pursued, for getting the agreement of both sides to the neutralization of the treaty ports.

Yet although the main trend in British policy was towards making the best of things as they were, there was also a strong tendency towards helping to change the situation by aiding the Manchus in some way. But no sustained attempt was made to do this in fact, as happened in 1862, and for a full year after the ratification of the treaties, British policy was experimental and uncertain. The experiment lay in treating with the rebels as a *de facto* power in the Yangtze valley; the uncertainty lay in whether this was a really workable policy and also in whether its alternative, helping the conservative and suspicious Manchu government defeat the rebels, was likely to further long-term

87

British interests in China. By the early months of 1862 the experiment in treating with the rebels was held to have failed, while on the other hand the Manchu government, although still not exactly inspiring confidence, seemed at least a rather better prospect as an ally than at the end of 1860. The major question in British policy then became not whether to intervene but how far to do so.

The movement of British forces in China during 1861 provides convincing evidence of the absence of any positive intention to intervene against the rebellion as soon as the Manchus had given way over the Treaty of Tientsin. The argument of some writers that the large forces used to defeat the Manchus were kept conveniently at hand, first to ensure that the Manchus observed the treaty and then to help crush the Taipings, is one of those less than half-true arguments which seem convincing enough at a distance (after a hundred years there is not much difference between 1860 and 1862) but which hardly tally with the dull but relevant day-to-day administrative facts and figures of the time to which they refer.[1]

About 21,000 British troops, one-third of them Indian, were concentrated in China during 1860. Of these 16,000 were in the expeditionary force which conducted the campaign in the far north, but immediately following the ratification of the Treaty of Tientsin 10,000 men of this force were embarked to return to India and England. Thus, at the end of 1860 there were about 11,000 British and Indian troops in China, 4,250 of them in the garrisons retained at Tientsin and the Taku forts, 1,200 at Shanghai and the remainder at Hong Kong and Canton.

Even the maintenance of a force of this size, the War Office pointed out in April 1861, absorbed a considerable part of the indemnity payments received under the treaty, especially since the presence of Indian troops meant that special rates of pay were made to the British troops.[2] Although admitting that, given the disturbed and uncertain conditions in China, the question of evacuation could not be peremptorily settled at home, both the War Office and the Foreign Office, not to mention the Treasury, were anxious to reduce the number of troops retained there as quickly as possible. In September it was down to 9,500 and the War Office was instructing the commander, Sir John Michel, to send back to India without delay all troops from that country.[3] These orders were temporarily withdrawn a few weeks later, after news of the death of the Hsien Feng emperor was received, but by the end of the year, the total force had been reduced to about 6,000. A suggestion made by Michel that barracks be built at Shanghai and a permanent garrison established there was rejected, partly on the advice of Elgin, now appointed Viceroy of India.[4] Commenting on this suggestion, Bruce wrote to Michel that although he was of 'decided opinion' that it was not safe to leave Shanghai undefended, even if arrangements were made with the rebels, yet he thought that the total force retained in China should not be calculated to perform 'any other service than the retention of Taku and the protection of Shanghai'.[5]

The naval strength of the British East India and China station was also considerably reduced over this period, from 66 ships with a total complement of nearly 8,000 men in March 1861 to 38 ships with a complement of little over 4,000 twelve months later.[6] Thus both the detailed figures of British forces in and around China during 1861 and the comments of British authorities upon the general question of military establishments there show that, although there was a concern to provide for the adequate defence of Shanghai, there was certainly no intention of maintaining or building up a large force for a future offensive campaign against the rebellion.

Lord Elgin, who had actually negotiated and later forced the ratification of the treaty which is said to have 'sealed the fate' of the rebellion, certainly did not advocate keeping large forces in China for this purpose. On his return to England early in 1861 he told the War Office that he thought that a force of 5,000 British and French troops combined should be enough to enforce the treaty and to secure indemnity payments, and that the garrison at Tientsin then being maintained could dispense with 'as much force as is necessary to garrison Shanghai and Canton, if it is decided to maintain troops at those places'.[7]

How far Elgin was from imagining that, the Manchus having now been dealt with, the next step was to settle the rebels is further indicated by his correspondence with his brother about this time. At the end of 1860 he was taking a far more sympathetic view of the rebellion and its prospects than he had done two years earlier, after his voyage up the Yangtze. In December

1860 he told Bruce that he inclined to the opinion that 'there is more of "avenir" on the Rebel than on the Imperialist side—bad as they both are', and he saw evidence 'both of honesty and power' in the rebel administration of the countryside. He warned that 'it will never do to come under any obligation not to communicate with them on the Yangtze. It would be wrong in principle to do so, and impossible in practice to carry out such an engagement.'[8] In February 1861, writing from Ceylon, he described the system of keeping Shanghai out of rebel hands by a permanent European occupation as 'an evil of great magnitude', though for the present he confessed he saw no alternative. But he disagreed with Bruce about the probable rebel attitude to the payment of the treaty indemnities should they occupy the port and argued that 'they would always be ready to purchase our neutrality by undertaking all the obligations enjoined on the Imperial Government by the new Treaty and Convention'.[9] For Elgin as he left China there was no question that negotiation, not intervention, was the proper attitude for the British to adopt towards the rebellion.

It would be false to suggest that, had Elgin remained as British minister in China instead of Bruce, later British policy towards the rebellion would have been very different from what in fact it became, for his rather favourable view of the rebels at this stage was certainly largely a reaction from his recent experience of the Manchu government's duplicity. But these letters indicate quite plainly that there was no predetermined British policy towards the rebellion ready to swing into operation as soon as the treaties with the Manchu government were finally settled. There was clearly more than one opinion about the future prospects of that policy among its leading agents in China.

On the later working out of that policy Elgin himself had little influence, while Bruce certainly never shared Elgin's kinder, second thoughts about the rebellion.[10] But even Bruce did not go to Peking, early in 1861, ready to plan a joint campaign with the Manchus against the Taipings. In January, while he himself remained for a time at Tientsin, he sent Thomas Wade, the Chinese Secretary to the Legation, on to the capital for preliminary talks with Prince Kung who, in the continued absence of the Emperor, was still the chief representative of the

Manchu government there. Kung was soon to be appointed first head of the Tsungli Yamen, the new board of experts on 'barbarian affairs' which was to become the Chinese equivalent of a Foreign Office. But despite this move towards setting diplomatic relations with the treaty powers on a more 'normal', that is to say a more Western, basis, the refusal of the Hsien Feng emperor to return from Jehol to Peking after the conclusion of peace or to acknowledge in any way the presence of non-tributary foreign representatives in his capital naturally fed British doubts that the new settlement had still not been accepted in good faith by the Manchu government.[11] Therefore Bruce, although certainly himself hostile towards the rebellion and anxious to conciliate and reassure the shaken Manchu government, felt it necessary to instruct Wade 'not to press the rebel question too much'.[12]

It was for the Manchu government to adopt such measures for its preservation as the means at its disposal allowed, he told Wade, 'but we are not going to furnish them directly with aid to put down this insurrection, and I do not wish them to infer from any apparent anxiety on our part, that our interests are much involved in a solution favourable to the existing government'. Once tranquillity was restored China's natural industry and commerce would quickly revive, whoever triumphed, but meanwhile 'our business is to work the Treaty through with this Government while it stands, to avoid committing ourselves to either party as partisans in the conflict, and to treat the rebellion, in conversation with the members of the Government, as an affair with which we have nothing to do and in which we cannot, consistently with our respect for the independence of foreign states, take any part. The "hundred names" and they only must settle the question.'[13] At the beginning of 1861 British policy towards the rebellion, as defined in these instructions from Bruce to Wade, had really not moved essentially from what it had been since 1853, a wait-and-see policy of limited neutrality.

Wade reported a discouraging apathy and indifference among officials in the capital towards 'the disease of the south'. Their main concern was not with the distant Taiping rebellion, 'which they evidently regard as next to chronic', but with the Nien rebellion in the Shantung area, so much nearer the capital.

He received what he called 'the usual query as to whether we would and how we could help them', but he was careful to insist that any aid given would be 'moral rather than material', and contingent upon the commencement of diplomatic relations in earnest. 'The Prince did his best to prove that the hindrance the rebels offered to our trade justified our action against them, but this I could not either allow' [sic].[14] The new era in British relations with the Manchu government under the Treaty of Tientsin was far from beginning with joint plans for the suppression of the Taipings.

It was always possible, however, that such plans might be made by the Manchus with other powers and British action be prompted as a counter to these. About the turn of the years 1860–61 there was much discussion among high officials of the Manchu government of a Russian offer of naval aid against the rebels, but this possibility was met by British officials in China not by offering similar or better terms but by warning the Manchu authorities of the dangers involved in using foreign forces at all.[15]

Among the Chinese, arguments in favour of accepting the Russian offer were advanced most vigorously by the Imperial Commissioner in charge of commercial affairs at the treaty ports, Hsüeh Hüan. Hsüeh maintained that although the expenses involved in using the barbarians might be great, so also were the expenses of the present campaigns against the rebels, and with foreign aid the issue might be more speedily settled. Further, the British and French were fearful of the Russians, and if the Chinese made an alliance with the latter this could help to curb the pride of the others, especially the British. This, said Hsüeh, falling back upon a hoary cliché of Chinese officialdom, was 'the method of using the barbarian to control the barbarian'.[16] Tseng Kuo-fan was much more qualified in his support, pointing out that China's weakness was on land rather than on water and that it would be of little use for Russian vessels to attack Nanking before Chinese land forces were in a position to co-operate effectively. When China's armies were better placed, Tseng suggested, the Russian offer might be accepted, but the terms should be clear and precise, and agreed upon well beforehand.[17]

Opposition came most strongly from the Director-General of

Grain Transport, Yuan Chia-san, who expressed the fear that the barbarian might ally himself with the rebel, with whom he had religious affinities, and that his covetousness would only increase. Yuan also raised practical difficulties, such as the problem of supplies, and questioned whether the barbarian would accept orders from the Chinese. Altogether, the harm was likely to be great and the advantage slight.[18] These opinions were reviewed in an Imperial edict issued early in January 1861 ordering Prince Kung and other officials in the capital to look further into the question, and although Yuan's objections were judged to have some reason it was considered that the Russian offer should not be rejected outright, that there was possible advantage to be had from it.[19]

That in the end it was not followed up seems to have been due in part at least to the advice of Wade. On January 24, just a few days after having talks with the British official, Prince Kung and his chief assistants in handling foreign affairs at this time, Wen-hsiang and Kuei Liang, submitted a memorial reviewing the question and the opinions received upon it, and advising strongly against the acceptance of direct foreign aid. The Russians were described, in another well-worn official cliché as, 'unfathomable' and the French, from whom a vague offer of assistance had also been received, as crafty and covetous. Both would make demands even before doing anything, and there was always the possibility of fresh 'border troubles' breaking out with them before the trouble in the heart of China was settled. Altogether little trust was to be put in them, as Russia's recent usurpation of territory in the north showed. Wade was then quoted as having told the Chinese officials very frankly that 'the suppression of the rebels is really something for China to handle. If others lend aid, what profit will there be in it for them if they do not occupy territory? It is not only that Russia and France might recapture territory and be reluctant to give it up, but even if England also did so he would not dare to say that she would not occupy it for herself. The seizure of India by England was a case in point.' Kung and his colleagues observed that although Wade's words could not be taken absolutely at face value, they felt that his warning should be heeded, and they went on to commend Yuan Chia-san's viewpoint rather than Tseng Kuo-fan's or Hsüeh Huan's and to suggest that, rather than use foreign forces directly, munitions and ships might be purchased as a means of 'ensnaring' the barbarian and preventing him from turning to the rebels.[20]

The edict which followed this important memorial stated that, given the suspicious nature of the barbarians, their overtures should not be too brusquely rejected lest they create new troubles. 'All we can do is tell them that (at present) China's military strength is enough to handle the task of suppressing the rebels, but if in future the occasion for assistance arises, we shall naturally borrow help from them. In order to control them', the imperial edict continued, echoing the recent memorial, 'we should devise means of entrapping them, enticing them to us by petty gain.'[21] Tseng and Hsüeh were accordingly instructed to look into the question of buying or hiring foreign arms and vessels. But the idea of the direct use of foreign forces, among whom the British were not mentioned as possibilities, was for the time being dropped. Besides a deeply ingrained suspicion and fear of the foreigner, Wade's warning was surely an important influence in reaching this decision.[22]

Apart from Bruce's instructions to Wade and the latter's talks with Manchu officials in Peking, developments elsewhere also indicated no intention to change British policy towards the rebellion immediately following the treaty settlement. In December 1860, during the first of many panics at the prospect of a rebel advance on Ningpo, Bruce told the consul there that he did not feel authorized to order the defence of that port and instructed him that, in the event of an attack, British naval forces should not interfere beyond protecting British subjects.[23] In other words, the defence of Shanghai in August 1860 was not to be taken as a precedent for defending other lesser treaty ports. In fact, British policy at this point had retreated somewhat from the stand taken by Clarendon in September 1856 when he had instructed Bowring to warn the rebels to respect 'the Ports in which British Commerce is carried on', for this had seemed to imply an intention to defend all the treaty ports and not only Shanghai. Later in 1861 Russell was to suggest to Bruce that it might be expedient to defend the Treaty Ports if the Chinese would consent not to use those ports for 'purposes of aggression', but it was not until March 1862 that the defence of all the treaty ports was explicitly ordered.[24] During 1861, with the exception of Shanghai and Tientsin, where garrisons were placed, only the foreign settlement areas were to be defended by British forces. At the end of the year Ningpo was in fact captured by the rebels without any opposition being offered by British naval forces there or, for that matter, by the Imperial forces.

Again, at Shanghai itself in January 1861 Meadows, who had been acting consul there since July 1859, refused to co-operate with a French suggestion that allied forces be used to clear the rebels from a 12 to 15 mile radius around the port, and his stand on this point was approved by the Foreign Office.[25] Further, both the Foreign Office and the War Office insisted that no payment should be exacted or accepted from the Manchu government for the expenses incurred in the defence of Shanghai in August 1860, as Bruce had at first proposed, lest this lead to misapprehension and 'induce the Imperialists to suppose that we are prepared to quit our neutral position and to take part with them in the Civil War'.[26] There was still an almost meticulous insistence on remaining neutral within the limits laid down.

The main trend in British policy at this stage was, in fact, towards treating with the Taipings as the power in actual occupation of territory of vital importance to British trade. This is clearly shown by Rear-Admiral Hope's first expedition up the Yangtze in February. In December 1860 the Chinese authorities had agreed to a British request that the river be opened to trade, despite the provision in Article X of the treaty withholding this right until the rebellion was settled, on condition that the Imperial government be not held responsible for the protection of British trade and subject to regulations designed to prevent the smuggling of arms to the rebels.[27] Wade believed that in agreeing to this concession the Manchu government hoped that the British would get involved in difficulties with the rebels.[28] Prince Kung merely argued that it was a concession worth making to prevent possible grievance and treachery by the barbarians. 'If we placate them adequately now, not only will we not have to worry about their being harmful to us, but they could even be of use to us.'[29]

Thus Elgin, as almost his last official act before his departure from China, requested Hope's assistance in 'the establishing of an understanding with the rebel leaders at Nankin which may secure British vessels passing up and down the river from being molested or interfered with by persons acting under orders from them'. It was not easy, he admitted, 'to determine how to communicate with them as we go up the river on an understanding with the government to which they are opposed', but he was confident of rebel co-operation on condition, as he told Parkes, who went as interpreter, that an attitude of strict neutrality was maintained. To Hope he also wrote privately: 'I rather think better of the rebel prospects since I came here; at any rate it is clear that we must not become partisans in this civil war.'[30] This official British expedition of February 1861 was certainly not planned as a reconnaissance preparatory to intervention against the rebellion.

Hope took ten ships with him, the large number being partly determined by his intention to establish consulates at Chinkiang, Kiukiang and Hankow, and to station vessels to regulate the trade at each of these ports, as well as at Nanking. He left behind two of the largest vessels available, partly on account of their draft, but partly also to avoid imparting to the expedition 'a belligerent aspect, which I think it very desirable to avoid'.[31] As a result of this expedition three new consulates were established and an agreement was concluded with the rebels permitting British vessels to pass through the territory under their control if holding river passes, copies of which would be sent to Nanking. It was also agreed that a British naval vessel might be stationed at the rebel capital to help regulate and protect the trade, and further that if in future the rebels should attack any of the river ports or any other places where British trade was carried on they would not molest British subjects, while the British authorities at those places would be instructed not to interfere in any hostilities. In addition, although less readily, the Taipings agreed that during the current year their forces would not approach nearer than two days' march (about 30 miles) to Shanghai. This promise later gave rise to what seem to be unwarranted charges of bad faith against them when they did attack Shanghai again in January 1862. But for the time being a satisfactory working arrangement had been reached on the basis, as Hope expressed it in his report on the expedition, 'that in the districts of country of which they hold possession, the Taiping authorities must be regarded as those of the *de facto* government, and must be dealt with accordingly'.[32]

Provisional Regulations, permitting British vessels to trade freely upon the Yangtze as far as Hankow, subject only to inspection designed to prevent any trade in arms, were published on March 18, and the river was then thrown open to trade.[33] British policy at this stage was not being based on the assumption that it was necessary to get rid of the rebellion as the condition for the development of the river trade, but rather on the assumption that it was possible, or at least that it was worth trying, to get round it without conflict.

It remained an unwelcome obstacle, of course, and official reports upon it were still almost wholly condemnatory. In the same despatch in which he defined his *de facto* approach to the rebels Hope also stated that he could regard them 'in no other light than that of an organized band of robbers'. Parkes, at greater length, reported that their government, in so far as they could be said to have one, appeared to be 'a pure military despotism' without any settled system of administration. Soldiers and slaves were the only two classes of population in Nanking, which was more of an armed camp than a seat of government. 'It is clear', Parkes added, 'that the behaviour of men of this stamp towards foreigners cannot always be counted on.'[34]

Against such views Meadows still argued in favour of the rebels. The Manchu dynasty had received its 'death blow' in the recent war, he declared, and it was of the utmost importance to find 'some other power in the nation to take its place'. The Taipings, Meadows held, were the obvious alternative, and although he thought no direct steps to encourage them should be taken, action against them would be disastrous to British interests in China and very expensive to boot. The usual criticisms levelled against the Taipings by foreigners, for example that they fired on white flags, were based on Western conditions and assumptions, not Chinese, Meadows insisted. The general attitude of the rebels towards foreigners was more encouraging than that of the Manchus, and there was 'a long succession of irrefragable proofs that the Tae-pings do earnestly desire friendly commercial intercourse with us'.[35]

In addition to Meadows, a more recent recruit to the consular service, R. J. Forrest, presented a report in March 1861 which is worth noting. Forrest travelled overland from Shanghai to Nanking, in order to join Hope's expedition. He therefore passed through a considerable tract of territory recently conquered by the rebels, and may be assumed to have had better opportunities for observation than interpreters who merely descended from ships to parley with rebel chiefs at a few river towns, which were usually in a state of siege. The picture Forrest drew of the countryside under Taiping control was not one of chaos or anarchy. He heard much of the melancholy effects of the Taiping advance into Kiangnan in 1860, but things were returning to normal by March 1861. Rebel authorities paid a visit to the rural districts once a month, and exacted a tribute of cash or rice from the inhabitants, he reported. Regularly appointed officers were appointed in all important places, and the people seemed to have confidence in them, so that unless some new military operations disturbed Nanking 'the villages around it will soon become peopled, and the land resume its fertile appearance', Forrest believed. At Nanking itself, he added, building was going on, 'and people who have known the place before say that a marked improvement is taking place. . . . The authorities assert, with some show of truth, that the rulers are now giving their attention to the formation of a fixed order of government, and to the improvement of the condition of the people; measures impossible before because of the Imperialist army'.[36]

There were, then, two views on the rebellion and its prospects still to be found in official British reports, but only just two views. Meadows and Forrest represent what was very much a minority opinion which did not seriously disturb or qualify the judgments of their superiors. Which was right is a question beyond the scope of this study. The rebellion had many faces, but although the prevailing British consular view of it can reasonably be criticized as too ready to assume the worst, and as making insufficient allowance for the military exigencies of the movement, it was nevertheless a view based upon a great variety of reports, first-hand and second-hand, official and non-official which, by the middle of 1861, were nearly unanimous in condemning the rebellion as purely destructive from practically every point of view.

Certainly for Bruce, now established at Peking, the weight of evidence was overwhelmingly against the rebellion. 'All classes of observers', he told Russell in June, 'seem unanimous both as to the destructive nature of the insurrection and as to the blasphemous and immoral character of the superstition on which it is based.' If the rebels succeeded, China 'would be reduced to a mass of agriculturists governed by a theocracy supported by armies collected from the most barbarous and demoralized part of the population', and the commercial prosperity of the country, including foreign trade with it, would receive a fatal blow. It was in no sense a popular, national rising and was, indeed, irreconcilable not only with the Manchu dynasty but with the whole traditional fabric of Chinese civilization. The difficulty was that the Manchu government, 'though undoubtedly more generally acceptable to the Chinese people, properly so called, than its competitor the Taepings', was so supine and inefficient that, despite its superior resources, no confidence could be felt in its ability to triumph. The logic of all this would seem to be that it should be given some sort of assistance, but Bruce did not as yet suggest this to the Foreign Office.[37]

Bruce in fact was in a considerable dilemma as to the best policy to follow in the circumstances. He complained in a letter to his brother in August 1861 that 'the ignorance and arrogance of this Government combined make it impossible to act with safety on the calculation of what is for their interest, while the effect of falling back on the Taepings will only be to ruin our trade. The mind gets weary and stale in attempting to solve a problem which admits of no solution, except that of events.'[38]

Events indeed, rather than Bruce's own will, were to resolve his dilemma, which was well illustrated by a long letter he wrote to Hope in June. In this he switched from one to another possible alternative policy without firmly settling upon any. The strict non-intervention usual in cases of civil war was attended in China 'with far more than ordinary hazard and risk to our trade', but he thought that the home government would 'probably abstain from rendering active assistance to the Imperial Government, both on account of the assurances of neutrality we have given to the insurgents, and on account of the serious and indefinite consequences to which such intervention would in all probability lead'. Another possibility was to take all the treaty ports, or at least the chief ones, completely under foreign protection, but this had its difficulties also. 'The insurgents would naturally object that in leaving the revenue and administration of these places in Imperial hands we do in reality assist the Imperialists', while there was little prospect of persuading the Emperor to regard them as completely neutral cities and to abstain from using them as bases for offensive operations. In any case, Bruce asked, how could such a principle be enforced upon the rebels? Could a purely naval force keep them in check, 'with chastisement at their capital in case of hostile movement on any of the ports?' This suggestion of possible direct action at Nanking was, it may be noted here, decidedly rejected by both Hope and the Foreign Office. Thus three possible lines of policy were outlined by Bruce—strict non-intervention, active assistance to the Imperial government, and the neutralization of the treaty ports backed by a readiness to use naval force at Nanking to enforce this—and none of them seemed completely acceptable or practicable.

Bruce concluded his uncertain analysis by stressing the importance of avoiding 'partial collisions' with the rebels, lest this create a feeling of animosity in them towards foreigners, 'which does not seem to exist at present'. Moreover, were such collisions to lead to a serious blow being struck by British forces without instructions from home, 'on the one hand Her Majesty's Government would not approve of being committed without being consulted, and on the other we should lose a favourable opportunity of placing our relations with the Emperor on a satisfactory footing, if we were deprived by some incidental event of the power of making our aid a matter of bargain with the Imperial Government'.[39]

Bruce obviously felt that aid to the Manchu government was the ultimately logical policy for Britain to follow, but also that it should not be involuntary or unconditional aid. He wanted it to be given in such a way as to achieve more than simply the suppression of a troublesome rebellion. At this stage, however, he was not prepared to take a strong initiative himself in the direction of intervention, both for fear that the Foreign Office would not approve and because of his doubt whether, given the attitude of the Emperor to the recent treaty settlement, it would effect any fundamental improvement in British relations with the Manchu government. Other men were to make the decision for him early in 1862.

Rear-Admiral Hope, the other main influence in China on the shaping of British policy towards the rebellion at this time, had greater faith than Bruce in the possibility of negotiating effectively with the rebels. One of the reasons in addition to tactical considerations that he gave for rejecting the idea of a naval attack on Nanking was that so long as the rebels held that city as the seat of their power they would be easy of access, 'and from such experience as our short intercourse has afforded, I see a fair prospect of our acquiring sufficient influence with them to enable us to carry all points which are essential to our commercial interests, even to that of eventual abstinence from the Consular ports'.[40] Hope believed that it was, in any case, unwise to provoke the rebels, since they were in a position to cut off tea and silk supplies coming down to Shanghai. Despite one or two incidents, large supplies of these commodities continued to reach Shanghai, and many merchants shared Hope's views on the dangers of interfering against a rebellion which, for all its unwelcome aspects, yet allowed trade to continue. Bruce, however, was 'not so sanguine as to our influence with Tae-pings being sufficient to save our trade from injury'.[41]

It was Hope also who had first urged the neutralization of the treaty ports as the best approach from the British point of view, arguing that so long as they continued to function as trading centres, 'the ingenuity of the Chinese would not fail to devise modes by which the produce of the country would be brought there in defiance of every obstacle'.[42] The Foreign Office was attracted by this idea, and in July Bruce was instructed to try to negotiate the neutrality of all the treaty ports with both sides. The Peking government, Russell believed, on what grounds it is not at all clear, would 'probably make no difficulty' in abstaining from using the ports as bases for operation so long as the rebels agreed not to attack them, while it was hoped that the rebels would see that it was not in their interests to run the risk of collision with foreign powers at the ports.[43]

But obviously, so long as the Manchu government was left free to continue to collect the rich customs revenues of these ports, especially Shanghai, and to obtain foreign arms through them it was hardly reasonable to expect the rebels not to attack them in return simply for a guarantee that they would not be used as Imperialist military bases. Bruce was well aware of this, and thought Hope's suggestion impracticable. He seems, therefore, to have made no very serious effort to win Imperial acceptance of the idea, despite Russell's instructions. He held firmly to the view that the Manchu government was still the legitimate and established government in China, to which alone he was accredited and with which alone treaties had been made.[44] Britain had no right to attempt to deprive the Imperial government of its claims upon the treaty ports, whether as sources of revenue or as bases of operations, and he rejected all suggestions for doing so, as for example a consular plan put forward in July 1861 for placing Shanghai under an Allied Commission which should collect the customs duties and place them in trust 'on account of the future government, whatever it might prove to be, whether rebel or Imperialist', after deductions had been made for indemnity payments and administrative expenses.[45]

Thus the idea of putting the treaty ports completely outside the field of conflict, either by getting the agreement of both rebels and Imperialists to their neutralization or by the Allies taking them over themselves, came to nothing. By the end of 1861 the 'neutrality' of these ports meant simply a demand by the British authorities that the rebels stay clear of them without any compensating guarantee that the Manchus would be prevented from making use of them. Bruce really held to this view all along; Hope and the Foreign Office came to accept it without argument later. It was, virtually, a denial of belligerent rights to the rebels so far as certain key cities in China were concerned, and as such, quite inconsistent with a profession of strict neutrality.[46]

Certain other aspects of British policy at this time also show that, although the main emphasis was upon still avoiding direct involvement in the struggle and upon testing the possibilities of a *modus vivendi* with the rebels, there was a strong inclination towards helping the Manchus in some way short of active intervention. For example, in May 1861, naval forces under Captain R. Dew were sent to Ningpo to help reorganize the defences of that port. Although British forces were still not to be committed beyond the defence of British subjects and property, advice was given to the Imperial authorities as to the best use of their resources, guns were mounted on the walls and Imperial soldiers trained in their use. Acting upon instructions from Hope, Dew also obtained a promise from the rebel chiefs in the vicinity that they would not attack Ningpo during the current year. This served to confirm Hope's belief that, although the Taiping movement 'can only be viewed as that of a banditti bent on free quarter and plunder, yet sufficient organization exists among them to admit of the hope that, by a due admixture of firmness and conciliation in dealing with them, they may be deterred from interfering with our Consular ports and trade'.[47] The fact that the rebels did attack Ningpo within the year, despite this promise, was one of the main reasons for Hope and the Foreign Office coming to the conclusion that the Taipings 'did not appreciate the nature of bonds and obligations'. That they were any worse in this respect than the Manchus or, some would no doubt wish to add, the British, is not very apparent.[48] But for the time being, Hope continued to believe in the possibility of negotiating the security of the treaty ports and of foreign trade. The negotiations were, however, very one-sided. The rebels were half-persuaded, half-warned to keep away from the ports, while the Manchus on the other hand were advised about their defence.

There was also apparent in the latter half of 1861 some sign of a milder view being taken of the enlistment of British volunteers on the Imperialist side. In the early part of 1861 the American filibuster, F. T. Ward, began recruiting the mercenary force which was later to receive Imperial recognition under the name of the Ever Victorious Army, and which was later still to pass under the command of Major Charles Gordon. Ward's activities were at first strongly disapproved of by the foreign consuls at Shanghai, both as a breach of neutrality and because he encouraged seamen to desert their vessels. Bruce reported, 'with satisfaction' but prematurely, the disbandment of this force at the beginning of July.[49] Russell, on the other hand, wrote in August that since the Chinese people appeared to be better off under the Manchu government than under 'the so-called National Party', if the Emperor were to establish an Imperial Legion of Foreigners there would be no reason to object to British subjects entering it.[50] The Neutrality Ordinance of 1855 was still being enforced in China at this time, and under its provisions nine British subjects who had been enlisted by Ward were sentenced to terms of imprisonment at Hong Kong. But since a similar charge against other men for serving on the rebel side had been dropped, these men appealed for a remission of sentence and in this they were supported by Bruce.[51] At this stage the legal position of British subjects serving either side in the struggle was, in fact, rather uncertain, but Russell's despatch of August 1861 indicates the existence of a readiness to release British subjects in favour of the Imperialists which was to become quite explicit a year later.

The issue of Revised Regulations for British trade upon the Yangtze at the end of 1861 also illustrates how Bruce's general policy of seeking to win the confidence of the Manchu government and its willing co-operation in implementing the new treaties made him ready to approve measures which weakened the prospects of the rebellion. The original regulations issued in March 1861 had thrown the whole river open as far as Hankow, and had not set any limits to the trade beyond making provisions against arms-running. The result was that trade with rebel centres soon developed. Elgin had apparently expected this to happen but had not seen it as a reason for holding back the opening of the river to foreign trade. He had told Hope that, although strictly speaking only certain ports, all of which were in Imperial hands, were opened to trade under the treaty, 'we can hardly prevent our people from traficking [*sic*] at those held by the rebels if the latter invite them to do so'.[52]

The Imperial authorities, however, were naturally disturbed at the river trade becoming a source of foreign supplies to the rebels. As early as July 1861 Tseng Kuo-fan was complaining that the capture of Anking might be delayed, since supplies were reaching the beseiged rebels from vessels flying foreign flags.[53] Prince Kung accordingly began negotiations with Bruce for the stricter control of British trade upon the river, and new regulations were issued in December. These specifically limited the right of British vessels to trade to only two ports above Chinkiang, namely Hankow and Kiukiang, and shipments of goods classified as war supplies, including hemp, oil, timber, steel and iron, were subject to inspection, as were all arms carried.[54]

These stricter regulations, of course, aroused the complaints of British merchants in China, who saw them as an invasion of established treaty rights, But Bruce insisted that the presence of British trade upon the Yangtze at all, while the rebellion still continued, was an extension of those rights and an act of favour on the part of the Manchu government, which had every right to demand that the trade should not become a source of strength to the rebels. The original regulations of March 1861, Bruce later told Russell, 'would certainly have done much to perpetuate the disorder prevalent in the centre of China, which it is as much our interest as that of the Chinese to see put down'.[55] The Foreign Office supported Bruce against the complaints of British merchants, so that, although British trade on the Yangtze continued still, it became one of the avowed objects of British policy from the end of 1861 on to help the Manchu government prevent the rebels benefiting from it in any way.

British policy was thus strongly weighted in favour of the Manchus during 1861, but was still one of neutrality in the sense that there was no active intervention against the rebellion. The change in that direction came about in the early part of 1862, primarily as a reaction against the renewal of rebel attacks upon Shanghai. But before then certain other events helped provide the conditions for the abandonment of the former policy. The first of these was a change, more apparent than real, within the Manchu government itself after the palace revolution of October-November 1861. The Hsien Feng Emperor died at Jehol in August, refusing to the last to recognize the presence of Western diplomats in his capital and surrounded by advisers of conservative, strongly anti-foreign viewpoints.[56] From among these a Regency Council was appointed to govern for his successor, a child of only five. A struggle for power quickly developed between this Council and the child's mother, Tzu Hsi, the famous 'Old Buddha' as she was later called, who received the support of Prince Kung. The return of the court to Peking at the end of October, a move long advocated by Prince Kung, became the occasion for a *coup d'état* which replaced the original Regency Council by a smaller Council, dominated by Tzu Hsi and of which Kung also was a member.

In a decree issued to justify this coup, members of the former

Council were condemned among other things for their part in the seizure of the allied emissaries in 1860 and for their alleged misrepresentation to the Emperor of the attitude of the foreign powers towards China. It naturally appeared to Bruce and other Western observers, therefore, that the more enlightened and conciliatory party in Chinese counsels had triumphed over reaction, and they greeted the change with high approval. It constituted 'the most favourable incident that has hitherto taken place in the course of our relations with China', Bruce reported to Russell, and in a private letter he called it 'a real ratification of the treaty'. He was encouraged to hope that the old-style difficulties which had stood in the way of easy diplomatic relations with the Manchu government would soon disappear.[57]

Like most palace revolutions, the struggle was over power rather than principle, and it by no means represented complete success for a party of reform and conciliation. At the time, however, this was the British hope. The emphasis in British comments and reports was upon the triumph of 'Prince Kung's party', and the argument was quickly advanced that more direct support should now be given to the existing government of the empire.[58] Bruce himself was far from advocating such aid immediately. Indeed, in January 1862, after receiving reports of the fall of Ningpo, he complained vigorously of a government still 'too enervated to act and too proud to beg assistance openly'.[59] But on the whole there was a real if rather short-lived improvement in official British opinion about the Manchu government. 'The new administration does certainly manifest a disposition to grapple in a more bold and practical spirit with its difficulties', Bruce reported at the end of February, while in the House of Commons in March the Under-Secretary of State for Foreign Affairs, Layard, assured members that within a very short time 'a very great change' had taken place in the government at Peking, and used this as an argument to help justify the abandonment of neutrality.[60]

While the prospects for effective co-operation with the Manchu government seemed thus improved, the possibility of maintaining a working arrangement with the rebels was weakened, in the judgment of British officials, first by events at Ningpo and later, more decisively, by events at Nanking and

106

Shanghai. In December 1861 the long-feared rebel attack on. Ningpo took place, and a treaty port passed for the first time under Taiping control. The official British reaction to this was twofold. On the one hand it was regarded as disturbing evidence that the rebels could not be relied upon to keep clear of the treaty ports, even when they made an agreement to do so; on the other hand it was seen as providing a useful test case, an opportunity 'of ascertaining by positive experience whether it would be possible to conduct trade from a seaport held by the Taipings'.[61] Bruce instructed the consul at Ningpo to seek answers to such questions as 'Do they show any disposition to govern and organize the country? Do they wish to encourage trade? Are the orders of their leaders obeyed? Do the respectable and wealthy classes of Ningpo return to the city and resume their avocations? Are property and life respected, or is the city treated as an orange to be squeezed dry and then thrown away? In short, is their administration a hand-to-mouth affair, or is it conducted so as to show that they understand that to form a government, the wealth and the industry of the country must not be destroyed? For information on these points I look with anxiety.'[62] From the British point of view, Ningpo became an experiment in direct relations with the Taipings.

It was hardly a fair test, unless the rebels were to be given some time in which to consolidate their gains from the threat of an Imperial counter-attack. Furthermore, the consul, Harvey, for all his protestations to the contrary, appears to have been a far from unprejudiced observer and his reports, although commended by Bruce, illustrate the official British view of the rebellion by this stage in its most extravagant form.[63] In March 1862 he told Bruce that after three months of occupation 'not one single step in the direction of "good government" has been taken by the Taepings; not any attempt made to organize a political body or commercial institutions; not a vestige, not a trace of anything approaching to order, or regularity of action or consistency of purpose, can be found in any of their public acts; the words "government machinery" as applied to Taeping rule, have no possible meaning here; and in short, *Desolation* is the only end obtained, as it always has been wherever the sway of the marauders has had its full scope, and their power the liberty of unchecked excess'. The rebellion, Harvey concluded, was 'the greatest delusion, as a political or popular movement, and the Taeping doctrines the most gigantic and blasphemous imposition as a creed or ethics, that the world has ever witnessed. . . . I look in vain in the darkest ages for a similar faction and upheaving of men; but there is nothing in past records so dark and bad. . . . The ravings of John of Leyden and his impious Münster adventurers in 1534–36 are left far behind in the race of folly by the Tae-ping madmen. . . . Taepingdom is a huge mass of "nothingness". . . . There is nothing to lay hold of in it. It is a gigantic bubble, that collapses on being touched, but leaves a mark of blood on the finger.'[64]

It is hardly surprising that Harvey's reports were challenged by sympathizers with the Taipings, but they were accepted by his official superiors as proving beyond all question the impossibility of looking to the rebels to provide a government under which trade could develop profitably. Their highly coloured phrases confirmed what many more sober reports had already suggested.[65]

While these conclusions were being drawn from the situation at Ningpo a crisis had developed in British relations with the rebels after a second visit to Nanking by Hope at the end of December. Hope's object in making this visit was to secure firmer guarantees from the rebels that they would not attack any of the treaty ports not already in their possession, whether on the coast or along the Yangtze. But his approach on this occasion was far less accommodating than in March, for he made his demands without offering any guarantee in return that the Imperialists would be prevented from using these ports as bases. Parkes, who again accompanied Hope as interpreter, confessed himself in some perplexity about the matter in a letter to the Permanent Under-Secretary of State for Foreign Affairs, Hammond, and felt that 'nothing less than hostilities would appear to have been resolved on unless the rebels do just as they are directed'.[66]

In threatening to defend all the treaty ports against rebel attacks Hope was indeed going beyond any instructions received up to that time, as was pointed out by Hammond in a memo attached to Parkes' letter. But Palmerston, the Prime Minister, added a second memo to the effect that 'these Rebels are

Revolters not only against the Emperor, but against all laws human and Divine, and it seems quite right to keep them away from the Treaty Ports. That is all that it is necessary to say to them. Those Treaty Ports are under the authority of the Imperial Government, and we have no right to prescribe in what way the Emperor shall use them.' Thus Hope's initiative in adopting a tougher line towards the rebels was readily approved and confirmed by the government at home.

The rebels refused to do just as directed by Hope and insisted that the agreement made in March 1861 to keep their forces two days' march from Shanghai was not binding beyond that year.[67] This claim, although questioned by Parkes, seems to have been justified. They refused to extend the agreement in any way, but on the contrary made plain their intention to advance upon Shanghai. To this Hope replied by warning them that they would incur 'not merely a repulse, as on a former occasion, but such further consequences as your folly will deserve'.[68] Nevertheless, shortly after Hope's return from this unsatisfactory interview, large rebel forces under Li Hsiu-ch'eng, the Loyal King, approached Shanghai in the middle of January 1862 and, without actually storming the city itself, overran the countryside around, including Woosung and Kaokiao, which commanded the approach to Shanghai from the Yangtze river. Their object, Hope believed, was to reduce the city by depriving it of supplies. By the end of February, in co-operation with Ward's force and the French, he was leading the available British forces to clear the Taipings from the immediate vicinity of Shanghai, and was recommending still more extensive action.[69] By the beginning of March Bruce also was justifying the need for offensive action, and by the beginning of May, the Foreign Office, necessarily several months behind developments in China, was giving its formal approval to these developments.[70]

Thus, under the immediate pressure of a Taiping threat to Shanghai at the beginning of 1862, the attempt to get round the rebellion, which was the basic feature of British policy during 1861, was abandoned in favour of an attempt to destroy it. There is no single, clearly marked point at which this can be said to have taken place, nor was the change in policy complete and consistent in every detail. A British consular representative remained stationed at Nanking at least until the end of 1862, and there were suggestions, never followed up, for a possible renewal of negotiations with the rebels.[71] But, broadly speaking, the early months of 1862 saw the real and decisive change in British policy towards the rebellion. The policy of neutrality laid down in 1853, qualified and imperfect as it was in the first place and applied as it was in a manner increasingly favourable to the Manchu cause, was now more or less explicitly abandoned in favour of a policy of deliberate intervention against the Taipings. The major issue during 1862 became how far and in what manner to help towards their defeat.

7

Intervention
(1862-64)

FEW NOW ARGUE, as most Western writers on the subject once did, that foreign intervention was the decisive factor in the defeat of the Taipings. Nevertheless, it continues to be recognized as of considerable importance, and it is often assumed that, being important, it was also quite extensive aid. Thus Lo Erh-kang, after suggesting that the English and French forces which had been retained in China to enforce the new treaties were reinforced by additional troops from India following the defeat of the Mutiny there, states that 'in the Spring of 1862 England began big scale military action against the Taiping state and a new phase in her interference began'.[1] It is certainly correct to suggest that a new phase in British policy began at this time, but in so far as Lo's argument infers that the British government was prepared to make a heavy commitment of its forces to the struggle it is quite contrary to the evidence. A primary objective of British policy during these years was to keep the scale of direct foreign involvement as small as possible, to the minimum necessary to ensure a Manchu victory.

Bruce in particular urged strictly limited intervention, for he was thinking far beyond the immediate question of the suppression of the rebellion, major problem though that was. His grand design, while British minister at Peking, was to win the adherence of the Manchu government to the new treaty settlement in spirit as well as letter. His approach, as he defined it to

111

a Foreign Office official shortly before he moved to the Chinese capital, was to convince that government 'that our objects are essentially pacific, that our demands are reasonable and that we are inclined to be moderate and conciliatory if we are met in a corresponding spirit'.[2] In this way he hoped gradually to create a situation in which the treaties would be fulfilled not under the constant threat of superior Western force, though he recognized that for a long time to come this must remain their ultimate sanction, but under a Chinese government able and willing to co-operate to this end.[3]

It needed to be a reasonably efficient as well as a reasonably willing government. Bruce certainly did not wish to see preserved in Peking a weak and incapable government which could be easily browbeaten into giving way to every Western demand. Such a government would simply invite rebellion from its own subjects and, ultimately perhaps, partition by ambitious Western powers. China would then become a second Turkey, a field for imperial rivalries of the most dangerous kind rather than a field for peaceful and mutually profitable trade. He told Russell in March 1862 that he was 'fully convinced that we, who neither seek territory nor promote by arms religious conversion, have little to apprehend from any success that may attend our efforts to raise the Chinese Executive out of its present helpless condition. Nor do I consider that it will be a matter of regret or hostile to our interests, that China should be encouraged by a consciousness of her strength, to use bolder language in defence of her just rights. The weakness of China, rather than her strength, is likely to create a fresh Eastern Question in these seas.'[4]

The basic object of Bruce's policy was simply to provide for the future security of British interests in China with as little trouble and expense to the British home government as possible. He wanted to see Great Britain relieved of the need to maintain large naval forces in Chinese waters, in fact to end the era of gunboat diplomacy. Any aid given the Manchu government against its domestic enemies should therefore contribute to its regeneration, not to its mere survival. It was an enlightened, far-sighted and humane policy, even if inspired by fundamentally self-interested motives.[5]

As the later history of China sufficiently shows, Bruce failed in his main objective. The Manchu government was neither effectively reformed in itself nor greatly reconciled to the presence of the West. The 'break-up of China' remained a constant possibility throughout the later nineteenth century, and the maintenance of British treaty rights there was always ultimately dependent upon the presence of British gunboats. The difficulties in the way of success for Bruce's plans were indeed formidable, as was the opposition he aroused. British merchants and missionaries who looked for quick returns under the new treaty settlement were critical of a policy which seemed to them more concerned to protect Chinese interests and sensibilities than their own. He had also to curb consuls brought up under the old dispensation, who were quick to call upon the nearest gunboat to force satisfaction from the local Chinese authorities when faced with what they considered an infringement of the treaties. If grievances were to be handled in this way, Bruce objected, not only might it lead to general hostilities, as in 1856, but there was little point in having a diplomatic representative to the central government in Peking.[6]

There was also little point in having such a representative if the Peking government itself was incapable of enforcing its authority upon its own subordinate officials in the provinces. Bruce wanted to strengthen the hand of the central government and to help make it the sole effective military and political power in the Chinese state.[7] His attempts to do this ran quite counter to the realities of the political situation in China by 1860, a fact of which he was not completely unaware. The failure of the regular Imperial armies to crush the Taiping rebellion during the eighteen-fifties meant that effective military and political power in central China and, through the new *likin* tax,[8] a great measure of independent financial power also was passing into the hands of the great provincial officials. Chief among these were Tseng Kuo-fan and his nominees, Li Hung-chang and Tso Tsung-t'ang, who became governors of Kiangsu and Chekiang respectively in 1862. These were the men who actually created the armies and devised the strategies which defeated the rebellion. Given their growing power and authority, any attempt to bring about changes in the government of China which did not win their support and co-operation was bound to fail. Indeed, it could be said that it might have served Bruce's long-term plans better had the final campaign against the rebellion organized by these provincial governors failed, like the earlier campaigns of Hsiang Jung and Chang Kuo-liang, for then the central government might have mounted another and more efficient campaign with Western help, and have emerged from the rebellion militarily and politically stronger, at least in relation to its own provincial officers. Thus late in 1863 he could argue, against all the apparent aims of British intervention, that 'every consideration of sound policy indicates that Nanking is the *last* place we wish to see taken, as while in the hands of the Taipings it gives us a hold both on them and on this recalcitrant government'.[9] Such statements make no sense at all unless one remembers the larger objectives of Bruce's policy while British minister at Peking.

There was perhaps little sense in making them in any case, at least at that late stage, for the protraction of the rebellion could equally well have led to the actual partitioning of China by the Western powers as to the effective regeneration of the central Manchu administration. It is difficult to see that there was ever much prospect of success for Bruce's plans, especially since they ignored the deep-seated social origins of revolt in nineteenth-century China.

But however unsuccessful in the long run, this major objective of reforming and strengthening the government in Peking conditioned Bruce's approach to the question of aid against the rebels and made him the chief spokesman in British counsels for limited rather than extensive intervention. The problem, he told Russell in February 1862, was to render assistance 'in a shape which will strengthen and not weaken the authority of the government'.[10] To this end the approach he recommended was indirect aid which helped organize the resources available to the Manchus. Thus foreign assistance in the organization of the Imperial customs and the training of Imperial forces by European officers was desirable, but the direct use of Western forces against the rebels was not, at least beyond the defence of the treaty ports themselves. In April 1862 he told Brigadier General Staveley, the commander of British forces at Shanghai, that 'whatever the risk to our trade it had better be incurred than that we should fight the battles of this Government for it, or afford it more than casual and temporary assistance, which is all that will be required to enable the Imperialists to triumph, if they can be induced to turn their own resources to proper account . . . '.[11] The aid actually rendered to the Imperialist cause by Britain over the next two years cannot be accurately described as 'casual and temporary', but the phrase accurately reflects Bruce's own approach to the question.

Such an approach is not altogether what one would expect from Bruce's earlier reports on the rebellion and his scepticism during 1861 as to the possibility of making effective arrangements with the rebels. It must be said that Bruce was not remarkable for the steadiness and consistency of his views on the question of aid, for despite his general objection to British forces fighting the battles of the Manchu government, he showed a recurrent urge to deal the rebels a 'deadly blow' at Nanking, while at other times he became so exasperated with the Manchu government as to threaten to withdraw aid altogether and even, on certain conditions, to hand over Shanghai to the rebels. But basically he did hold to a policy of limited and indirect aid, to be applied through the central government, not the provincial authorities. Bruce found his post at Peking a wearying and frustrating one,[12] but he brought to it a breadth of vision and a sensitivity of outlook which is worthy of respect, even though it sometimes led him into inconsistencies of attitude and uncertainties of policy.

The Foreign Office approved Bruce's moderate and conciliatory approach to the Manchu government.[13] It agreed also that direct British intervention against the rebellion should be strictly limited in extent, though it showed itself readier than Bruce to approve the tendency of service officers to go beyond the limits set. The rational course for Britain to pursue, Russell told Bruce in July 1862, was to avoid any extensive engagements, to protect the treaty ports and to encourage the government to improve its armed forces so that it could itself reduce the rebels to subjection.[14] The British government did 'not propose to give to the Chinese government the whole force of the British Empire for their support', he assured the House of Lords, after quoting this despatch.[15]

The motives which made the home government insist on the limits of the commitment it was prepared to make on this issue were somewhat different from those uppermost in Bruce's mind. Considerations of economy were very important,[16] as were considerations of domestic politics. In 1857 the first Palmerston government had won an election precipitated by the outbreak of the *Arrow* war in China, and Palmerston's second government launched the campaign of 1859-60 after the Taku repulse. For this government to become embroiled so soon in yet another large-scale war in China was likely to prove too much even for John Bull himself to carry off successfully with parliament and the electorate. The possibility of just such a war developing was a main point in the arguments of the numerous critics in England of the policy of intervention, and the government was always at some pains to insist that it was only going so far and no further.

In any case, the British government was not urged to commit its forces deeply by the government it was supporting. The Manchu authorities maintained a decidedly ambivalent attitude on the question of foreign aid against the rebellion. The need for it, within limits the desirability of it, was recognized, but it was accepted with many misgivings as the lesser of two considerable evils. After the rejection of the Russian offer at the beginning of 1861 there was no further discussion of the question among high Manchu officials until the beginning of 1862, although plans for acquiring foreign arms and vessels were developed. The initiative in reopening the question of direct foreign aid came from the local gentry and officials at Shanghai. The former were particularly active, one of them, P'an Tseng-wei, even writing to Tseng Kuo-fan and travelling himself to Peking in order to urge the need for hiring foreign troops, not only to protect Shanghai but to help recapture inland cities such as Soochow.[17] Leading Manchu officials were, however, chary of these proposals for the extensive use of foreign aid in the interior. Tseng Kuo-fan argued that, whereas at ports such as Shanghai and Ningpo Western and Chinese interests were bound up together and should be defended in common, this was not so in the interior. If foreign troops were hired to help recapture cities such as Soochow, Changchow or Nanking, 'failure would lead to ridicule and success to unpredictable difficulties later'.[18] Prince Kung raised practical objections to the use of foreign troops in the interior. They moved much more quickly than did the Chinese, yet would be dependent on them for supplies; they were impatient and always anxious to advance, but China would have to supply the garrisons for the places they recaptured. Altogether, the value of using foreign troops beyond the treaty ports was questionable, he argued.[19]

In addition, although this was no doubt partly a face-saving formula, such aid as was accepted was to be on a temporary basis, necessary only in a period of acute crisis. 'The English ambassador says it is possible to send troops to help suppress the rebels, but only temporarily, not permanently', an Edict of February 25, 1862, read. 'He should be informed that after the alarm was sounded at Shanghai, troops were despatched from every quarter. But since this relief has not yet arrived it is necessary to borrow the help of foreign countries; but once our strength has been concentrated there, and put under competent command, naturally there will be no need of help.'[20] There was no anxiety to see large numbers of foreign troops brought to China to help suppress the rebels. In the middle of 1862, after the failure of the first combined attempt to clear a thirty-mile radius around Shanghai, there were reports that the British proposed to get more troops from India to assist in a later campaign. Both Tseng Kuo-fan and Tso Tsung-t'ang, who was leading the Chinese forces in Kiangsu and Chekiang, expressed their opposition to this, Tso being sceptical of their value on the ground that recent reverses near Shanghai showed that the barbarians were as much afraid of the rebels as China's own forces, and Tseng arguing that China's own resources were adequate to the task in hand. Many cities had been recaptured, Tseng wrote, 'the means for subduing Kiangsu and Chekiang exist, and if our policies do not succeed and the rebel conflagration die out, China should bear the burden herself.... How can we lightly hire foreign forces and so become an object of scorn to later generations?' China, in suppressing the rebels, should not plant the seeds of future complications, he concluded.[21]

When criticized for being too accommodating towards the foreign powers in the interpretation of the treaties, a situation in which Bruce could sympathize with him, Prince Kung vehemently defended the policies of the Tsungli Yamen and indicated another aspect of the official Manchu attitude towards foreign aid. 'As for the opinion that foreign help in putting down the rebels is not trustworthy, I am very far from saying that it is', he insisted. 'It is just that there is a danger that if we do not make them our allies, they may be used by the rebels. The harm in that would be immeasurable.'[22] Aid accepted in this spirit was, needless to say, readily abandoned when the need for it was felt to have passed. Foreign-officered forces, such as the Ever Victorious Army, were a constant source of apprehension to the Manchu government, for it was difficult to keep control over them or to be sure of their later loyalties. There were no regrets among Chinese officials when the Ever Victorious Army was disbanded in May 1864, before the final capture of Nanking, for it had long been regarded as a troublesome encumbrance.[23]

Altogether, the official Manchu view on the extent to which foreign aid against the rebels should go paralleled, on the obverse side of the coin, the official British view. Limited assistance, at the ports rather than in the interior, given indirectly by provision of arms and equipment rather than directly with foreign troops—all these points were common both to Bruce and the high Manchu officials in their approaches to the question. This is not to say that the aid actually given was exactly on this pattern. The local pressure at Shanghai in favour of more extended intervention was strong on both sides, while the Foreign Office was less insistent on the precise limits to be observed than was Bruce. But although there were differences in detail, there was agreement on fundamentals. In the circumstances foreign intervention was necessary, but it should be limited and it was better given indirectly.

Limited intervention was, in any case, all that was possible with the military forces Britain had available in China by 1862. Although her naval forces in the station were increased by about a third on what they had been in March 1861, her military establishment in China remained around the five-thousand mark and was not increased in the last years of the rebellion. There was, however, a very considerable relative increase in the British force stationed at Shanghai. In January 1862 this was between six and seven hundred men, to whom should be added four or five hundred French, two hundred and fifty volunteers and perhaps the same number of marines, a total European force of about fifteen hundred. During March and April the number of British and Indian troops at Shanghai was considerably increased from the garrison then being withdrawn from Tientsin, and by the middle of the year the regular British force there numbered about two thousand five hundred. With other additions the total force available was probably in the region of four thousand.[24] In the circumstances this was certainly a formidable force, especially when the great superiority of its arms and training are taken into account. But it was not of a size, nor was it ever intended, to be used much beyond the defence of Shanghai and its immediate vicinity. In fact one of the arguments used by Rear-Admiral Hope in favour of defending a radius around Shanghai rather than simply the city itself was that it would take fewer troops, using them in flying columns to support Chinese garrisons, than to man walls four and a half miles in extent. The object was to keep the size of the force needed at Shanghai as small as possible.[25]

The British military commander in China during most of 1862, Brig.-Gen. Staveley, was authorized to send for additional troops from India if he felt it absolutely necessary, but he was certainly not encouraged to do so. When he did call for them, upon what the War Office regarded as the inadequate ground that Indian troops stood the Shanghai climate better than British, he was reprimanded and told that it was the opinion of the government that 'the British military forces at Shanghae may safely be reduced'.[26] In March 1863, over twelve months before the capture of Nanking, Bruce also urged upon him the desirability of making arrangements with the Chinese authorities for the defence of the port 'which would gradually enable us to reduce the number of troops at Shanghae, and consequently the expenses of the occupation; for I look with dread at the consequences of the financial difficulties that must result from the present state of expenditure'.[27] In the middle of 1863, by which time the threat to Shanghai was safely past, the British force there was reduced to about fifteen hundred. The British forces maintained at Shanghai during 1862–63 were never capable of an extensive campaign against the rebellion.

The occasions on which regular British naval and military forces were engaged in direct action against the rebels were confined to the year 1862. The manner in which these engagements were first undertaken illustrates the quite unplanned nature of the change in British policy in the first part of that year, for they were begun well in advance of any Foreign Office approval or instruction. At the beginning of 1862 British policy, as understood by the Foreign Office, did not go beyond the defence of the foreign settlement areas save at Shanghai, while negotiation with the rebels where necessary was still an accepted part of it. 'It is true that the accounts we receive on all sides show the Taepings to be little better than Banditti organized on a large scale and bent on free quarters and plunder', a Foreign Office memorandum of February 22 read, 'and we have abundant evidence of the destructive nature of the insurrection and of the blasphemous and immoral character of the superstition on which it is based; but our efforts in the various interviews which our agents have held with the Rebel leaders have been directed chiefly to securing the persons and Property of British subjects, and maintaining our rights to trade as secured for us by Treaty.'[28] A few days after this was written Rear-Admiral Hope's report telling of the refusal of the rebels to extend the agreement not to approach the treaty ports was received, and early in March his instructions were extended to provide for the defence of all the ports not already in rebel hands by the naval forces under his command. There was no instruction about the use of military forces, and any need for action beyond the ports was not yet envisaged by the Foreign Office.[29]

At Shanghai, however, action beyond the walls of the city had already been taken and more was being planned even before these instructions were sent. Early in February consul Medhurst had urged the need for action by British forces beyond the walls on the ground that it was necessary to clear a belt of country around the city in order to maintain supplies for its population, now swollen by refugees. He saw such action as essentially defensive, and quite consistent with a policy of strict neutrality.[30] On February 21 Hope used naval forces to co-operate with Chinese troops under Ward in clearing the rebels from the immediate vicinity of Shanghai and to recapture the towns of Woosung and Kaokiao (which commanded the river approaches to the port). He also urged upon Bruce the need for more extensive action, and suggested clearing the country within a line running through towns approximately thirty miles out. Bruce thought this project 'within the scope of the intentions of the Government', but insisted that the Imperial authorities must provide adequate garrisons to hold the line, 'for I do not think Her Majesty's Government would approve of our being committed to hold any other position than Shanghae itself'. Hope was confident both that the Chinese would provide forces capable of holding the towns when recaptured, and that the projected campaign was merely anticipating the wishes of the home government.[31]

At the end of April 1862, therefore, substantial British, French and Chinese forces began their attacks on the rebels within the line proposed. It proved easier to capture the towns than to hold them for, as Bruce had feared, the Chinese garrisons to which they were handed over proved incapable of defending them against renewed rebel attacks. By the beginning of June the situation around Shanghai was back much to what it had been before this clearing campaign started. Despite the urgings of Hope, Staveley refused to renew it during the summer months, and was content to hold Shanghai itself and the river approaches, concentrating meanwhile on training Chinese forces for a new campaign in the autumn.

The pressure on Shanghai in fact eased considerably without further British action, and by mid-July Staveley was able to report that 'the rebels have ceased to give any annoyance in the vicinity of Shanghae'.[32] From information received from Europeans in the silk districts, he added, the bulk of their force appeared to have gone towards Nanking, 'which city is pressed by a force of Imperialists'. This was in truth the situation, the Loyal King having been recalled urgently by Hung to assist in the defence of the capital. It therefore proved a much easier task to clear and hold the thirty-mile limit when the campaign was renewed in October.[33]

It is apparent that the thirty-mile-radius policy was very much the creation of the officers stationed at Shanghai. Bruce gave it qualified approval before it was first applied in May, but the idea certainly was not his, and he was later very critical of it.[34] The Foreign Office really did nothing more than acquiesce in the scheme. On May 6, a week after the campaign had actually started, it agreed that action by British forces up to fifteen or twenty miles from the forts was allowable, and by July 10 it had got as far as permitting action 'not extending

beyond thirty miles from the Port'.[35] Neither the Foreign
Office nor Bruce ever took the initiative in directing that offensive operations beyond the ports be undertaken, and they were
agreed in rejecting a suggestion that the whole of the silk
district around Shanghai be occupied.[36]

At Ningpo also, service action outran Foreign Office instructions. On July 7 Russell told Bruce that 'Ningpo ought to be
recovered by the Imperialists'.[37] In fact it had been recovered
for the Imperialists as early as May 10 by the combined action
of British and French naval forces. Friction with the rebels in
occupation of Ningpo had quickly developed over their refusal
to give up a claim to jurisdiction over the foreign settlement
area, which had been hastily defined and proclaimed by the
foreign consuls there soon after the Taiping capture of the port,
apparently without any prior reference either to Manchu or
rebel authorities. The situation was greatly aggravated when
the rebels began strengthening the defences on the city wall
opposite the foreign settlement. This was interpreted as the
prelude to a rebel attack on the foreign settlement, though it
could as readily have been interpreted as a purely defensive
measure, for the foreign settlement area was unfortunately
placed in the direct line of fire between the city and any forces
advancing up river to attack it. 'Incidents' over firing from the
wall by the rebels endangering foreign ships and residents
naturally occurred. Altogether it was a thoroughly explosive
situation, especially since the foreign settlement area was
crowded with refugees from the city.

Early in May the Imperial forces, based on Chusan Island,
were ready to attempt its recapture, and the British and French
naval commanders thereupon issued a remarkable warning to
the rebels to the effect that 'we maintain a perfect neutrality,
but if you fire the guns or muskets from the battery or wall
opposite the settlement on the advancing Imperialists, thereby
endangering the lives of our men and people in the foreign
Settlement, we shall feel it our duty to return the fire and
bombard the city'.[38] This was certainly a very peculiar kind of
'perfect neutrality'. After the inevitable shots from the wall had
been fired, the city was bombarded by the two British and the
one French naval vessels there, between 10 a.m. and 4 p.m.
with a two-hour break for lunch, according to Capt. Dew's

report of the action. It was then stormed, captured and handed over to the Imperial authorities on the same evening, their forces having taken virtually no part in the battle.

In the following months the British naval forces in the area helped to clear a thirty-mile radius around Ningpo as had been attempted at Shanghai, but foreign assistance to the Manchus in this area became mainly a French affair. The actual recapture of the city was, however, carried out with considerable aid from British naval forces which, strictly speaking, had never received instructions from the Admiralty going beyond those ordering the defence of the treaty ports not in rebel hands. The action at Ningpo hardly came within the scope of those orders, but it was nevertheless in harmony with the trend in official British policy towards the rebellion by this time. On June 6, Bruce expressed his approval of it to Russell, arguing that a collision at Ningpo was bound to come sooner or later, and on July 22, a fortnight after writing that the recapture of Ningpo ought to be left to the Imperialists, the Foreign Secretary was approving its recapture by Her Majesty's forces.[39]

These two campaigns, at and around Shanghai and Ningpo, were all in which regular British forces were engaged against the rebels. But in addition to this direct intervention, assistance was given to the Manchu cause in a number of other important ways. The training of Chinese troops by British officers was begun at Tientsin early in 1862 and extended to Shanghai after the failure of the first thirty-mile-radius campaign. The co-operation of the Imperial authorities in this project was not altogether wholehearted, from their fear that the troops trained in this way would become difficult for Chinese officers to handle, and Staveley complained at the number and quality of the troops provided for training at Shanghai. Bruce was fearful lest British action of this sort provoke the jealousy of other powers, and would have preferred to see military officers from a smaller treaty power, such as Prussia, carry it out, but it was actually done by British and French officers during 1862 and 1863.[40]

Again in March 1862, in order to assist in the defence of the treaty port and its perimeter, a large body of troops from Tseng Kuo-fan's forces were transported down the Yangtze through rebel territory to Shanghai in British trading vessels chartered for the purpose by the Chinese authorities. This appears to have been the main occasion upon which aid was given in this way. Hope approved the firms owning the vessels undertaking the commission, 'provided the permission is looked upon as entirely exceptional', and Medhurst asked for Bruce's approval of what would, he noted, amount to 'a violation of the Neutrality Ordinance'. Later attempts by British shipowners to charter vessels to the Manchu authorities at Ningpo for similar purposes appear to have been discouraged.[41]

Aid was also given by supplying Manchu forces with arms. Early in 1862 Ward's force had been provided with arms and supplies at cost price, while Bruce applied on their behalf for muskets and field-guns from India. The arms supplied seem to have been chiefly of the kind going out of use in the British army at this time—smooth-bore muskets and old-fashioned field-guns, not the new Enfield rifle or the Armstrong shell-firing gun.[42] As to their extent, it is difficult to get any precise idea, but it would seem to have been fairly substantial. Staveley reported in November 1862 that the Ever Victorious Army had recently received '10,000 stand of arms, 12 twelve-pounder guns and 1,000,000 round of ammunition', and at the same time reported his intention to sell to the Manchu authorities at Shanghai, 'at a valuation', the arms and accoutrements of two regiments leaving for India.[43]

Quite as important as the provision of arms for the Manchus were the measures taken to prevent their reaching the rebels. In July 1862 Staveley called attention to the large smuggling trade in arms being carried on by Western traders, and reported that deserters from rebel forces claimed that ten per cent had muskets or rifles, though these were later said to be of 'inferior description'.[44] Bruce thereupon requested that action be taken at Hong Kong and Singapore to stop supplies of arms being acquired by traders at those ports, and this was accordingly done by the Colonial and India Office at the request of the Foreign Office.[45] Further, new regulations for trade on the Yangtze came into force on January 1, 1863, which specifically forbade foreign trade at any point on the river apart from Chinkiang, Kiukiang and Hankow, under pain of confiscation of both ship and cargo. There was no question of stopping the foreign river trade altogether, but a stronger determination to see that the rebels did not benefit from it was now apparent.[46]

Very important to this end was the scheme to provide the Manchu government with a modern flotilla of ships, capable of enforcing these trade regulations on armed Western trading vessels. This had been suggested to the Manchu government by members of the foreign-officered Imperial Customs Service. While its head, H. N. Lay, was absent on long leave in England in 1862 he was commissioned to buy suitable vessels and recruit officers and men. Bruce gave the scheme his encouragement, while the home government facilitated the buying of the vessels and removed the legal obstacles in the way of recruitment by an Order in Council on August 30, 1862. This authorized Lay and the chosen commander of the flotilla, Capt. Sherard Osborn, to enlist British subjects for military and naval service under the Chinese Emperor. The chief purposes of the fleet referred to in these early negotiations were the suppression of piracy in China waters and the policing of trade. For Bruce and the British government these were certainly major reasons for their support of the scheme, for they were anxious to reduce the naval forces maintained in China waters to protect British trade. But there is no doubt that the flotilla was regarded by many as also, and indeed primarily, intended for action against the rebels, to be in effect a substitute for the direct use of British naval forces against the rebels on the Yangtze.[47]

In fact the Lay-Osborn flotilla was never used in any capacity at all in China waters, being dispersed soon after its arrival because of disagreements over the terms under which Osborn would serve. The main point at issue was whether he should be required to act on orders from provincial governors and commanders as well as from the central government. According to a prior agreement drawn up between Lay and Osborn, the Chinese government was to issue orders to the flotilla only through Lay, who would as it were, censor them. Not surprisingly, both the Peking government and the provincial authorities refused to approve such conditions of service, while Lay and Osborn also refused to give way. Lay's argument was that 'a European force in the hands of local authorities would be infallibly misapplied and, its immediate object accomplished, would be cast aside, without any permanent good either to China or Europe'.[48]

Bruce characteristically played a rather wavering role in this crisis, which strictly speaking was one between the Manchu government and officers in its employ. He saw the point of view of the government but also approved of Osborn's refusal to accept orders from provincial Chinese authorities. Lay was blamed for the contretemps and was dismissed from the Customs Service. The affair provides a clear illustration of the difficulties in the way of attempting to by-pass the authority of the great provincial officers in any plans either for the suppression of the rebellion or for strengthening the government of China.[49]

More successful, though hardly more harmonious, was the use of British military officers, notably Gordon, to serve in the Ever Victorious Army. This is much the best-known aspect of British action against the Taiping rebellion. As with the thirty-mile-radius scheme, the initiative in this matter came from some of the British authorities, civil and military, serving at Shanghai and not from Bruce or the Foreign Office. Bruce, in fact, never approved this kind of aid at all, but his objections were over-ruled by the support given to the idea by the Foreign Office itself.

The original commander of the force, Ward, was killed in fighting near Ningpo in September 1862. Consul Medhurst and General Staveley were quick to advance proposals for replacing him by a British officer who might improve the quality and discipline of what was a far from model army. Bruce dis-approved of these proposals, thinking it preferable that 'the successor should be taken from among the officers of the corps', while Rear-Admiral Hope, just returned to Shanghai from a visit to Japan at the beginning of October, 'put a stop to' these early moves to place the Ever Victorious Army under a British officer. Hope and Bruce both backed the claims of Ward's second-in-command, another American adventurer named Burgevine, and he was for the time appointed.[50] By the end of the year, however, the Foreign Office had learned, through the War Office, of Medhurst's and Staveley's proposals of September, and gave its approval to these. On January 9, 1863, a second Order in Council was issued authorizing British military officers to take service in the armed forces of the Emperor of China, without making this dependent on recruit-ment by Lay or Osborn.[51]

Before the new Order in Council was received in China

difficulties had already arisen between Burgevine and the Chinese authorities at Shanghai over the payment of his troops and a proposal to transfer them to assist in the siege of Nanking. Burgevine was dismissed by Li Hung-chang, who then applied to Staveley for an officer to replace the American, and on January 22, 1863, an agreement was drawn up for the joint command of the force by Chinese and British officers. The latter, however, were still not to serve beyond the thirty-mile limit.[52] At the end of February news of the second Order in Council had been received in China. The misnamed Ever Victorious Army had meanwhile suffered a severe repulse at Taitsan, just outside the thirty-mile limit, partly because of uncertainties over its leadership. Staveley then reported his intention of putting Gordon in command, and asked how far restrictions on his movements would apply. The Foreign Office replied that British officers under special licence (they were placed on half-pay, but retained their regimental rank) might serve anywhere in China.[53] But this was as far as it was prepared to go. When Staveley proposed that it might be well to take over the force altogether and make a British contingent of it, officered and paid for by the British government from funds derived from the Shanghai customs, the Foreign Office refused to entertain the idea.[54]

Bruce disapproved of the whole principle of using any British officers to lead Chinese forces in the field. 'I cannot be a party, in any way, to the employment of these officers beyond the radius, either at Ningpo or Shanghae', he told Major-General Brown, Staveley's successor, in June 1863, at which time he was also engaged in upbraiding the Peking Government for its failure to exact strict observance of treaty terms from its provincial officers.[55] Indeed, the core of his objection to the system was that, apart from being likely to arouse the jealousy and suspicion of other treaty powers, it encouraged and strengthened provincial rather than central government independence and authority. The Ever Victorious Army was a force employed by and responsible to the local Chinese authorities at Shanghai rather than to the Imperial Government at Peking. It was officered by Europeans, mostly Americans, while its rank and file, who numbered between three and five thousand, included many captured rebels as well as Chinese volunteers.[56]

Although a troublesome and potentially dangerous force, quite capable of deserting *en masse* to the rebels, by 1863 Bruce thought it should be held together for a time on account of its undoubted military value and the dangers involved in precipitate dissolution.[57] But he did not wish to see provincial control of it underwritten by British officers, especially through agreements with the local Chinese authorities which ignored the central government at Peking. He particularly resented the support given to Li Hung-chang early in 1863 by the British military authorities at Shanghai in refusing to reinstate Burgevine, despite Bruce's own advocacy of that adventurer's claims. It embarrassed his good relations with the United States minister at Peking, Burlinghame, by making it appear that the British were anxious to unsurp a position formerly held by an American, while by thwarting an arrangement agreed upon between foreign ministers and the government in Peking it tended to weaken the central executive, 'which it is our true policy to strengthen, and thereby to render more difficult the restoration of Tranquillity, and less effectual our means of enforcing the observance of Treaties by remonstrance at Peking, instead of by violent action at the ports'.[58] The system, he complained a few weeks later, had 'invigorated the pernicious system of provincial independent Government'.[59] As with the Lay-Osborn scheme, the forces of regionalism had proved too strong for Bruce's long-term policy in China.

Russell did not share Bruce's objections to British officers leading provincial Chinese forces, and saw no reason why they, rather than other foreigners or adventurers, should not do so.[60] It is difficult to avoid the conclusion that the Foreign Office, and still more the service officers in China, with the possible exception of Hope, who in any case left China at the end of 1862, never fully appreciated the objectives behind Bruce's insistence on giving only strictly limited aid to the Manchus. For them the suppression of the rebellion tended to be an end in itself, and they were always ready to stretch the limits a little when a good opportunity presented itself.

Gordon assumed command of the Ever Victorious Army in March 1863 and thereafter the main British contribution to the defeat of the rebellion was made through the very considerable support given him and any other British officers who joined the force.[61] The campaigns and difficulties of Strachey's 'faintly smiling Englishman' have been described many times at length elsewhere. The main point to be emphasized here is that his victories, the chief of which was the capture of Soochow at the end of 1863, were the more readily gained because of the support provided by the regular British forces around Shanghai. The thirty-mile-radius area provided him with a sanctuary, a safe base and source of supply. In September 1863 some British forces were temporarily moved up beyond the thirty-mile limit to provide him with advanced support when it was feared that Burgevine, who had deserted to the rebels, would succeed in fomenting a mutiny within the ranks of his force. This affair led Bruce to complain to Elgin that 'admirals and generals have gone Taeping mad', but the Foreign Office proved once again willing to condone service initiative.[62] Gordon went on to capture Soochow and, in May 1864, Changchow also, after which the Ever Victorious Army was hastily disbanded, to the relief of nearly all parties. By that time the Orders in Council authorizing British service in the Emperor's forces had also been withdrawn.

The repeal, in March 1864, of the two Orders in Council was prompted by reports of the execution, on the orders of Li Hung-chang, of the Taiping Wangs who had surrendered Soochow to Gordon after he had promised them safe conducts. Gordon himself was so outraged by this affair that for a time he threw up his command, but eventually resumed it again, on the ground that 'however ungrateful or hopeless it may be to try and redeem the Mandarins, do we better matters by having the Rebels back again? The one has some Government, the others have none.'[63] But a considerable outcry had been raised among foreign observers, and a meeting of consuls at Shanghai condemned Li's action as one of 'extreme treachery, abhorrent to human nature'.[64]

The British government had already faced a great deal of criticism at home over its policy of intervention and had several times shown itself anxious to avoid the charge of implicitly condoning atrocities. In May 1862, when first approving a policy of direct aid, Russell had insisted that it be impressed upon Prince Kung 'that if he sanctions cruel and indiscriminate punishments he will entirely lose the support of the British authorities', and there was more than one enquiry into charges of this kind before the Soochow incident occurred.[65] This provided the occasion, in March 1864, for the repeal of the Orders in Council, the first of which had in any case become pointless after the collapse of the Lay-Osborn scheme. In doing this the British government does not appear to have been anticipating the imminent defeat of the rebellion, though its eventual defeat was becoming clear. The reasons given in the House of Commons by Palmerston were simply the 'disgraceful' conduct of the Manchu officials and the fact that only Gordon and 'one or two other persons' had taken advantage of the Orders in Council.[66] They were accordingly repealed, but without first advising or consulting Bruce, who was quick to point out 'the grave complications that may arise if orders that amount to a change of policy are based upon the conduct of a provincial governor without awaiting the result of a reference to the Government at Peking through Her Majesty's Representative'.[67] The 'change of policy' was not complete, since the British government was presumably still ready to use its own forces to defend a thrity-mile area around the treaty ports. But the withdrawal of the Orders in Council represented a sort of half-step backwards towards the old policy of limited neutrality. Intervention had not been a popular policy in Britain itself, and the government appears to have been glad to begin to contract out of it before the rebellion was finally destroyed.

By the time of the repeal of the Orders in Council the rebellion was in fact facing destruction. The armies of Tseng Kuo-fan, actually under the command of his brother, Tseng Kuo-ch'uan, had begun their siege of Nanking in May 1862 and were slowly tightening their grip upon the city. Other armies, of which the Ever Victorious was one, were pushing the rebels back from the coastal provinces they had overrun in 1860 and 1861. The rebellion was slowly contained within a shrinking area of territory between Nanking, Soochow and Hangchow. The wisest policy to have attempted in such a situation would have been to stage another 'Long March' to some other area and establish a new base, but Hung Hsiu-ch'üan refused to abandon his proclaimed capital and the rebels no longer possessed the kind of *élan* which had carried them northward from Kwangsi in 1852. With the fall of Soochow in December 1863 and of

Hangchow in March 1864 the main rebel force was bottled up in Nanking and destroyed there with great bloodshed in July. A few remnants escaped and maintained the struggle a little longer, but to all intents the Taiping rebellion as a serious threat to Manchu rule ended in the middle of 1864.

The main British contribution to this had been the denial to the rebels of any chance to capture Shanghai and its rich revenues or to establish themselves firmly in the coastal provinces after their expulsion from their bases further inland. It is impossible to deny the great importance of this aid to the Manchus, who would at least have had a longer struggle to defeat the rebellion but for it. Yet it should also be said that there were limits set to the extent of this aid by the British government, even though it was indulgent towards the tendency of some of its agents to go beyond those limits; that it was aid given and withdrawn in an unplanned, unco-ordinated and at times almost haphazard fashion; and that it was aid intended in part to serve as a stepping-stone towards stronger government in China. In so far as it can be said to have had ends beyond merely helping to crush the Taiping rebellion, the British policy of intervention was a failure. It helped in fact to preserve a reactionary and fundamentally hostile government in China, not to create a more efficient and enlightened one. But it is a great over-simplification to suggest that it was a policy designed to preserve the Manchu government *because* it was weak and reactionary. Results are no sure guide to motives.[68]

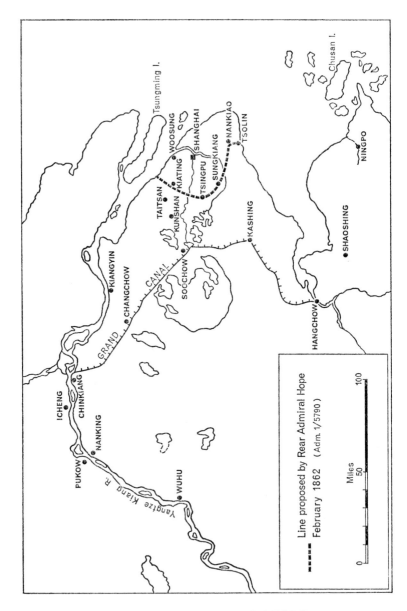

THE THIRTY MILE RADIUS

8

The Public Debate
(1860-64)

LIMITED THOUGH IT WAS, the policy of intervention provoked considerable public debate both at home and among British residents on the China coast. After some renewal of hope in the rebellion during 1860 and 1861, agreement on its destructive and heretical character was virtually unanimous by 1862, but the question of the proper policy to follow towards it remained an issue of some public concern, though never of vital import, during the years 1862 to 1864.

As in the earlier chapter illustrating the public reaction, it seems appropriate to begin with the missionaries, since their reports did most to stimulate renewed interest in the movement about 1860 and their own involvement in its fate remained peculiarly strong. The Treaty of Tientsin had strengthened the tendency, already apparent in missionary circles by the mid-fifties, to ignore the rebellion as a prospective ally in the task of Christianizing China. Article VIII had explicitly recognized the Christian religion as 'inculcating the practice of virtue' and guaranteed its professors, foreign and native alike, from persecution. In welcoming these provisions, the directors of the London Missionary Society observed that the hopes of a few years earlier that 'the providence of God' was about to open China through the influence of internal insurrection had not been realized, 'but God has now answered our supplication by other means, with the prospects of happier results and greater security'.[1] The continued existence of a native movement of such heretical tendencies as the Taiping was, indeed, now more likely to be an embarrassment rather than an aid to the missionary cause in China.

There was still no overt missionary hostility towards the rebellion, however. But whereas in 1853–54 they had urged a policy of neutrality, confident that the overthrow of the Manchus was certain if no foreign intervention was forthcoming, by the late fifties the missionaries appear to have been much more dispassionately neutral. Given the 'decrepitude, cruelty and corruption of the Manchow Tartar Dynasty' on the one hand and the 'degeneracy and decay' of the rebels on the other, the once very pro-Taiping Bishop of Victoria was convinced that 'non-intervention in the civil convulsion of China was clearly the course for British statesmen to pursue'. In the earlier stages of the movement, the Bishop admitted, the presence of Protestant missionaries at Nanking might have given 'a sounder character' to rebel practice and belief. But now the missionaries could only 'patiently abide the issue, moderating excessive hopes and repressing undue despondency and fear. However much a nearer view of the rebel movement may hereafter repel our minds', the Bishop continued, 'it must at the same time be remembered that doubtless, in the hands of Providence, it will have accomplished a good result.'[2] The rebellion had perhaps helped prepare the way, but little more could now be said for it. By the end of the decade British missionaries in China seemed no longer to place any great hopes in the rebellion; they were almost above the battle.[3]

In the middle of 1860, however, there was a temporary renewal of hope among some of their number stationed at Shanghai. In July of that year three representatives of the London Missionary Society and one of the Baptist Missionary Society visited the rebels at Soochow, and reported that it was 'evident that the religious element enters very powerfully into this great revolutionary movement'. The Scriptures were still their standard of faith as at the beginning of the movement, and 'as long as they receive them as the word of God, we have reasonable grounds to hope that their errors will gradually be corrected', these missionaries insisted.[4] This report led the

London Missionary Society to issue a special circular expressing 'sanguine hope' in the movement once again,[5] while in a joint letter sent to the Foreign Office in November 1860 representatives of all the major missionary societies save only the Church Missionary Society urged the continuance of a policy of neutrality upon the government. The writers of this letter stated that they watched the progress of the insurrectionary movement 'with lively interest not unmixed with hope' and discerned a 'decided attachment to Christianity' in the leaders of the movement, despite their confused and imperfect acquaintance with the truths of Revelation.[6]

The strongest advocate of the Taiping cause among British missionaries on the China coast at this time was the Rev. Griffith John. He had been one of the London Missionary Society representatives on the first visit to Soochow just noted, and with the Rev. Joseph Edkins of the same society he paid a second visit there in August 1860, while in November he went with a Baptist missionary, the Rev. Z. Kloeckers, to Nanking itself.[7] On the basis of these journeys, John published a pamphlet in which he gave a very detailed and favourable description of Taiping religious and political institutions, and argued strongly for a continued policy of non-intervention. He was convinced that the rebels, notwithstanding all their 'errors', were 'the chosen instruments to relieve China from the darkness and thraldom of idolatry and, in connection with foreign missionaries, to bless her with the light and liberty of the Gospel'. The interests of religion, commerce and civilization all pointed to neutrality as 'the one legitimate ground for Western nations to take'.[8] To the secretary of the London Missionary Society John was able to report that on his visit to Nanking he had secured an Edict of Toleration promising freedom of movement and of preaching in Taiping territory to all Christian missionaries, so that the way at last seemed open to repair the deficiencies and heresies of the rebel faith. 'They have doubtless gross defects', he concluded, 'but in every respect, religious, political and social, they are centuries ahead of the Imperialists.'[9]

Even in 1860, however, not all the British missionaries in China shared such convictions. The Church Missionary Society's representative at Shanghai, the Rev. J. Hobson, warned against the reports of the London Mission's representatives, whom he described as 'to a man, red hot Rebels'.[10] In London Mission circles also there were those who doubted. James Legge wrote from Hong Kong that he could not 'make the same apology for the errors of the rebels which our brethren at the north seem disposed to do, nor be equally sanguine as to the prospects of their ultimate success. Unless they can attach the people to them they will never get the empire, and thus far they have failed to establish in any place a vigorous and righteous government.'[11]

During 1861 such scepticism and doubt, rather then John's optimism and faith, increased among the British missionaries, and the tone of their comments upon the rebellion became steadily harsher. As the Bishop of Victoria had anticipated, a nearer view of the rebellion served to repel, on political as well as on religious grounds. The Rev. W. Muirhead, who joined Hope's first expedition up the Yangtze in early 1861, reported after some three weeks in Nanking that, 'in a secular point of view the movement at present is only destructive. It breaks up all domestic and social ties; it annihilates trade . . . and blasts the peace and prospects of the empire. . . . In a religious point of view the movement at present is no less destructive. . . . It is proposed to Christianize the empire by a process truly Chinese and perhaps effectual in a mere nominal light. The means in operation will, we fear, be productive of vast mischief, and only serve to introduce a spurious kind of Christianity.'[12] After the same expedition, the Rev. J. Hobson reported to the Church Missionary Society that the religious men among the rebels were 'but a very small portion of the whole, and the religion of the religious is but a cross between Mohommedanism and Mormonism'.[13]

Most disappointing to the British missionaries was the realization that, despite the Edict of Toleration granted to John at the end of 1860, there would be considerable difficulties in the way of attempting to establish mission stations in Taiping territory. Edkins and John seriously considered making such a move, but after a further visit to Nanking in March 1861 they became convinced that 'the design of converting the Taiping chief to correct scriptural opinions was a hopeless one'. What Hung chiefly wanted was recognition from foreign missionaries who would not challenge, and by their presence would implicitly acknowledge, his claim to special revelation and supreme religious authority.[14]

Edkins, although disappointed, did not become hostile to the rebels, and seems to have retained a sort of affection for them. But he concluded that they were 'not statesmen' and that, although they had 'a certain system and strong convictions regarding some great religious truths', they had 'entered upon a political enterprise too great for them. Under the influence of these convictions and undaunted by difficulties which they cannot surmount, they are careless of the future, and indulge in imaginary recreations of a reconstituted China, modelled by themselves, or rather by some force of fate, which is to work the change for them.'[15] After much debate with themselves, therefore, Edkins and John abandoned the idea of a mission in Nanking, the one to go north to Tientsin and the other inland to Hankow. 'It was our hope at one time that the Tai Ping movement was destined to be a direct means to the evangelization of China', John wrote in March 1862. 'In this we may be disappointed. Be that as it may, there can be little doubt of its indirect influence for good.'[16] He could not turn his back entirely on the rebels, but the high hopes of 1860 had gone.

More hostile in his disappointment was the Wesleyan missionary, the Rev. Josiah Cox, who went on Hope's second voyage to Nanking at the end of 1861. In reply to his query whether he should come and live in Nanking he was told by Hung Jen-kan that 'missionaries ought not to come, for the doctrines are different and the Heavenly King will not allow other doctrines than his own'. Cox, who in 1853 had hailed the glimmering dawn, was now thoroughly disillusioned and reported that he had not expected that 'on a nearer view of these insurgents they would appear to my judgment so bereft of hopeful elements. I certainly at present fail to discover amongst them any party which promises to be capable of administering a government, and can only regard them as marauding hordes.'[17] By 1862 the Taipings appeared to some missionaries to be 'more hostile to Christianity than the Imperialists themselves', an attitude found especially among those Church Missionary Society representatives at Ningpo who witnessed the rebel occupation of that city during 1862.[18]

Presented with such reports, the home societies naturally

abandoned their remaining hopes in the movement also. The last years of the rebellion were passed over without much comment in missionary records and there were no obvious stirrings of regret at its final defeat, or doubts lest perhaps a great opportunity had passed. It was left to the later historian to ask 'did ever Christians have so golden an opportunity of winning a great heathen nation for Christ?' Speculation as to possible lost opportunities seems rather pointless, however, for it is difficult to see that either the fate of the rebellion or the course of British policy towards it would have been very different even had the Protestant missionaries given it strong and consistent support throughout.[19]

The missionaries of the time, busily establishing new stations in the north and in the interior of China under a treaty promising them full toleration, had no difficulty in finding some place for the rebellion in their conception of God's plan for China. Griffith John was sure that 'this wonderful movement had not been permitted to rise and progress so far without some great productive end'. For others the work of the rebels had been one of judgment alone, 'sent on this miserable land for the long night of gross idolatry and fearful iniquity'. The Rev. Hudson Taylor of the China Inland Mission, saw their influence 'in shaking the confidence of the people in their gods of wood and stone, and in leading them to feel the need of something better' as one of the factors favouring the future work of evangelization in China. The Baptist Kloeckers felt that 'whether the Taepings get the whole of the country or part of it, or whether the whole be regained by the Imperialiste, in either case we have good prospects before us'. Since his work was God's work the missionary could not lose.[20]

Despite their disappointment in the rebellion, however, most of the missionaries seemed to have favoured the continuance of a policy of neutrality towards it. James Legge, for example, argued in July 1862 that 'the Manchous have had their time in China as the Stuarts had in Britain and the Bourbons had in France. It is not ours to hasten their downfall by interfering against them in the struggle between them and the Taepings, but neither are they worthy that we should interfere on their behalf. . . . There was one fair course for us to pursue—a real, impartial neutrality.'[21] This letter was widely published, the secretary of the London Missionary Society forwarding it to the Foreign Office and at the same time expressing the hope that, if an 'honest return to neutrality' was impossible, the British government should at least lay down limits within which its action would be confined. 'Let the severity of our dealings with the Taepings be tempered with mercy', he wrote. 'It should not be ours to co-operate in their extermination.'[22]

The British government was not so sympathetic to the work of the Protestant missionaries in China as to be ready to adapt its policies to suit their views, and if it did confine itself to limited intervention, such as was suggested in this letter from the secretary of the leading missionary society in Britain, it did so for reasons of its own. But if the missionaries cannot be said to have influenced government policy in any direct way they surely communicated something of their own ambivalent feelings about the rebellion to the public at large. Opposition to the policy of intervention during the years 1862 to 1864 drew strength from a variety of quarters, one of which was undoubtedly a wide body of opinion influenced by the more sympathetic missionary reports of 1860–62 in such a way as to be disappointed in but not vindictive towards the rebellion.

Apart from the missionaries, many merchants were also opposed to intervention against the rebellion. Although this policy was officially justified in terms of the protection of British trade interests in China it does not follow as the night the day from this that the merchants themselves all thought it the policy best designed to serve those interests. It would be an exaggeration to suggest that the majority of British merchants concerned with the China trade were opposed to this policy, as would probably be true for the missionaries, but it is clear that there was at least a substantial body of merchants of whom this could be said.

Once again the Jardine, Matheson correspondence provides a useful touchstone of merchant views. During 1861 this correspondence reflected considerable hostility towards the rebels, together with impatience at the 'half measures' adopted by the government towards them.[23] By the middle of 1862, however, the emphasis was upon leaving them alone. In June of that year the then Hong Kong head of the firm, Alexander Perceval, told a correspondent in India that he thought Great Britain should not interfere in the struggle without the assistance of at least ten thousand men and if, as Perceval clearly expected, the government was 'not prepared to undertake the matter properly, it would be much better to come to terms with the *de facto* rulers near Shanghai'.[24] In July the firm wrote a circular letter to its business correspondents in England calling their attention to the fact that, since the aggressive measures taken against the rebels during the first unsuccessful campaign to clear a radius around Shanghai had ceased, the market for imports had 'assumed a much healthier appearance'. The letter went on to express the conviction that the long period of stagnation for the import trade at Shanghai would have been avoided if a policy of strict neutrality had been persisted in, and that 'both the Import and Export trade in China cannot fail to be seriously threatened by a renewal of hostilities'. Several of their home correspondents expressed agreement with these strictures on government policy.[25]

A more favourable view of the rebels also began to be taken by Jardine, Matheson as it was found that, despite their encirclement of Shanghai, they offered 'no serious impediment to the passage of Silk', and little credit was attached to the stories of atrocities committed by rebel forces, 'the Imperialists being the real oppressors and devastators of the country'.[26] The departure of Rear-Admiral Hope, who was regarded as the chief architect of the policy of intervention, was greeted with the hope that 'the aggressive policy of our authorities will be considerably modified'; Bruce was condemned as 'imperious and inaccessible', and as not exerting 'any salutary influence whatever' in Peking, while it was hoped that the failure of the Lay-Osborn scheme would make ministers in England 'come fully alive to the folly of the course they have been pursuing'.[27] Jardine, Matheson & Co., the greatest of the opium-trading firms in China, certainly cannot be counted as among the supporters of the official policy of intervention against the Taipings. They were, in fact, pro-rebel if anything by 1862–63.

Strong criticism of government policy also came from the chairman of the Hong Kong Chamber of Commerce, James Mackenzie, in a letter sent to Russell in October 1863. This long letter was mainly concerned to rebut alleged imputations by H. N. Lay of a general proclivity towards smuggling among merchants in China, but in his last paragraphs Mackenzie turned to consider the policy of intervention. It was necessary to do this, he said, because of 'confident but erroneous statements by imperfectly informed parties at home that the foreign merchants as a body are well satisfied with and approve of that policy'. On the contrary, Mackenzie asserted, 'the great majority of the responsible commercial classes [foreign] in this country strongly disapprove of the present action of our authorities, and many persons even, who at an earlier period gave all their influence to the opposition to the maintenance of neutrality, have seen reason materially to modify their opinion'. The reason seen was not sympathy for the rebel movement as such, but opposition to the larger objectives behind the policy of limited intervention. 'The commercial body for the most part has no faith whatever in the regeneration of China by such foreign aid as is now afforded', Mackenzie wrote, instancing the Imperial Customs Service, the Lay-Osborn flotilla and the military reorganization of Chinese forces. He concluded with the suggestion that, though it might now be too late to withdraw with honour or safety from the defence of Shanghai, there should be no difficulty in restraining British activity within the defined thirty-mile limit, but the extension of the Shanghai system to other treaty ports 'would, in the general opinion of foreign residents in China, be a most serious mistake and one much to be deprecated'.[28] In short, he argued for de-escalation of the British role in the struggle.

Views more sympathetic to government policy than these were certainly to be found among British merchants in China and in the coastal press. In March 1861 a deputation of merchants representing the Shanghai Chamber of Commerce had accompanied Hope on his first expedition up the Yangtze and reported on the commercial possibilities of the places visited. Although hopeful of a city such as Hankow, at least while it remained in Imperial hands, the deputation saw no prospects of trade with centres under rebel control. Of Nanking it stated, 'The people are enslaved. The soldiery unpaid, but habituated to plunder, are little likely to engage in any industrial pursuits. The rulers, so far from being able to govern the country, do not even admit within the walls of their capital the shopkeepers necessary for the supply of the daily wants of the residents.'

The rebel movement, it was claimed, could 'in no just sense be considered political, still less patriotic or constructive', and the report concluded by expressing the fear that the advantages reasonably to be expected from the opening of the Yangtze to foreign trade would be counteracted by the anarchy and disorganization it entailed.[29]

Although an implication in favour of action against the rebellion can be read into this report, there was in it no definite statement of opinion about the best government policy in the circumstances. But at least one of the members of this deputation, Alexander Michie, soon emerged as a strong advocate of the policy of intervention, so much so that he was more than once quoted in debates in the House of Commons as illustrating merchant support for such a policy. Thus, at the end of 1862 he told the Parliamentary Under-Secretary for Foreign Affairs, Henry Layard, that 'the British merchants most largely connected with China are in favour of the British Government giving such assistance to the Chinese Government as will enable them to keep the Taepings out of the treaty ports; nor do I think there is any difference of opinion as to the advisability of pushing our assistance to the ultimate crushing of the rebellion. The *modus operandi* may have been questioned, and I know some merchants have considered the Government might with advantage have gone a step further than it has done. But all feel and acknowledge the delicacy of the position. . . . The great majority, however, have been in favour of the plan pursued as being the most economical to this country and the soundest in policy, not compromising the British Government more than necessary and teaching the Chinese to help themselves. . . .'[30]

Despite the rather cautious tone of Michie's assessment, Layard quoted these views in the Commons as providing 'remarkable and complete testimony' of the success of the government's policy and of its acceptability to British merchants in China. But although Michie may have been correct in his claim that 'the great majority' supported the policy it is clear from the Jardine, Matheson correspondence and the Mackenzie letter to Russell that there was a significant body of merchant opinion in China hostile to that policy, especially as it developed after 1862.

The English language coastal press, however, was fairly

definitely favourable, although again dissident voices were to be heard. The *Friend of China* continued throughout to assert the superior virtues of the rebels and to oppose intervention, while another Hong Kong published paper, the *China Overland Trade Report*, maintained a vigorous if not very consistent attack on a policy which it claimed would neither conciliate nor destroy the rebels. The *Trade Report* had no such regard for the rebels as had the *Friend of China*, but it argued that the injury they were capable of inflicting on British interests 'should make it our policy to conciliate them', and it accused British representatives in China of foisting their views upon the home government 'by a vast amount of misrepresentation'.[31]

On the other hand, the most substantial and influential papers on the China coast by this time, the *China Mail* and the *North China Herald*, were violently anti-rebel and pro-intervention by 1862, though both had advocated continued neutrality during most of 1861. By March 1862, however, the *Herald* was asserting that the time was past 'for entertaining any wavering opinions of neutrality, clemency or expediency', and by March of the following year was urging direct intervention beyond the thirty-mile limit, as the *Mail* was to do also.[32] It is probable that these views had widespread support, especially among the residents of Shanghai, who were most exposed to the danger of rebel attack.

In Great Britain the question of the merchants' attitude to official policy emerged most sharply out of a debate in the Commons in July 1863. In this Lord Naas roundly attacked the policy of intervention, claiming that many London merchants engaged in trade with China looked upon it with alarm and were 'almost to a man' opposed to the Lay-Osborn scheme and 'against an interference calculated, as they believe, to damage the commercial interests of England'. Later in the debate Samuel Gregson, chairman of the East India and China Association but himself an India rather than a China merchant, claimed that 'our merchants were perfectly satisfied in the policy pursued by Her Majesty's Government'.[33] Lord Naas thereupon took the question further in a letter to *The Times* in which he gave the sources of his information about merchant feeling as Mr. J. Dent, of Dent & Co., and Mr. Walkinshaw, of Turner & Co., who had called upon him and informed him that he was 'at liberty to state, on their authority, that the China merchants as a body were opposed to the new policy of the Government'. A week later Walkinshaw, writing from Glasgow, supported Lord Naas and contradicted Gregson's claim with the counter-claim that the merchants considered the policy 'fraught with the most dangerous consequences, and one far more likely to prejudice than benefit the trade between the countries'. The defence of the treaty ports, but beyond that non-interference between the Manchu government and the rebels, was, Walkin-shaw wrote, the policy wanted by the mercantile community in China. Gregson replied, referring in general terms to his con-versations with 'several gentlemen largely engaged in trade with China and some of them recently returned home', but without naming names. On the whole the honours of the exchange would seem to have gone to Lord Naas.[34]

Appropriately enough, the division of merchant opinion in England on this question was best reflected in the House of Commons. There were several debates on the issue there, as there were also in the House of Lords, and on July 8, 1862, a vote was taken on a resolution calling for British officials in China to be directed 'to avoid any intervention beyond that absolutely necessary for the defence of those British subjects who abstain from all interference in the Civil War now raging in that country'.[35] This was defeated by a large majority (197 to 88) but it is to be noted that the resolution was moved by James White, who had been for many years a merchant in China and who was described in a parliamentary guide as being 'a merchant in London chiefly engaged in trade with China'. White criticized Russell's recent instruction that all the treaty ports should be defended against the rebels on the ground that this was a potentially 'stupendous task', and he rejected the govern-ment argument that its policy of intervention was the best for the protection of British trade interests in China by pointing out that tea and silk exports from China were still increasing, including the particular types of silk produced in the rebel-held areas.

White was supported in the vote by a number of other merchants and manufacturers, as was the government also, of course, but the weight of merchant opinion in the House, in so far as it was expressed in this division list, would seem to have been fairly evenly divided. Of about forty members listed in parliamentary guides as being either merchants or former merchants twenty-three voted on this issue, fourteen for the government and nine against; and of twelve listed as manufacturers seven voted, three for the government and four against.[36] There was certainly no unanimous cry from trading and manufacturing representatives in parliament for active measures against the Taipings.

In a later debate, after a Dundee merchant, W. E. Baxter, had attacked the policy of co-operating with what he called the 'cruel and corrupt government of the Mantchou Tartars', Palmerston complained rather testily of the 'inconsistency of these mercantile gentlemen' who were constantly urging the government to make treaties and extend commercial opportunities yet were reluctant to accept the necessity for action to maintain those treaties. 'We have interfered with great success in the affairs of other countries, and with great benefit to the countries concerned', Palmerston claimed, listing Greece, Belgium, Portugal, Turkey and Egypt as examples.[37] To these he was quite ready to add China. His aristocratic government certainly did not feel it necessary to wait upon the approval of middle-class merchants before interfering in what it conceived to be the true commercial interests of Great Britain, especially when those merchants spoke with so divided a voice as they did upon the question of helping to suppress the Taiping rebellion.[38]

It is not apparent that this division reflected any very precise division of interest among the China merchants, whether on the China coast itself or at home. Some contemporaries saw the opium merchants as the great opponents of the rebels, and merchants engaged in gun-running activities as the chief opponents of any policy designed to end the rebellion. These were probably often the same people. In any case, as the Jardine, Matheson correspondence has already indicated and as will be argued further in the following chapter, the opium merchant was not invariably pro-interventionist. Gun-runners, and also land speculators in Shanghai, were probably among those happiest to see the rebellion continue, but these categories seem inadequate to account for the extent of publicly expressed merchant opposition, especially in parliament.[39] Some of the evidence suggests that on the China coast the Hong Kong based merchants were more critical of intervention than the Shanghai based, but this is rather tenuous. What is clear is that the merchants engaged in the China trade did not constitute a monolithic interest group whose attitudes on this question can be confidently lumped under one large generalization.[40] Their interests, or at least their own assessment of their interests, varied. So too did their opinions, if not about the rebellion itself then certainly about British policy towards it.

Merchants and missionaries were, apart from the official policy-makers, the British interest groups most directly concerned with the rebellion. But behind all was that amorphous, generally feeble but sometimes compelling thing, public opinion. In the last years of the rebellion this was never so deeply stirred as it had been for a time during 1853, yet by force of circumstances it was more persistently involved, especially over the question of government policy, than in the earlier, halcyon years of the movement.

Under the influence of the favourable missionary reports of 1860, strengthened by mistrust of a Peking government which, it was believed, had so perfidiously sought to avoid acceptance of the Treaty of Tientsin, there was a renewed tendency towards a sympathetic view of the rebellion during 1860–61.[41] In an article entitled 'The Truth about the Taepings', the *Spectator* noted in April 1861 that 'that stratum of society—a very large one—which derives its information from religious periodicals, begins to be again permeated with accounts of the great Chinese movement'. After summarizing what it conceived to be changes in public opinion since 1853 from 'rapturous credulity', through annoyance at finding it had believed too much, to the extreme reaction that the Taipings were 'criminals unworthy of anything but the rope', the *Spectator* saw evidence of another swing back towards recognizing some virtues in the movement. It went on itself to give a fairly favourable picture, based on missionary reports. 'A great intellectual movement of some kind is taking place among the largest section of human beings', it suggested, and although it was clear that the rebels were not really Christians, yet 'neither are they a gang of mere marauders of unintelligible tenets and villainous cruelty'. Under Taiping rule considerable reforms were being implemented, including the prohibition of opium-smoking, the setting up of institutions for the poor, the compelling of the rich to work and, above all, the encouragement of respect for foreigners. The ancient system of China was breaking up, and ideas at least as opposed to Confucianism as to Christianity were permeating that 'apparently immovable mass'. Change had begun 'in the only region where change ten years ago seemed impossible.'[42]

This kind of favourable view of the movement was echoed in articles in other journals about this time, although their authors seemed to have felt it necessary now to take the offensive against an opposite view.[43] The ready assumption behind much of the comment made in 1853, that here was a reforming and progressive movement clearly worthy of support, had to be reasserted and proved by 1861. By the early months of 1862, however, with the falling away of missionary hopes once more and with the publication of further Blue Books containing many official reports on the rebellion, there were few ready to raise their voices in praise of the Taipings. There were still plenty, however, who were ready to do so in condemnation of the change in government policy towards them.

Although it never became an issue of major political importance, as the *Arrow* war had been in 1857, the policy of intervention against the Taiping movement nevertheless provoked considerable debate in the years 1862 to 1864 and was at least as widely opposed and criticized as it was accepted and supported. There was frequent editorial comment in the press, while in parliament the issue was debated on seven occasions in the House of Commons and twice in the Lords between March 1862 and May 1864. It seems reasonable to suggest that this largely hostile public debate, while not occasioning any great danger for the Palmerston government, helps explain its rather precipitate withdrawal in March 1864 of the Orders in Council permitting British subjects to serve in the Chinese Imperial military forces.

With few exceptions, by 1862 the parliamentary critics of the government on this issue were concerned only to question the wisdom and necessity of any British intervention in the struggle, not to defend or praise the Taiping movement itself. Virtually the only spokesman for the superior virtues of the rebels over the Manchus by this time was the member for Aberdeen, Col.

W. H. Sykes, who consistently presented them as 'Reformers and Puritans' and as 'the National Party' in effective control of one-third of China.[44] Other critics, however, saw the rebellion, both as a religious and as a political movement, in very much the same terms as did the defenders of government policy, differing only in their emphasis upon the expense and possible danger of deeper involvement inherent in any policy of intervention.

Lord Naas, in a lengthy speech on the question in the Commons on July 6, 1863, stated firmly that he was no advocate for the Taipings but warned that 'the further we proceed in the present direction the greater will be the probability that we shall find ourselves embarked in a Chinese civil war only to end in an Anglo-Chinese protectorate or even perhaps an Anglo-Chinese empire. . . . What has happened repeatedly in India is certain to happen in China if we persist in our present course'.[45] Others expressed alarm at the actual and potential expense of such a policy. James White stated that he 'had no sympathy with the Taipings, but he had an earnest sympathy with the taxpayer of this country who would, no doubt, be called upon to defray the cost of a gigantic scheme of interference'. Another speaker calculated that the maintenance of British forces in China was already costing a million a year, 'which amounted to an additional penny on the income tax'. Cobden and Bright, in speeches which hardly mentioned the rebels, argued that British trade in China did not need, nor did its current volume justify, the commitments the government was making. On a familiar theme, Bright insisted that trade with China, 'the most miserable trade in the world when compared with the magnitude of the population', would best develop by being left to make its own way. Wars in China had been and still were unnecessary for its advancement.[46]

The government's main answer to these criticisms was simply to insist that the rebellion was a completely destructive force. Unless China was to be allowed to drift into a state of anarchy in which there would be no prospects whatever for trade, it had to be put down, and it was sound policy to help 'the enlightened Government of China', which Palmerston facetiously described as having now been 'rendered' friendly to the West, to do this. But, government spokesmen insisted, there was no intention of undertaking more than limited intervention, which in any case the Taipings had brought upon themselves by their attacks upon the treaty ports. The warning analogy of India was simply rejected as irrelevant.

Palmerston, who seems to have taken a rather lighthearted view of the whole issue, answered Cobden's general attack upon the past and present China policy of his governments with the ironical argument that, having weakened the Manchus and helped create favourable conditions for rebellion against them by defeating them in war, 'then, on the principle that there is a just Providence which inflicts retribution upon those who commit wrong and refuse redress, we are bound now to do everything in our power to make amends to the Imperial Government for the injury they then sustained . . .'. The next speaker complained that Palmerston had spoken 'with even more than his usual hilarity and vivacity', while the *Spectator* described this speech as containing 'nothing less than an assertion of his own will, and his intention to persevere in a particular policy whether the country likes it or not. . . . It was a hilarious song of defiance, heard with disgust even by members who feel that the alternatives are Lord Palmerston or a Tory administration.'[47]

It is plain from all this that intervention against the Taipings was not an issue upon which the Palmerston government felt very seriously challenged. Certainly there was no sense of urgency about these fairly frequent debates which, with one or two exceptions, were held before thin and disinterested houses and which only once resulted in a division.[48] To some extent the issue seems to have been deliberately kept alive by the opposition in the absence of any great domestic issues of dispute. Pending a new reform bill, which had to wait for Palmerston's departure from the scene, foreign policy provided the chief openings for attack on the government by the rather heterogeneous and disorganized opposition of these years. In a private letter to Bruce on June 10, 1863, Russell observed that 'the absence of any great internal questions has drawn the House of Commons wild upon foreign questions, of which few know anything'. Intervention in China was one of these questions, but Russell was confident that the 'disease' would not become an epidemic. 'It only requires a sedative and a silencer, which

Palmerston can well administer', he assured Bruce.[49] Although *The Times* might assert that Great Britain had almost as much at stake in the civil war in China as in that in America, no import of this is apparent in these debates.[50]

By 1862 *The Times* itself was in full cry after the rebels, calling them, in a style it seems now to have abandoned, 'the blood-thirsty and rapacious Taeping, the Thug of China, the desolator of cities, the provider of carrion to the wild dog, the pitiless exterminator, the useless butcher'. Intervention in some shape or other against this 'travelling anarchy' had become 'indispensable to our position in China', and it gave wholehearted support to every aspect of government policy, including the Lay-Osborn flotilla which aroused the criticism of many of the usual supporters of intervention.[51] The *Morning Post* also gave steady support to the government, and dismissed the arguments of its parliamentary critics as 'simply impracticable and impossible'. Non-intervention as a general principle in foreign relations was only intelligible towards countries which had reached 'a certain grade of political, moral and philosophical development', it argued. The U.S.A. was such a country, but China was not. The *Manchester Guardian* agreed that it was 'mere pedantry' to apply this principle to countries 'which know nothing of international law and customs', and judged the policy of the British government to be 'faithful, straightforward and friendly, and calculated to prove eminently advantageous both to China and Great Britain'.[52]

Public opposition, however, was considerable. During the latter part of 1862, after the change in the government's policy had been made plain by debates in Parliament, a number of memorials were sent to the Foreign Office urging that British representatives in China be instructed 'to withdraw as speedily as possible from this untimely intervention in Chinese affairs'. In them, no judgment was passed on the merits of either side in the struggle in China, but only upon the impolicy of British interference in it. These memorials were all nearly identical in wording, and were clearly the result of an organized campaign by Peace Societies.[53]

Strongest opposition to what it called 'Lord Palmerston's clandestine war' came from the radical *Daily News*. During July and August 1862 it attacked government policy in several leaders, in one of which it reprinted from the *Times of India* a particularly horrific account of alleged Imperialist atrocities in the treatment of captured Taipings. This account prompted enquiries from the government, which always felt vulnerable to the charge of condoning atrocity by becoming involved in this struggle. The *Daily News* kept up its attacks, printing several letters from Sykes without itself directly praising the Taipings. 'The best thing we can do is to take China as it is and carry on the best trade we can with it, instead of attempting to create it anew in the hope of doing better', it was still arguing in mid-1864.[54]

Among other newspapers the *Daily Telegraph* favoured mediation, while the conservative *Standard* was inclined to take Metternich's view of revolt in Greece and advise that the whole affair be left to burn itself out beyond the pale of civilization. The *Liverpool Daily Post*, while chiding the House of Commons for its apathy on the question and attacking the government for approving the 'extraordinary conduct' of Rear-Admiral Hope, believed that the Taipings had 'always shown themselves more willing than the Mandarin party to foster trade, [and] are in a position to offer far greater facilities and far greater rewards'. The *Manchester Daily Examiner* felt no doubt that 'substantially, [China] is now divided into two *de facto* empires. Let us recognize both and do our best to trade with both. . . . At all events let us not gradually commit our honour to the impossible task of resuscitating an empire which bears the stamp of inevitable decay.' The *Morning Herald* asked, in a nineteenth-century brand of tabloid journalism, why Britain should 'crusade to keep the Yellow Dwarf of modern times on his goblin throne? Why are we bound to cement up every crack in the obsolete willow pattern plate?'[55] More earnestly, the *Spectator* asked: 'What is the Mexican adventure which is now embarrassing France compared to a task like this? It is the very process by which we conquered India begun over again.' England was in danger of blundering into the government of a third of the human race through 'a war nobody ordered, or wanted, or pretends to understand'.[56]

In all this debate on government policy between 1862 and 1864 there was no longer much discussion of the nature of the rebellion itself. In its review of Brine's *The Taiping Rebellion in*

151

China, which it considered to be the most impartial and balanced study of the movement which had till then appeared, perhaps, rather too impartial and judicious, the *Athenaeum* observed at the end of 1862 that 'the Taipings in the sight of England are angels or demons, honey or vitriol, civilizers or exterminators, just as we choose; for it is perfectly easy to cram dogmatism in abundance on either side from books, pamphlets, speeches and leading articles'.[57]

Even by the time the *Athenaeum* was making this comment, however, there were few left in Great Britain to praise the rebels. In July 1863 a writer in the *London Quarterly Review* noted a strong revulsion of feeling against them while himself maintaining that 'the present antipathy is as unreasonable and absurd as was the former sympathy'.[58] But there was no swing of the pendulum back again in favour of the rebels. Soon articles in praise of Gordon's exploits began to appear and the legend to take shape that 'the Taeping monster has been crushed by British skill and valour'.[59]

British public opinion then, in so far as it can be pinned down with any precision, may be summed up as shifting from eager support for the rebels as liberal, patriotic, quasi-Christian reformers in 1853, through several years of growing dis-illusionment, indifference and hostility to a partial revival of interest and hope about 1861, and finally to virtually complete rejection by 1862–63, but with the rider that there was widespread and consistent disapproval of the policy of active intervention against it throughout 1862–64.

It seems altogether in keeping with the ignorance and un-certainties out of which this opinion was largely compounded that, no sooner were the rebels defeated at Nanking, than doubts began to be expressed as to whether this would be altogether a good thing for British interests in China. 'We are not at all sure we ought to congratulate ourselves on the news', the *Standard* commented late in 1864. 'With an enemy in the field against him, occupying a portion of his empire, threatening new conquests, a standing menace to his throne, the Emperor of China was wonderfully complaisant to the English, upon whom he relied for something more than sympathy in his troubles.'[60] Even *The Times*, which had called loudest for the destruction of the rebellion after 1862, agreed that Great Britain might expect to find the Chinese government 'much less tractable'. On December 31, reviewing the events of 1864, it could only say that with the defeat of the rebellion 'it remains to be seen whether the Government of Pekin will maintain the friendly bearing to Foreign Powers which has hitherto found a motive in the need of counsel and assistance'.[61] The last half-century of Manchu rule in China makes one question, indeed, whether in the long run Britain gained anything of substance from her involvement in the struggle against the Taipings.

9

Why Intervention?

AT A VERY GENERAL LEVEL the answer to this question is agreed upon by all historians of the subject, whatever view they may take of the rights or wrongs of that intervention. Deeply-felt commitments of political principle and ideology, such as bedevil our own age, were not involved. It was a simple issue of commercial advantage. Great Britain intervened in defence of the treaty rights she had exacted from the Manchu government since 1842 and of the trading interests which had developed and it was believed would develop under their sanction. The real question is why these rights and this trade were felt to be so seriously threatened by 1862 as to justify involvement in what was, as we have seen, a far from universally popular cause in Britain.

Some of the answers which have been given to this question attempt to force nineteenth-century issues too rigidly into twentieth-century categories of thought. Others, although pointing to the kinds of reasons which might well have operated in the minds of those responsible for British policy at the time, appear to be based more upon calculations of general probability than upon precise historical evidence. It seems appropriate therefore to approach the question posed by way of a critical examination of the kinds of answers that have been given to it.

The argument that the British government acted against the rebellion because it feared that, as a popular national movement, it would establish a strong government upon which British demands would be less successfully pressed than upon the weak and unpopular Manchu government, is open to objection on several counts.[1] Whether the Taipings would in fact have been able to establish such a government had they succeeded in overthrowing the Manchus, British officials in China at the time certainly did not believe that they were at all likely to do so. Not the political strength or the nationalism of the movement but its anarchy was what they most feared. Thus Bruce wrote in May 1862 that the overthrow of the Manchu government by the insurgents as then constituted would be 'the commencement of a state of anarchy and disorganization by the side of which the condition of China during the last ten years, will appear to have been one of prosperity and peace. Its unity as an Empire will disappear, and the disjointed members will turn to foreign protection for the tranquillity which they will look for in vain among contending native factions'.[2] Indeed, it was the conviction that the Taiping movement had by this stage lost any popular support it may once have enjoyed that became one of the grounds justifying intervention against it. After receiving reports of the repulse by the mass of the populace of an attempt by the rebels to capture the island of Chusan early in 1862, Russell wrote, 'It was obvious that unless the Chinese would themselves act, it was useless for foreigners to try and rid the country of the Taipings; but now that a spirit of resistance to these scourges is shown we ought to help the people and encourage their Government to resist their destructive progress'.[3] Bruce and Russell certainly thought of themselves as fostering rather than opposing popular objectives in China by helping the Manchus to defeat the Taipings.

In any case, as has already been argued, the British objective was not to keep the Manchu government as weak and supine as possible but to make it at least strong enough to preserve internal order and not invite external aggression. The British would, of course, have been opposed to the emergence of any government strong enough to denounce the treaties effectively, but this seemed a very remote prospect in the eighteen-sixties. The Taipings were certainly suspect from the British standpoint as being hostile to the treaties and as likely to obstruct their operation, but the root of probable Taiping obstructionism was seen in their religious pretensions rather than in any surging tide of nationalist support such as the nineteen-twenties were to witness.[4] In any case, the difference between the rebels and their Manchu rivals was, in this respect, merely one of degree. The British were never faced with the simple choice of supporting a government fully reconciled to the treaties against rebels implacably opposed to them.

Further, it should not be assumed, as it generally seems to be by those who put forward this Taiping nationalism kind of argument, that the attitude of mid-nineteenth-century British administrators of empire towards national movements in major areas of economic penetration was necessarily one of opposition, as may be true for the twentieth century. About 1860 Utilitarian views on empire and trade still predominated in British political and economic thinking. Formal empire was not actively sought and, although the turn of the tide towards imperial protectionism was not far off, an optimistic belief in the existence of a natural world market was still general. The main obstacles in the way of the free working of this market were not so much nationalist as mercantilist ideas, which survived in the policies of autocratic, out dated governments such as that of the Manchus. On every count, whether of natural justice or of economic self-interest, popular movements of revolt against governments of this kind were to be regarded sympathetically, as had been done in the case of the South American republics and Italy, rather than with hostility and suspicion.[5] The Taipings had appeared in something of this light in 1853, and if they failed to win consistent British approval this was not on account of any suspected modern-type economic nationalism in their movement but on account of their failure, in the eyes of the British government, to give promise of being likely to guarantee the basic political and social conditions for trade.

The extension of this argument from emerging nationalism in China to the suggestion that the Taipings were also feared as the vanguard of other nationalist movements in Asia is even more difficult to accept. Whether or not the mutiny in India in 1857 was in any sense an 'echo' of the rebellion in China, as Lo Erh-kang suggests,[6] no connection was suspected at the time by British policy-makers. A fear that India might be stirred by events in China was expressed by *The Times* in September 1859, after the repulse of British forces by the Manchus at

Taku,[7] but the Taipings were never credited with having this kind of influence. The usual line of argument was, indeed, not from events in China to their effects in India, but rather the reverse. As we have seen, Britain's expensive military and political commitments in India, acquired in the first place by interfering in the internal struggles of that country, were frequently cited as warnings against becoming involved in a similar way in China, and at the beginning of 1861 Wade even used this parallel to warn the Manchus themselves of the dangers of foreign intervention for China. Within the perspective of the last hundred years the modern historian may see these two great uprisings as among the first waves of a rising tide of Asian nationalism, but the Taiping rebellion at least hardly looked like that from the standpoint of those responsible for British policy in China about 1860.

Another anachronistic argument is that which suggests that British hostility was provoked in part by some element of socialism in the Taiping programme.[8] This feature of the rebellion was certainly observed by British officials, at least in its early years. Bowring, for example, noted in 1854 that 'an absolute community of goods and no right of property' was reported to exist among the rebels, while in 1856 Alcock wrote of 'a saturnalia of social anarchists' as likely to result from success of the rebellion.[9] But for the most part official reports did not credit the rebels with having any sustained and organized social system at all. The few which indicated otherwise did not suggest that the economic system of the rebels was in practice fundamentally different from that prevailing under the Manchus. Robertson in 1857 reported that under the rebels 'the Husbandman cultivates his land and the produce accrues to himself', while Forrest in 1861 simply reported monthly exactions of tribute from the villages, but not more.[10] Bruce expressed the fear that if the rebels triumphed China would be 'reduced to a mass of agriculturists governed by a theocracy', and in so far as he credited them with any kind of distinctive social system it was its agrarianism, not its socialism, which alarmed him. There would simply be no place for trade and industry in a Taiping state. Bruce was, it may be added, sceptical of the sincerity of the proposals brought forward by Hung Jen-kan for the introduction of Western science and technology, and thought these merely a move to win Western sympathy.[11]

Also difficult to accept, save as a very general consideration in the minds of British officials, is the argument that fear of action by other powers prompted British intervention. Had such action actually occurred before 1862 it is probable that it would have been a sufficient cause for British action also, but the suggestion that the mere prospect of Russian intervention at the beginning of 1861 was a major reason for the change in British policy[12] is not supported by the evidence of Wade's talks in Peking nor of Bruce's despatches at that time. Bruce, in fact, rather discounted the danger of extensive aid from the Russians, arguing in July 1862, for example, that they were not likely to be active in promoting any serious improvement of the Chinese forces in the north of China because 'I think there is a feeling among them that the Chinese, well disciplined and armed, would require to be treated with *ménagement*, and that territorial questions would not be so easy of settlement if her national forces were more developed'.[13] Bruce certainly counted both France and Russia as powers less inclined than Britain to look upon the extension of Western empires into China as dangerous and undesirable, but the conclusion he drew from this was that British involvement in the Taiping struggle should be kept to a minimum lest it provoke the ambitions of these powers.[14] The Foreign Office was advised about possible Russian moves by the British Ambassador in St. Petersburg, and was naturally interested in the question, but the practical difficulties in the way of effective Russian assistance in the Yangtze area were recognized, and there was no alarm expressed at the idea of the Russians ousting the British from their trade on the river.[15] In so far as fear of other powers stealing a march on her existed, it was a general rather than a specific fear on Britain's part, and was not an immediate or major reason for the adoption of a policy of intervention in 1862.

Religious considerations did not count for much in British policy towards the rebellion. The 'blasphemy' and 'superstitions' of the rebels were sometimes denounced in official reports and statements, but it can fairly be said that the British government was not very deeply concerned whether a 'Christian' or a 'heathen' government ruled in China, so long as it was a stable and reasonably friendly government which offered no obstacles to the development of trade. One of the points made against the rebels by Bruce was that their religious principles made them quite unacceptable to the mass of the Chinese people, and therefore the less likely ever to establish a stable government. In Bruce's view the Manchus, though hardly popular, were at least more acceptable to the Chinese people, because they preserved Chinese traditional beliefs.[16] As far as possible Bruce wished to dissociate the British government from the activities of the Christian missionaries in China, being convinced that 'foreign Governments will most effectually serve Christianity in China by abstaining from protecting it as if it were a matter in which they have an interest'. Russell approved these views.[17] There was thus no tendency in British policy, as there was in French, to set out to serve the interests of Western Christianity in China,[18] and suppression of the rebellion was certainly not undertaken in that spirit on the British side.

But if the advancement of Christianity was no part of British policy on this question the advancement of trade certainly was. The opium trade in particular has been singled out by many as of prime importance in determining British policy towards the rebellion, and the argument that intervention was undertaken largely in defence of this trade and of the revenues derived from it by the British government in India would seem obviously to have much force in it.[19] About one-sixth of the British revenue in India at this time came from the sale of opium, and the prohibition of opium-smoking was a prominent feature of the Taiping programme whereas the Manchu government had agreed to legalize the trade into China in 1858. It is when one comes to look for detailed evidence to support these general arguments that difficulties arise.

In the first place, it is to be remembered that the rebel prohibition of opium-smoking under severe penalties was no new thing in China and not in itself likely to cause great alarm to opium-traders who were well used to smuggling in the drug with the connivance of many Chinese. In June 1854 Bowring considered that the general social and political disorganization occasioned by the rebellion would tend to promote rather than diminish sales of the drug, adding that 'the severe penalties proclaimed by Tae-ping-wang against the use of the drug will probably be just as inoperative as all the Imperial thunderings have been'.[20] In May 1856 the head of Jardine, Matheson & Co. reported to one of his correspondents that, although it was somewhat difficult to form any very decided opinion as to future trade prospects because of the contradictory reports current on the strength and disposition of the rebels, he was himself 'inclined to think that the demand for opium will not be materially interfered with for any length of time', since dealers were very experienced in finding alternative routes and outlets.[21] A few months later the comment of the firm's agent at Shanghai on reports that opium was in fact smoked at Nanking was that this would 'probably swell their numbers considerably'.[22] In the early and middle years of the rebellion neither British officials nor opium-traders appeared to have been greatly troubled by the effects, actual or probable, of the rebellion upon the market for opium.

In later years, when many more British observers visited the rebels, friend and foe alike agreed upon the continued prevalence of the opium habit among them. Griffith John, after one of his visits to Soochow in 1860, observed that 'though the use of opium is strictly forbidden, yet we know that it is largely consumed by them. Both the common soldiers and many of the chiefs partake of it freely. . . . Continued applications were made for opium and arms.'[23] Less sympathetic observers made the same kind of observation. In 1859 Wade reported a conversation with a Cantonese at Nanking who smoked opium still, 'and so, he said, do one-third of the people of Nanking; not openly, however, for indulgence in the vice is forbidden by law, nor is the drug openly sold'.[24] In May 1861 Parkes reported that opium was freely smoked outside the walls of the rebel capital, while the military observer Wolseley, in his *Narrative of the War in China in 1860* published in 1862, wrote that 'to say that the [Taipings] deserve any praise for their proclaimed laws prohibiting the use of opium is absurd . . . it will be laughed at by every man who has lately paid the Yangtsekiang a visit at any point where the rebel territories touch upon it. We visited many such places and at all, as at Nankin, the great cry was for opium and arms.'[25] By the time that British intervention against the rebellion actually occurred, therefore, there was considerable scepticism, not to say outright disbelief, in the anti-opium aspect of the rebellion among British observers, both official and non-official.

Nor does there appear to be any evidence to show that British officials concerned with the administration of India advocated intervention in defence of their opium revenues. India Office correspondence for the years 1860 to 1863 certainly reveals concern among some of these officials for the future of the trade and the revenues derived from it, but this concern had its roots in quite other considerations than the rebellion in China. Sir Henry Bartle Frere, for example, was alarmed by growing evidence of the production of opium in China itself, and in October 1861 wrote gloomily to Sir Charles Wood, Secretary of State for India, expressing his conviction of 'the utter insecurity of at least half our opium revenue'. The Taiping rebellion, however, was seen by him not as a cause of this insecurity but as one of the few temporary alleviating factors in the situation, for he continued: 'The recent recovery in price in China is owing to purely temporary causes—a taste among opium epicures for a particular flavour which the Indian drug possesses and which the Chinese growers have not yet learned to imitate, and the insecurity of life and property in some of the districts where the poppy cultivation was most popular (this insecurity is also temporary) owing to the rebellion.'[26] For at least this member of the Council of the Governor-General of India in 1861 the rebellion was helping rather than impeding the export of opium to China.

The two Financial Members of Council in the last years of the rebellion, Samuel Laing and Sir Charles Trevelyan, felt little concern for the future of the opium revenues. Laing wrote to Wood in April 1862 that, since Chinese expenditure on the drug had risen steadily 'in spite of Wars, Rebellions and fluctuations of prices and supply . . . I see no reason to doubt it will keep up as we give them a larger supply at a moderate price'.[27] Trevelyan wrote a year later: 'On all main points I concur with Mr. Laing's view on the Opium Revenue. We have gone on calling it precarious long after the contrary has been demonstrated by actual experience. It is *anomalous* but it is not *precarious*. . . . The Chinese will no more go without opium than certain classes of our fellow subjects will forgo the use of spirits. The idea of the Chinese becoming independent of us by growing their own opium is a mere chimera. . . .'[28] Wood himself was less optimistic than Laing or Trevelyan about the future prospects of the trade, but he was also rather fatalistic about it. He is certainly not to be found urging intervention against the Taipings as a means of protecting it. However much to be regretted, a fall in revenue from this source was, he feared, 'beyond control'.[29] Laing, in a pamphlet he published in 1863 entitled *England's Mission in the Far East*, did advocate intervention, but only on the grounds that the rebellion was destroying the prospects for British trade in general in China, not that it was threatening the opium trade in particular.[30]

Thus, in so far as there were fears for the opium trade among Indian government officials in the early eighteen-sixties, these fears sprang from such considerations as the development of native production of the drug and the agitation of anti-opium groups in Britain itself,[31] not from rebellion in China. Indeed, it seems to be no overstatement to say that, despite the kind of general arguments that have been advanced to prove a connection, opium interests had nothing whatever to do with the British decision to intervene against the Taipings, not because British merchants and officials were unconcerned about protecting this valuable trade, but simply because they did not see the rebellion as a serious threat to it.

If not the opium trade in particular, however, British trade prospects in general were certainly felt to be seriously threatened by the rebellion. Yet it is not apparent from the trade figures that, down to 1862 the rebellion had inflicted any very serious damage on British trade with China, a fact which helps explain why so many China merchants opposed intervention. It may be, as T. R. Banister argued in his *History of the External Trade of China*, that the total effect of the rebellion on the foreign trade of China is 'incalculable', and that this trade might have developed much further and faster but for the impoverishment it caused.[32] But as later years were to show, the real potentialities of China as a market for foreign trade had been exaggerated, and the end of the rebellion did not see the beginning of any great boom in such a trade. During the fifties and early sixties it continued to grow slowly, apart from a temporary drop at Shanghai in 1853–54, and Banister himself concedes that 'it is remarkable that, even in spite of the fact that ... this terrible and ruinous civil war was at its height, so much progress in foreign trade has actually to be recorded'.[33] Contemporary critics of the rebellion were also obliged to recognize this. In October 1861 Bruce found it 'rather a matter of surprise that trade should continue at all than that occasional losses should be suffered. The export of silk between June 1860 and June 1861 has, in spite of these disadvantages, amounted to 85,000 bales.'[34] In July 1862 General Staveley also reported from Shanghai that 'Europeans continue to visit the rebel country for the purpose of trade and are treated with civility; large quantities of silk have been brought into Shanghae during the last fortnight, and trade seems in a thriving state'.[35]

In 1863 British exports of silk from China did in fact drop sharply after the destruction of the mulberry trees in the fighting around Soochow, but this could be said to be more a result than a cause of intervention. Save for the slump in trade at the relatively minor port of Ningpo during its occupation by the rebels, the immediate trading position in China seems to have been little affected by the rebellion before 1862.[36] British officials however, were less concerned with the immediate prospects for the import of opium and the export of tea and silk, the staples in which China coast firms like Jardine, Matheson were mainly interested, than with the future market for British manufactures. In this respect the rebellion, by impoverishing the country without holding out any real prospect for its future regeneration, was for most British official policy-makers totally destructive. So, despite the criticisms of those local merchant houses who found their trade continuing strong despite the rebellion and who had no liking for any policy of aid which might strengthen the central government, intervention seemed justified. Palmerston, defending this policy in the House of Commons in May 1864, argued that 'those who view this question only in the aspect which it bears upon the particular merchants who export in China, and who have establishments in that country, take a very narrow and limited view of the question. These merchants in reality only form the outfalls by which the thousand rills of upland industry in this country find their way to the great oceans of the markets of the world.'[37] The Taiping rebellion was, by its alleged anarchical character, an obstacle in the way of the free flow of British manufactures into the 'great oceans of the markets of the world', and if it could not be easily got round, as had been attempted in 1861, it must be swept aside.

As an explanation for British intervention against the Taiping rebellion then, the general proposition that it was undertaken in defence of British trade interest in China seems to mean essentially that it was undertaken in defence of the supposed future prospects of those interests, rather than in defence of any major current interest which was demonstrably jeopardized by the rebellion before 1862.

The crux of the problem from the point of view of the British government was not opium or any other particular interest, but the general destruction and disruption which accompanied the rebellion and was believed to be central to it. It was basically a question of law and order. 'I do not think that any grounds exist for assuming that a regular government can spring out of the anarchical and disorderly elements which constitute the physical force of the insurrection. An impassable gulf separates it from the orderly and industrious part of the population', Bruce wrote in April 1862.[38] The correctness of this view of the rebellion is not the point at issue here. This was, by 1862, firmly established as the consular Foreign Office view, the product of a whole series of reports and observations going back at least to 1854 and confirmed into dogma by the experience of 1861.

It is, I believe, inadequate to dismiss this official British characterization of the rebellion as a mere pretext advanced to justify an opportunist determination to maintain Manchu rule in China, however corrupt and oppressive, just because this was the government with which such advantageous treaties had been made in 1860.[39] Apart from virtually dismissing as historically irrelevant and even dishonest a considerable mass of detailed evidence, such a judgment ignores the considerable complexities and uncertainties in British policy on this question after 1860. In any case the fact of being in rebellion against a government which had made or, more precisely, had been forced to make treaties advantageous to Great Britain was not in itself sufficient grounds to provoke intervention, as the situation in Japan about this time may serve to illustrate.

There also, during the eighteen-fifties, Britain had concluded treaties with a government reluctant to make them and which was soon to be faced with serious domestic rebellion. Despite the fact that the rebels in Japan were avowedly and actively much more opposed to these treaties than the Tokugawa government which had signed them, Great Britain remained neutral in the struggle which followed, and was even disposed to favour the rebels. Apart from the much smaller British interest at stake, the main difference with the situation in China was in the assessment of the quality of the rebel movement in Japan. In contrast to the Taipings, the rebellious western fiefs in Japan came to be regarded as capable of establishing more effective government than the ruling Tokugawas. By 1867 the British were quite prepared to see come into power a group whose popular slogan included the phrase *jo-i*, 'expel the barbarian', although it should be added that the then British minister in Japan, Parkes, recognized that the anti-Tokugawa leaders themselves no longer regarded this slogan as practical politics. The parallel is not perfect, but it is close enough to support the argument that, had the Taipings been regarded as comparable to the Japanese rebels in point of political capacity and organization, the simple conclusion of a favourable treaty with Great Britain in 1860 would not have guaranteed active British support for the Manchu government in China, any more than it did for the Tokugawa government in Japan.[40]

Thus, in seeking an explanation for the British involvement in the Taiping rebellion after 1862 one is ultimately forced back to the kind of argument advanced by H. B. Morse half a century ago, when Taiping studies were far less advanced than now. Writing of the Western powers in general, but certainly with Great Britain chiefly in mind, Morse concluded that 'in defence of their own interests, the Western powers were impelled more and more to intervene in the measures taken to suppress the rebellion, and were driven from step to step in supporting the imperial government which, with all its faults, was yet the power to which they were bound by treaties, and in resisting the rebels, who brought only rapine and devastation in their train'.[41] In the light of modern studies on the Taipings, one may wish to qualify Morse's characterization of them as bringing 'only rapine and devastation in their train', but this was undoubtedly the official British view, honestly held, and the policy of active intervention against them which developed by 1862 can only be historically understood in terms of that view.[42]

It should be added that any explanation of the change in British policy which implies that it was the product of some kind of logical analysis and reassessment at a high level of government planning is, to that extent at least, misleading. In fact the change of policy came about as an unplanned and immediate response to the pressure of local events. This is not meant to suggest that it was simply the fortuitous result of such pressures and events, for it is plain that the tendency in British policy towards intervention was strong before 1862 and, in terms of the official British view of the situation in China, it was a logical development. But it was not a certain development. It is at least arguable whether direct British action against the rebels would ever have been taken but for the second attack upon Shanghai, although a large measure of indirect aid to the Manchus probably would have been given, and to some extent had already been given before that event. 'We had nothing to do with [the rebels] until they approached the treaty ports', a government spokesman claimed in the House of Commons, 'and they might have gone on fighting for centuries if they had not threatened those ports.'[43] Like most government apologies for policy, this puts the matter in too simple a way, but there was some force in the argument.

This claim raises a final consideration which should not be overlooked in any explanation of why Great Britain intervened against the rebellion. The rebel threat to Shanghai at the beginning of 1862 was to a considerable extent the result of their defeats in the central Yangtze valley during 1861. The victories of Tseng Kuo-fan's armies had, by the end of that year, deprived the rebels of their former main base in Anhui and virtually driven them back upon the coastal provinces, where conflict with the Western treaty powers was much more likely to develop. British intervention cannot be fully explained, therefore, without reference to the larger military fortunes of the rebellion, and in assessing the significance of that intervention in bringing about the final defeat of the rebels one must see it in the perspective of the overall decline of the movement after 1853. In that decline the inadequacies of Taiping leadership and the slowly mounting pressure of the provincial Chinese armies directed by Tseng Kuo-fan were of far greater importance than the limited intervention of Western forces, although that intervention undoubtedly helped to speed the process considerably.

British policy throughout the rebellion was very much the creation of government officials, with those in Whitehall by no means always in control of the process. The influence of interested groups outside the official circle appears to have been minimal, at best corroborative rather than creative, but the influence of the official on the spot, military and naval as much as consular, was often decisive, determining what British policy was to be in fact in a new situation well before the British government at home, or even the British minister in Peking, could lay down what it ought to be in principle. Such locally inspired changes of policy in detail had, of course, to be consistent with the main British objectives in China, which were laid down by Whitehall. But given the slowness of communication between China and Europe at this time a wide area of initiative remained for the man on the spot, and he might easily commit his government by the inexorable logic of action at least more quickly, and quite possibly more deeply, than its chief spokesmen would themselves have chosen to do. Bowring had done this at Canton in 1856, and essentially the same process was repeated by Hope at Shanghai in 1862. That simple-sounding concept 'British policy' was the product of the interplay of a complex of personalities, principles, long-term national objectives and short-term local needs and pressures, over which no one had more than partial control.

British policy towards the Taiping rebellion, then, seems to me to illustrate the uncertainties and hesitations rather than the cynical astuteness of mid-Victorian imperialism at work in China. The British government stumbled into action against the rebellion, was always anxious not to get drawn too far into the struggle, and had half-formed but unrealized theories about using its aid to improve the quality of the Manchu government. It did not deliberately set out to suppress what it recognized to be a progressive, nationalist, anti-imperialist rebellion in order to preserve a reactionary and conveniently weak government in China. In the light of later developments, it is not surprising that the issue has been presented in such terms, especially by modern Chinese historians. But the effective choice which the British government of the day saw before it was between the political break-up of China and limited support for an admittedly weak, inefficient and not very trustworthy government which it was nevertheless hoped might, with encouragement, become reasonably modern in outlook and practice.

British policy was, perhaps, based on a mistaken view of the real nature and potential of the Taiping rebellion. It was certainly based on motives of self-interest, although this did not preclude a genuine desire among some British officials in China to help that country to find its feet in the modern world community which it could no longer ignore. But despite superficial appearances, British policy on this particular issue does not provide a very convincing example of a cynically repressive imperialism at work. Too many assumptions both about what the Taiping rebellion was capable of achieving in nineteenth-century China and about the nature and development of British policy towards it have to be made for such a view to be historically acceptable.

Appendix

THE VISIT OF W. H. MEDHURST AND LEWIN BOWRING TO
NANKING, JUNE 1854

UNLIKE THE OTHER OFFICIAL British visits to Taiping
territory (Bonham 1853; Elgin 1858; Hope 1861) no report of
this visit was ever published by the British government. Since
the two reports submitted by Medhurst and Bowring (Medhurst
was almost certainly chiefly responsible for them) contain much
of interest, it has seemed worth while to reproduce them in full
here. They were forwarded in two separate despatches from
Sir John Bowring to the Earl of Clarendon, to be found in
FO 17/214. Clarendon's reply is in FO 228/169.

Appendix

1. DESPATCH No. 78 OF SIR JOHN BOWRING TO THE EARL OF CLARENDON

Shanghai 7 July 1854

My Lord,

My despatch No. 60, dated 15th of June, stated to Your Lordship that I had determined to send a Mission up the Yangtsze Keang, in order to obtain more accurate information as to the real character of the rebellion, of which Nanking is the Head Quarters, and to ascertain whether supplies of coal could be found in that Great River for the public service.

I have the honor to send copies of the instructions given to Messrs. Medhurst and Bowring, whom I nominated to the Mission.

They have returned today, and I have no doubt Your Lordship will agree with me that the business confided to them has been admirably managed, and that the reports they have made and the documents they have brought, are such as not to leave a shadow of doubt, either as to the political or religious nature of the movement.

More detailed reports will be ready for the next mail, but I have been exceedingly desirous that not a moment should be lost in furnishing Your Lordship with those authentic particulars which I am able to gather together in the few hours left me before closing the Despatches.

Your Lordship will see that the conclusions at which I have been disposed to arrive, are fully borne out by the facts now ascertained.

The course we are called upon to pursue under present circumstances, will require the most mature deliberation. In a few days, the question of the Custom House duties here will I hope be disposed of, (as I find the American Consular Court is to be opened on the 15th. instant for adjudication on the claims preferred against the merchants of the United States), and I shall then be more free to discuss with the American Commissioner the measures which it may be desirable to adopt.

I must apologize to Your Lordship for the irregular form in which I have to forward some of the accompanying documents, but there is no time to make official copies of them.

I have the honor to be,
    With the highest respect,
        Your Lordship's
            Most Obedient,
                Humble Servant,
                    JOHN BOWRING.

Appendix

Sir John Bowring's Instructions to Messrs. Medhurst and Bowring on Departure for Nanking.

Shanghae 13th. June 1854

Gentlemen,

His Excellency the Admiral has concurred in a suggestion of mine that it is desirable under existing circumstances that we should obtain more information as to the state of matters on the Yang-tsze Kiang, both political and commercial, and he has therefore directed Captain O'Callaghan, of Her Majesty's Steamer 'Encounter' to convey you up that river.

The especial object of your visit is to ascertain whether a supply of coals can be provided for the public service, and as it is understood that a considerable quantity can be purchased at Woohoo you will proceed to that place, or even further if needful, to accomplish this particular purpose. You will purchase such quantities of coal as Captain O'Callaghan may direct, and you will ascertain on what conditions, and to what extent supplies of coal can be provided. You will also gather all accessible information as to places of production, prices, markets to which sent, and every detail in this important matter.

You are authorized, either in proceeding up or down the river, to visit the great commercial depots of Chinkiangfoo, Nanking, and any other important cities or marts of trade. In them you will collect any facts which are calculated to throw light upon the probable demand for British manufactures, the disposition to trade with Foreigners, the supplies obtainable of Chinese produce, and in fine every detail which may assist to form a reasonable judgment as to the capabilities which these places may offer for the future extension of our commercial relations.

You will avail yourself of the present opportunity to collect all accessible information which may enable you to report on the position, plans, and prospects of the Tai-ping-wang party, their political views, their forms of government, their religious books, creeds, and observances, their domestic and social habits, and all facts respecting them which seem entitled to notice. You are authorized to state that I am at present at Shanghae, that I am desirous of establishing friendly relations with the Chinese people, that I have sent you up to make enquiries as to what is taking place and to purchase coals for the use of our people. I need not add that the higher the authority to which you can obtain access, the more satisfactory will be the probable result of your mission.

Appendix

I shall be glad if you will obtain specimens of raw materials, manufactures, works of art, or curiosities likely to illustrate the report of your mission. Information as to the occupations, dress, food, domestic and social usages, education and character of the inhabitants or occupiers of the Districts through which you pass, may in many ways be obtainable. I confide this interesting mission to your guidance in the hope that its results may not only add much to our knowledge but be instrumental in advancing those great commercial objects which are specially entrusted to my care.

I have the honor to be,
> Gentlemen,
>> Your most obedient Servant,
>>> JOHN BOWRING.

Enclosure 2

> *Sir J. Bowring to Messrs. Medhurst and Bowring naming the vessels with which they are to proceed to Nanking.*

Shanghae 15 June 1854

Gentlemen,

His Excellency the Naval Commander in Chief has appointed Her Majesty's Steamer 'Rattler', commanded by Captain Mellersh, to receive you on board and accompanied by Her Majesty's Steamer 'Styx', to proceed with you for the objects of your mission up the Yang-tsze keang.

His Excellency expresses his desire that the 'Rattler' and 'Styx' should return to this Port as quickly as may be consistent with the fulfilment of the duties committed to your charge, and I must instruct you to avoid all needless delay, so as at all events to return to Shanghae on or before the 6th proximo.

I have the honor to be,
> Gentlemen,
>> Your most obedient Servant,
>>> JOHN BOWRING.

Enclosure 3

> *Report by Messrs. Medhurst and Bowring to Sir J. Bowring of Proceedings on Mission to Nanking.*

Shanghae 7 July 1854

Sir,

We have the honor to report our return from Nanking, whither we proceeded in accordance with the instructions conveyed in Your Excellency's letter No. 35 dated the 13th. ultimo.

Appendix

As the immediate departure of the mail prevents our submitting a detailed report of our proceedings, we are compelled to confine ourselves on this occasion to a brief summary of what took place during our visits to the localities occupied by the Insurgents, and of the conclusions we have come to regarding their present position from the circumstances which came under our observation.

The first place we visited was Chinkeang Foo, on approaching which the insurgent garrison fired a shot across the bows of H.M.S. 'Rattler'. This necessitated our anchoring and landing the next morning to demand an apology, having at the same time in view the acquisition of information as regards the possibility of procuring coals. Our interviews with the chiefs were on the whole satisfactory, and such as to induce us to anticipate that at Nanking also we should be favourably received. The apology required was readily tendered, although in objectionable phraseology, which was however altered on its being pointed out, and one of their officers, who styled himself a commander of 15,000 men, was directed to accompany us to Nanking, with the alleged purpose of facilitating our introduction to the superior authorities in command at that city.

Our reception at Nanking was not such as we were led to expect. For though no actual insult was offered, beyond styling us 'barbarians' and issuing letters to us in the form of mandates, yet it was very evident that there was a great indisposition to hold any communication with us, which extended itself to a prohibition to allowing any of the insurgents to visit the ships, while we ourselves were restricted from penetrating beyond the outer suburb stockades. Finding ourselves baffled in every attempt to obtain an interview with any chief of standing, we addressed a letter in Capt. Mellersh's name through a subordinate to the Eastern King in which we informed him that the principal object of our visit was to obtain information on a number of points, as well as to procure coals, of which we had discovered a large quantity in store on the River side. The points on which we wished to be enlightened were enclosed in the form of questions, to which we insisted on having definite replies. After much evasion and delay we received a reply, translation of which is enclosed, containing answers to all our queries, and putting 50 questions for solution in return; our rejoinder to which will be found in enclosure No. 2.* We forbear for the present from commenting upon this extraordinary document, though we beg to call Your Excellency's special attention to it, as one very characteristic of the misguided and absurd pretensions, religious and political, put forth by the promoters of this remarkable movement.

* Enclosure No. 5 here.

Your Excellency will observe that our endeavour to procure coals was totally unsuccessful, so much so that an attempt on our part to anchor the 'Rattler' opposite a depot, where some 1000 tons were in store, was met by evident preparations to resist by force any movement in that direction. Finding them thus decidedly hostile, we begged Capt. Mellersh to return to his first anchorage rather than risk a collision.

The want of coal of course precluded our moving higher up the River to Woohoo, and other places whither no doubt instructions had been sent to treat us in a similar manner, a conclusion eventually justified by our unfavourable reception at Chinkeangfoo on our return. Being convinced of the inability of holding any further communication with the Nanking insurgents, we determined upon returning, and on our way back we visited E-ching Heen, (a large town on the left bank of the Yang-tsze-keang, and half-way between Nanking and Chinkeang Foo) and the Silver Island Anchorage (outside of Chinkeang Foo) both of them occupied by the Imperial Forces. Our reception at these places was most cordial and satisfactory.

We found the insurgents closely confined to the walls and immediate suburbs of Nanking and Chinkeang, also of Kwachow, which we passed at a very short distance. Each of these places is besieged by a large force of Imperialists who are constantly giving their occupants battle. The neighbouring districts are all in the hands of the Imperialists, who harass any parties of insurgents that attempt to communicate between their several posts. We saw no indication whatever of any popular demonstration of sympathy with the views of the insurgents. The interior of Chinkeang City, the only one which we entered, and the suburbs of the other towns are completely ransacked and utterly deserted by their former inhabitants. We saw no commerce or traffic of any kind going on, and how or where the insurgents procure their daily provision we could not ascertain. Large quantities of grain, we were told, are in their possession but the amount cannot last very long. They appear to have no money nor resources adequate to maintain a long protracted struggle, and their ultimate success appears, from what we saw, to be very problematical. We could not find in answer to enquiries that any properly organized form of government exists among them, although certainly implicit obedience is shewn to the commands of the higher authorities. We noticed a total absence of men of age, of education, or of respectability, and even the Eastern King, although possessed doubtless of great talent and an extraordinary influence over the minds of his followers, judging from the style of his 'Mandate' to Capt. Mellersh, must be a man of most ordinary literary attainments. His blasphemous assumptions of Divine Power, we may remark, shew him at the same time to be a man devoid of all moral principle.

Although so much hampered in our endeavours to obtain information, we happily succeeded in securing copies of all their latest publications, nine in number, and some of their proclamations, all containing many new and curious details which of course we cannot now give.

In consequence of our peculiar position, and for convenience sake, we deemed it advisable to request Captain Mellersh to permit us to make use of his name in all the correspondence that passed from first to last; but we hold ourselves responsible for the contents of the letters he addressed, all of which, with the exception of that we enclose, are of too commonplace a character to deserve transmission. Their chief end was to maintain our position against the absurd assumptions of superiority variously intruded upon us almost every day, and we hope that the plain manner in which we denied all such claims, as exemplified in the letter we enclose, will meet with Your Excellency's full approval.

In conclusion we beg to express our acknowledgements of the hearty and useful co-operation afforded us throughout both by Captains Mellersh and Woolcombe and the several officers under their command.

We have the honor to be
  Sir
     Your Excellency's most obedient
      humble Servants
        W. H. MEDHURST
        L. BOWRING.

Enclosure 4

  The Eastern King to Captain Mellersh, R.N., of H.M.S. 'Rattler'
  giving information regarding the Political and Religious Creed of
  *the Insurgents.**

Yang, the Comforter, the Holy Ghost, the Honae Teacher,† the Lord who redeems from disease, an Assistant Minister of State, and a Generalissimo of the Celestial Dynasty of T'aiping, truly commis-

---

* I have been unable to locate the Chinese original of this letter in the series FO 682 (Documents in Chinese from the Chinese Secretary's Office) in the Public Record Office. Lo Erh-kang quotes from this letter in the 1957 edition of his *T'ai-p'ing t'ien-kuo shih-kao*, p. 211, but it is not clear whether he is doing so from a Chinese translation of the English version or from a Chinese original.

† On this title, note T. Hamberg, *The Visions of Hung Siu-tshuen and Origin of the Kwang-si Insurrection* (1854), p. 46: 'Yang Siu-tshin is also known under the

sioned by Heaven to rule, issues this mandate for the information of the barbarian younger brethren.

On the 20th day of the 5th month (Sunday, 25th June) a General of our Celestial Kingdom reported (orig: memorialized) that you the younger brethren had brought two vessels and anchored them off the central station outside the capital, and that he had not ascertained the object of your visit, but had received from you several letters (orig: petitions) which he submitted for my inspection. These documents I have perused and understood, and I commend you for not having been deterred by distance, though dwellers beyond the ocean, from coming to do homage at our court, and for having exhibited so sincere a desire to conform to the laws and ordinances of our Celestial Kingdom. Your conduct has given me very great pleasure.

I observe, however, that you complain of our having employed several improper modes of expression towards you. In this you are in error owing to your not being conversant with our heavenly principles and doctrines, at which I am not at all surprised.

In your letters you make enquiries regarding the administration, the laws and ordinances of our Celestial Kingdom, and to enlighten you I have taken up each of your questions upon these heads, and given them distinct replies to which I demand your careful attention.

I am the Comforter, the Holy Ghost, the Lord who redeems from disease, an Assistant Minister, a Generalissimo and the Eastern Prince, whom the Heavenly Father, the supreme Lord, the Great God, and Jesus the Redeemer of the World, the Celestial Elder Brother, have of their great mercy personally commissioned to descend into the world in order to assist the true Sovereign in destroying utterly all imps and devils upon the earth, to redeem the inhabitants of the world from their diseases, and to bring together all the nations of the earth, so that the souls of all men may ascend to Heaven.

My Sovereign, the Celestial King, is God's own son, and the uterine brother of the Celestial Elder Brother. He is also the true Sovereign of Universal Peace over the myriad nations of the globe, specially commissioned to that end by the Heavenly Father, the Supreme Lord, the Great God, and by Jesus the Redeemer of the

---

name of Ho-nae teacher, which is derived from dividing the character of his name Siu into two 禾 乃, and does not seem to have any particular meaning.' The American interpreter E. C. Bridgman translated it as 'Universal Provider', but commented: 'it is not only new but, if literally rendered, would be utterly unintelligible to all but the initiated. It is an enigma, and would seem to be employed as a sort of counter-sign or watchword' (U.S. Congressional Papers, McLane Correspondence, p. 74).

world, the Celestial Elder Brother. My sovereign the Celestial King is the Celestial King of universal peace, the greatly gifted Prince, the supreme director of the world, who gives life to all people, enables them to conform to the truth, and preserves them from being ruined by imps and devils.

You barbarians have always had the credit of knowing how to worship the Heavenly Father. Are you aware that he is omniscient, omnipresent and almighty? So also you have always had the credit of knowing how to revere Jesus the Redeemer of the world, the Celestial Brother. Are you aware that he too is omniscient, omnipresent and almighty?

My sovereign the Celestial King has been commissioned by Heaven to extend the true doctrine. In all his doings he is just and equitable. He looks upon the inhabitants of the world as one great family, and cherishes them as his own flesh and blood. The myriad nations of the globe he looks on as the members of his own body. All our ceremonial laws and rules have been graciously communicated to him by the Heavenly Father and the Celestial Elder Brother Jesus, who have from time to time put themselves to the trouble of coming down from Heaven on purpose to make him acquainted with them.

Whenever the Heavenly Father is pleased to teach the common people his Divine Will he descends into and commissions me, the Generalissimo, to utter it with my mouth. And when the Celestial Elder Brother Jesus is pleased to communicate his Divine Will to the common people he descends into and commissions the Assistant Minister of State and Generalissimo the Western Prince to declare it to them.

Ever since our Celestial Kingdom took up arms in the good cause, all our proceedings have been guided by the Divine Will of the Heavenly Father and Celestial Elder Brother. In obedience thereto alone have we raised our vast armies in defence of the holy cause, destroyed the corrupt, saved alive the good, taught men to conform to the true doctrines of God and exterminated all that is depraved and false. The imps have set on foot their vile schemes in ten thousand different ways, but in every case the Heavenly Father and Celestial Elder Brother have vouchsafed to us their gracious countenance, and made it impossible for our enemies to do us harm. Even when slight indications of treachery have exhibited themselves among our own people, the Heavenly Father and Celestial Elder Brother have similarly looked down upon us and the traitors have been unable to escape their mighty hand.

I am ignorant whether you, our barbarian younger brethren, who dwell beyond the seas, do in like manner obey the commands of the

Appendix

Heavenly Father and Celestial Elder Brother. From what I have
seen of your letters I should judge that in many points you are
uninstructed in the Heavenly Principles and therefore think it right
to address to you this clear, distinct and detailed mandate, so that
you may learn to appreciate the proofs of the Heavenly Father's
power, and to obey his laws.

Let all implicitly obey this my mandate.

I annex replies to your thirty questions.

1. To your enquiry (whether after we shall have succeeded in
subjugating the country we shall be willing to trade with England,
and if so, at what parts and places, and under what conditions as
regards prohibited articles; and to your request that I should address
a letter on the subject to your Plenipotentiary for you to take to
Shanghai) I reply,

That after peace shall have been fully established we shall be
willing to trade not only with England but with the myriad nations
of the globe, for all the inhabitants of the earth are brethren. The
places of trade can be the subject of after arrangement. Only such
articles as are injurious to the human frame will be prohibited.

2. To your enquiry (as to what provinces, departments and districts
we have reduced) I reply,

That the Empire belongs to the Heavenly Father. He was able to
create the Heavens, the Earth and all things therein in 6 days. My
sovereign the Celestial King has in person received God's distinct
commission to be the true Sovereign of the myriad nations of the
globe, and to raise a vast army in the holy cause. This having been
effected the whole empire is at peace.

3. To your enquiry (as to what system of laws and statutes we
employ in the administration of our government, and to your request
to be supplied with copies of our codes) I reply,

That the Celestial Dynasty governs in accordance with God's ten
commandments, making them its code of morality. The destruction
of the wicked and the protection of the good is the law we obey.

4. To your enquiry (as to the number of our troops now in possession of the Celestial Capital and Chinkiangfoo) I reply,

That the soldiers of the Celestial Kingdom are innumerable. The
people of myriad nations in heaven above and on the earth beneath
are all the children of the Heavenly Father and soldiers of the
Celestial King. How then can they be numbered?

5. To your enquiry (as to our true object in subjugating the empire,
whether it be to exterminate the Tartars or whether to spread and
promote God's truth) I reply,

180

Appendix

That the Celestial King has been specially commissioned by God to come down from Heaven for the express purpose of exterminating the imps, and bringing the whole world to the knowledge of the truth and the worship of the Father. The destruction of all who do not obey God is the special object we have in view.

6. To your enquiry (as to whether and why I received the appellation of 'the Comforter', 'the Holy Ghost' and as to the meaning of the titles 'Honae Teacher' and 'Redeemer from Disease') I reply,

That the Heavenly Father appeared upon earth and declared it as his sacred will that the Eastern Prince should redeem the people of all nations upon earth from their diseases, and that the Holy Ghost should enlighten all their blindness. The Heavenly Father has now pointed out the Eastern Prince as the Holy Ghost, and therefore given him the title of 'Comforter, Holy Ghost, Honae Teacher and the Lord who redeems from disease', so that all the nations of the earth may know the confidence placed in me by the Heavenly Father in his mercy.

7. To your enquiry (whether we have introduced a new currency, and when the impish cash is no more to be current) I reply,

That the divine coin of the Celestial Kingdom is on the point of being put into circulation, when the cash with the impish stamp will of course be at once done away with and proscribed.

8. To your enquiry (where we are going to establish our Celestial Capital) I reply,

That the Celestial Capital has already been established at Kinling (Nanking) and the myriad nations of the earth are in consequence at peace.

9. To your enquiry (whether you are to infer by the designation given to Jesus of Celestial Elder Brother and that given to the Celestial King of Second Elder Brother, that the latter is actually the child of God, or that he is so only by allegory) I reply,

That the Celestial King is the second son of God, truly declared to be by the Divine Will of God. The Celestial King likewise ascended up to Heaven in his own person and there again and again received the distinct commands of God to the effect that he was the Heavenly Father's second son and the true sovereign of the myriad nations of the globe. Of this we possess indubitable proof.

10. To your enquiry (whether the Heavenly Father has appeared upon earth during the present year, and whether in his manifestation he is personally visible, or whether his voice alone is heard) I reply,

That when God the Heavenly Father appears on earth he descends into my person and through my golden lips enunciates his teachings for the benefit of the world, and he thus gives innumerable manifestations of his power and might.

11. To your enquiry (whether we levy taxes or duties of any kind) I reply,

That as a matter of course the customs and duties of every station, and the revenue of the country belong to and are paid in to the Celestial Court.

12. To your enquiry (why we have altered three characters in the horary characters and one in the names of the constellations) I reply,

That we have altered the characters you refer to in consequence of their unpleasant sound. (Note: In the Canton dialect the sound of the character 仒 is the same as that for 'the female organ of generation' the sound of 丑 is the same as that for 'bad' and the sound of 夘 is the same as that for 'have not'. The last character 鬼 signifies 'devil' and is on that account objectionable.)

13. To your enquiry (as to the individuals whose duty it is to preach and minister to the people, and whether we have any priests, elders or teachers) I reply,

That the official authorities make known the Heavenly Principles to the people in the manner enjoined by the Holy Scriptures.

14. To your question (regarding the mode of admission into our community, whether enquiry is previously made into the sincerity of the candidate, or whether he goes through a course of teaching before admission, or whether he takes an oath of initiation, or whether admittance is free to all without restraint) I reply,

That the rules of admission are to acknowledge that the Heavenly Father and Celestial Elder Brother have put themselves to the trouble of appearing upon earth to appoint the Celestial King as sovereign, and the Eastern, Western, Southern, Northern and Assistant Kings as assistants, to descend into the world for the special purpose of delivering the souls of all nations upon earth, and to sweep away every imp and devil, so as to teach all men to know forever that God is the Ghostly Father that the Celestial King is the true Lord, and to obey to all eternity the laws of the Celestial Kingdom. My sovereign the Celestial King loves all men as his own flesh and blood, and would not deter anyone (from joining him). The officers of the Celestial Kingdom confide in all men as brethren. Those who return to virtue and seek admission into our faith may do so without restraint. No reference is made to their antecedents and no oath of initiation is necessary. If any man be false at heart God is present to detect him.

15. To your enquiry (as to what number of wives we allow to each individual) I reply,

That as regards the taking of wives and concubines by the brethren, their unions are determined by Heaven, and upon Heaven depends the number they take.

16. To your enquiry (whether we have established literary examinations, from what classics we take our themes, and whether we have abolished the old impish literary titles) I reply,

That at the literary examinations of the Celestial capital we discard all classics and take for our themes fragments of the true doctrine of God. All literary degrees given by the Tartars we entirely abolish, as they are not Celestial honorary titles. Those who have talent may, if they please, contend for degrees at the Celestial Examinations, and if they prove worthy they will be employed.

17. To your enquiry (whether we are aware of the loss of a day in our Calendar, in consequence of which Sabbath days fall a day too soon, and to your question why we do not correct the error, and whether our names for the days are the same as those used by other Chinese) I reply,

That the Sabbath days in the Celestial calendar are those of old Chinese calendars in which they are made to fall in the constellations 星 昂 虛 房. Our horary characters are the same as the old ones, with the exception of the objectionable ones, which we have done away with.

18. To your enquiry (whether we have entered into any agreement with the Americans allowing them to trade) I reply,

That when the American steamer came to the Celestial Capital last month they received from me a mandate to the effect that not only would they be allowed to trade, but that the myriad nations of the globe should enjoy the same privilege on the express condition however that those who came to trade should implicitly obey the heavenly commands. Also that vessels bound for the Celestial Capital for trading purposes should anchor at Silver Island, below Chinkiangfoo, and there await the orders of the authorities of that city.

19. To your enquiry (as to the locality where the good coal we have in store is produced, the price at which it is obtained, and the practicability of your hereafter receiving it as an article of commerce) I reply,

That Heaven and Earth were created by the Heavenly Father. The earth produces myriads of things, and coal no doubt is found in all parts of it. The coal that is in store on account of the Celestial Court cannot be sold. I would prefer therefore that vessels which you intend to send here to purchase it should stay away.

20. To your enquiry (whether we possess our lands, houses and

other property in common so that no man may appropriate more than his share) I reply,

That our lands and their produce are equally divided. All men having been begotten by Heaven, they should together enjoy Heaven's good gifts. Hence all men are said to belong to one family.

21. To your enquiry (as to the individual at Canton who furnished the Celestial King with foreign translations of the Scriptures, and taught him religious truth; whether it was Lo Hosun* or no; and to your question 'what is the name of the Celestial King') I reply,

That after the Celestial King came down into this world he was again taken up into the high Heaven by the Heavenly Father, who sent a Celestial messenger to receive his soul into Heaven, where the Father took great pains to instruct him upon every subject, and commanded him to exert his utmost to bring mankind to the knowledge of truth. Subsequently the Celestial King heard that a foreign brother had established a place of worship in the province of Canton, in which he preached God's truth, whereupon the Celestial King went in his own person to the place of worship set up by the teacher Lo, in order to ascertain whether the truth of God which he taught agreed with that the Celestial King received. Has this teacher Lo come with you or not?

22. To your enquiry (as to what news we have received of the progress of the army despatched to subjugate Chihli, whether or not they have captured Shunteenfoo, and whether we have sent armies in any other direction) I reply,

That the subjugation of the impish dens is no doubt determined upon by the Heavenly Father and the Celestial Elder Brother has the power to effect it, so that the imps must certainly be destroyed. As regards our troops the Heavenly Father is daily advancing such of them as are worthy to subjugate the impish localities.

23. To your enquiry (as to the palace in which the Celestial King resides, and the locality in which his palace has been built, and to your question whether 'Teentih' is a former designation of the Celestial King or whether (as you have been told) Teentih is the name of the individual who established the dynasty and Taeping Wang that of the present monarch, his successor) I reply,

That the Celestial King now resides in the Golden Palace. He has also 'The city of the true God'. The Palace of the true God is our Heavenly Father's palace. 'The Palace of Christ' is our Celestial Elder Brother's Palace. 'The Palace of the Golden Dragon' is the Celestial King's Palace. 'Teen Kwo' (The Celestial Kingdom) is the true appellation and not 'Teentih'. 'Teen Wang' (the Celestial King)

* i.e. Rev. I. J. Roberts.

is the true sovereign and Ruler, Taeping. Besides him there is no other.

24. To your enquiry (whether we publish a Government Gazette and to your request to be supplied with a copy) I reply,

That no official gazette of Imperial Decrees has yet been published.

25. To your enquiry (whether we administer baptism or immersion to candidates admitted into our community and in what form we administer the rite, also whether we have the ordinance of the Lord's Supper) I reply,

That the worship of God consists in the washing clean of the heart, not in the immersion of the body. At every meal we offer up thanks to God. Morning and evening we pray to him, and at all times we remember to obey the ten commandments.

26. To your enquiry (whether we offer our sacrifices as mere thank-offerings or with any idea of atonement for sin attached to the rite) I reply,

That if we be free from sin when we sacrifice to and worship God, we then merely thank him for his mercy, but if sin be on us at the time we pray that it may be atoned for. These are, however, not the only ceremonials connected with our sacrifices.

27. To your enquiry (whether smoking tobacco and opium, drunkenness, lewdness etc. are strictly forbidden, and by what laws we punish these offences) I reply,

That all smoking of opium and every species of tobacco, all drinking of wine, lewdness etc. are punished by the Celestial King with decapitation in accordance with the express command of the Heavenly Father.

28. To your enquiry (what is our motive in separating the males from the females, and how long we intend to retain this law in operation) I reply,

That to prevent men and women from promiscuous intercourse is the true doctrine, a law which all nations should obey and not presume to set aside. The union of husbands and wives is subject to the direction of the Heavenly Father.

29. To your enquiry (whether the Canton and Fuhkeen factions in occupation of Shanghai have as yet given in their allegiance to us, and whether we will accept their submission) I reply,

That not only will we permit the factions at Shanghai to yield obedience to our rule, but we would wish the myriad nations of the earth to submit to our sway.

30. To your enquiry (whether we have any titular nobility and if so whether it is hereditary) I reply,

That meritorious persons receive bountiful rewards and high honours. These are similar to the hereditary celestial orders of nobility.

———————

The questions I have to ask are these—

You nations having worshipped God for so long a time, does any one among you know,

1. How tall God is, or how broad?
2. What his appearance or colour is?
3. How large his abdomen is?
4. What kind of beard he grows?
5. What colour his beard is?
6. How long his beard is?
7. What cap he wears?
8. What kind of clothes he wears?
9. Whether his first wife was the Celestial Mother, the same that brought forth the Celestial Elder Brother Jesus?
10. Whether he has had any other son born to him since the birth of Jesus his first born?
11. Whether he has had but one son, or whether, like us mortals, a great many sons?
12. Whether he is able to compose verse?
13. How rapidly can he compose verse?
14. How fierce his disposition is?
15. How great his liberality is?

You nations having worshipped God and Jesus for so long a time, does any one among you know,

16. How tall Jesus is, or how broad?
17. What his appearance or colour is?
18. What kind of beard he grows?
19. Of what colour his beard is?
20. What kind of cap and clothes he wears?
21. Whether his first wife was our elder sister?
22. How many children he has had?
23. Of what age is his eldest son?
24. How many daughters has he had?
25. Of what age is his eldest daughter?
26. How many grandsons has God at this moment?
27. How many granddaughters has God at this moment?
28. How many heavens are there?
29. Whether all the Heavens are of equal height?
30. What the highest Heaven is like?

Having worshipped God and Jesus for so long a time can you tell me,

31. Whether as the angels in the Heavens of Heavens constitute the army and power of God so also the ministers and people of those countries that worship God and Christ constitute the army and power of God?

32. Can you tell me whether the denizens of those countries whose people do not constitute the army and power of God are human beings or imps?

33. Can you tell me whether in your morning and evening devotions you entreat permission to enter the Celestial Kingdom, or pray not to be suffered to enter therein?

34. What meaning did Jesus intend to convey when he commanded his disciples saying 'The Kingdom of Heaven is at hand. Ye must repent of your sins'?

35. What meaning did Jesus intend to convey when he said 'I will destroy God's temple and in three days I will rebuild it'?

36. Why did Jesus come to life on the third day after having been nailed to the cross?

37. What did the angels mean when on the birth of Jesus in the Kingdom of Judea they sang praises in the sky, saying 'Glory to God on high, on earth peace (Taeping) and good will towards men'?

38. In your morning and evening prayers do you pray for the descent upon earth of the Holy Spirit, the Comforter, to transform your minds?

39. What meaning did Jesus intend to convey when he commanded his disciples saying 'At some other time the Comforter will come down into the world with very great power, not like me today'?

40. What is the meaning of the words in Scripture 'Your Lord bears the diseases of the people of the world'?

41. Can you tell me whether you nations collect in the Celestial Kingdom through the power of God imperceptibly protecting you in your journey hither, or is it by your own power that you are able to reach the Celestial Kingdom?

42. Can you tell me why you nations collect in the Celestial Kingdom? Is it that God imperceptibly deputes you to collect together here, and supports your sovereigns in presenting themselves at court, and uniting with us in the service of God, or does God expressly send you hither to trade?

43. Can you tell me whether you obey the will of God and the injunctions of Jesus, or do not obey them?

187

44. Do you nations hope to secure eternal life through obedience to the Divine Will and the injunctions of Jesus, or are you able to secure everlasting life without such obedience?

45. Does any one among you know whether the corrupt Gods, and the serpent the devil spoken of in the Old Testament are identical with the beings now called imps?

46. You know that God will listen to your petitions for the gift of the Holy Spirit to renew your hearts. Are you aware that he has sent the spirit into the world in the person of the Eastern King?

47. You all know that God has in his mercy accepted your petitions that he should greatly manifest his power in the destruction of imps and devils. Are you aware that he has already of his great mercy descended into the world, and for several years taken into his hands the guidance of affairs? That Jesus has for years guarded him in his descent, and that they have performed innumerable miracles and mighty acts, and destroyed numberless imps and devils?

48. May I enquire whether you are sincere in giving your aid to God and Jesus in exterminating the imps or whether you are assisting them in their rebellion against God and Christ?

49. You all know that God and Jesus are the arbiters of all affairs in the Celestial Kingdom, that the armies and powers of all the Heavens are concentrated in the Celestial Kingdom; that the people of all nations, when graciously enlightened by God, understand that it is their duty to collect in the Celestial Kingdom in order to pay their homage to the Supreme God, to the Holy Redeemer of the world, under the true Sovereign of all nations, and to become the armies and power of God. Are you aware that any nation which does not thus appear to do reverence at the courts of God, of the Redeemer, and of the true Sovereign of all nations, is a nation of imps?

50. God and Jesus having been served by you for so long a time, and they having for several years past descended into the world, and taken the lead in the extermination of the imps, why is it that your nations are not seen to come with a few offerings of holy things to pay tribute to God, to Jesus, and to the true Sovereign of all nations? You not only do not perform this duty but you have the audacity to presume to impose upon us in spite of ourselves, and without any sense of propriety to represent that your object in coming to the Celestial Kingdom is the desire to get coals. Ponder for a moment and consider how you are rebelling against God, against Jesus, and against the true Sovereign of all nations. Let me ask, is such conduct consistent with Heavenly principles. Think well of this.

The 23rd. day of the 5th. month of the 4th. year of **Keaying** (51st. of cycle) of the Celestial Kingdom of Thaeping. 28th. June 1854

```
┌─────────────────────────┐
│                         │
│      Seal of the        │
│                         │
│      Eastern King       │
│                         │
└─────────────────────────┘
```

Translated by W. H. Medhurst

Enclosure 5

Captain Mellersh, R.N., to the Eastern King in reply to his queries for information on English Creed.

Captain Mellersh, R.N., Commanding H.B. Majesty's vessels off Nanking makes this reply to the Eastern King.

I yesterday had the honour to receive your communication, which you were pleased to designate 'a mandate' and I have made myself acquainted with its contents.

I am at a loss to comprehend the opening remark of your letter to the effect that my reiterated objections to the improper language used towards me by your subordinates arose from my ignorance of Heavenly principles. As regards the term 'barbarian' I can only say that it has always been employed by the Chinese as an appellation of raw uncivilized tribes, and as for the terms 'mandate' 'petition' 'memorial' etc., they are never used but in correspondence between superiors and inferiors. Now I have repeatedly and distinctly informed your authorities since my arrival here, that England is not an uncivilized, nor even a second rate nation, and that moreover she is not subject to your dominion. For the future therefore in any intercourse you may have with the English, it would be well if you all, from your King to the meanest peasant, refrain entirely from the use of such disparaging terms as those of which I have had reason to complain, or you will most certainly bring about a collision similar to that of 1841/42, the result of which is by no means difficult to foretell.

I am extremely obliged to you for your replies to my thirty-one questions [*sic*]. But in reference to your closing declarations, such as that God has specially commissioned you and your people to exterminate the imps—that your sovereign is God's own son, and the

189

uterine brother of the Celestial Elder Brother—that he is the true sovereign of all nations—that you, the Eastern King, are appointed by God to the office of the Holy Ghost, the Comforter—I think it right to state to you distinctly that we place no faith in any one of your dogmas to this effect, and can subscribe to none of them. We believe only what is revealed to us in the Old and New Testaments, namely, that God the Father is the creator and Lord of all things— that Jesus is his only begotten son—that he came down into the world and became flesh—that he died on the cross to redeem us from our sins—that after three days he rose again from the dead, and ascended into heaven, where he is ever one with God—that he will appear once again hereafter to judge the world—that those who believe in him will be saved—and that those who do not believe in him will be lost—that the Holy Ghost is also one with God—that he has already been manifested among men, namely, shortly after the ascension of our Lord—that now those who pray for his influence will receive him in their hearts and be renewed thereby—and that these three, the Father, the Son and the Holy Ghost, are the one and true God.

Annexed to this letter you will find replies in detail to your 50 questions, and from these you will be able to judge wherein our creed differs from yours. It must be remembered however that human beings are not infallible and I would recommend you rather to consult the only revealed will of God contained in the Old and New Testaments. Study these humbly and carefully and you can never go astray. Such is my hope.

To Yang, the Eastern King of the Celestial Kingdom of Universal Peace.

Dated 29 June 1854

The following are my replies to your questions.

Answers to queries No. 1—8. God has no height nor breadth. In John I, 18 you will find it recorded that 'no man hath seen God at any time'. Again in John IV, 24 is written 'God is a spirit' etc. Again in John V, 37 it is written 'and the Father himself has sent me. You have neither heard his voice nor seen his shape'. How then can God be said to have height or breadth?

Answer to query No. 9. God is a spirit. How can he be said to marry? As regards his son you will find it written in Luke I, 35 'And the angel answered and said unto her, the Holy Ghost shall come upon thee etc., therefore that holy thing which shall be born of thee shall be called the Son of God'. The mother of Jesus afterwards married a

190

Judean named Joseph, and bore him sons and daughters, but was never called the Celestial Mother.

Answer to query 10. God has no other son but Jesus. In a scriptural sense believers are, in the New Testament, said to be the sons of God by adoption. This answer applies also to query 11.

Answer to query 12. There is nothing impossible with God. This answer applies to query 13.

Answer to query 14. Those who offend God and break his laws, he is fierce to punish. But if men repent of their sins and trust in the merits of our Saviour, he is very merciful to pardon.

Answer to query 15. There is no moment when human beings are not experiencing the goodness of God, and his liberality is infinite. How then can he be wanting in liberality?

Answer to query 16. The New Testament does not inform us what kind of a person Jesus was in his outward appearance. This answer applies to queries 17-20.

Answer to query 21. The Scriptures do not inform us whether Jesus married a wife while he lived among us. After he ascended to Heaven, he was a spirit and one with God. The allusion made in Revelations XIX, 7 to 'the marriage of the Lamb' refers to the union of believers with Christ, and is used figuratively. This answer applies to queries 22-27.

Answer to query 28. The Bible does not tell us how many tiers of Heavens there are. The sentence in 2 Corinthians XII, 2 'caught up into the *third* heaven' means simply taken up into the highest heaven, and does not convey the idea of there being several heavens one above the other.

Answer to queries 29, 30. I do not know, and can therefore give you no satisfactory reply.

Answer to query 31. The kingdom of God is not of this world. His power is infinite. The dwellers of this earth cannot be his soldiers.

Answer to query 32. Many nations on the face of the globe are ignorant of the truth, and know not God. Nevertheless he loves them all. In Matthew V, 45 it is written 'For he maketh his sun to rise on the evil and the good' etc. We mortals should not therefore presume to call our fellow mortals 'imps 'or 'devils'.

Answer to query 33. As regards our praying to be admitted into the Celestial Kingdom I have to reply that, if by this term you mean 'your territory' we certainly do not pray to be admitted into it. But if you intend by this phrase to designate Heaven, it is our duty constantly to pray for admittance there.

Answer to query 34. It was John the Baptist (not Jesus) who cried

'Repent ye, for the Kingdom of Heaven is at hand'. He said this in reference to Christ's coming.

Answer to query 35. In John II, 19 it is written Jesus said unto them 'Destroy this temple, and in three days I will raise it up'. This he said referring to his approaching death and resurrection.

Answer to query 36. Jesus' resurrection on the third day after his crucifixion was a fulfilment of the prophecy concerning him, and was intended as an evidence that death could have no dominion over him.

Answer to query 37. The sentence 'Glory be to God in the highest, and on earth peace, goodwill towards men' signifies that the Gospel of Jesus would rebound [?] to the glory of God, and by its diffusion among men be the cause of promoting peace and goodwill.

Answer to query 38. It is our duty every morning and evening to pray to God to give us His Holy Spirit to open and enlighten our hearts.

Answer to query 39. In John XV, 26 it is written 'But when the Comforter is come, whom I will send unto you etc. he shall testify to me'. These words were shortly after verified, as seen in Acts II, 4, where it is said 'and they were filled with the Holy Ghost'.

Answer to query 40. There is no such expression in the Scriptures as 'your Lord bears the diseases of the people'. In Peter II, 24 it is written 'who in his own self bore our sins in his own body on the tree etc. by whose stripes we were healed'. The meaning of this passage is perfectly clear.

Answer to query 41. We believe that God directs us in all our ways, as is written in the New Testament. 'Are not two sparrows sold for a farthing, and one of them shall not fall to the ground without your father' [*sic*].

Answer to query 42. We came here to ascertain the state of affairs with a view to the establishment of commercial relations hereafter. As regards homage, I reply that England pays no homage.

Answer to query 43. We are in the habit of praying that God will send his Spirit into our hearts, to aid us in doing His will.

Answer to query 44. We hope for eternal life only in dependence on the merits of Jesus' atonement, as it is written in Acts IV, 12 'Neither is there salvation in any other' etc.

Answer to query 45. The serpent, the devil, spoken of in the Old Testament, does not refer to the Tartars.

Answer to query 46. It is true that the Holy Ghost has already descended upon earth (see Ans. 39) but the Holy Ghost is one with God, and the Eastern Prince being a mere mortal, it is impossible that he should be designated by that appellation. It is written moreover as follows, see John XIV, 16-17, 'I will pray the Father, and he shall give you another Comforter, even the Spirit of truth whom the world cannot receive, because it seeth him not, neither knoweth him.' See also Acts II, 38, 1 Corinthians VI, 19, Acts X, 44-48 on the same subject.

Answer to query 47. We do not know that your people have received the express command of God to exterminate the Tartars, and we doubt such to be the fact. The rise and fall of nations is determined by God's providence. If they be found in the way of righteousness they flourish; if in the way of sin, they decline.

Answer to query 48. As we do not believe that you hold God's special commission to exterminate the Tartars, we take no part in the contest.

Answer to query 49. We do not believe that Thaepingwang is appointed by God to be the true sovereign of all nations. As regards doing homage at your court, I do not see what that has to do with being designated as imps or otherwise. Pray refer to my answer to your 32nd question.

Answer to query 50. God is the true King of Kings, but his Kingdom is not of this world, and we cannot therefore pay him tribute. T'aeping wang's claim to be the true sovereign of all nations is a most unwarranted assumption, and the sooner he drops the appellation the better, for thus only can he avoid offending other sovereigns, and involving himself in trouble. As to the coals, I regard them simply as an article of commerce, which considering the friendship you, the Eastern King, profess to cherish you ought at once to have supplied.

I have now replied to every one of your 50 questions, and I beg your particular attention to my answers. Let me however impress upon you the necessity of consulting the Scriptures for information. Christ tells us 'Search the Scriptures, for in them ye think ye have eternal life, and they are they that testify of me'.

Appendix

2. DESPATCH No. 85 OF SIR JOHN BOWRING TO THE EARL OF CLARENDON

Shanghai 14 July, 1854

My Lord,

I have now the honor to enclose to Your Lordship a more complete report of the observations and proceedings of Messrs. Medhurst and Bowring during their visit to Nanking, than they were able to furnish in time to accompany my somewhat hurried Despatch No. 78, dated 7th. instant.

It is not necessary I should reiterate the satisfaction I feel in conveying to Your Lordship the valuable contributions these gentlemen have brought to us, especially valuable for the future guidance of our diplomatic and commercial policy in this country.

I am disappointed in the expectation of being able to report to Your Lordship that an official foundation had been already laid for accomplishing the great object of opening the Yangtszekeang to Foreign Trade. The discovery that the regions in communication with this magnificent river are in a condition to furnish abundant supplies of coal to the steamers that may hereafter ride upon the surface of the 'Son of the Ocean' is of consummate importance, and I have no object more at heart than that we should avail ourselves of the popularity and influence we at this moment enjoy with the local Mandarins in order to obtain for the British Flag a right of access to the great commercial marts upon the banks or in the neighborhood of this mighty stream. The penalty attaching under Chinese Law to the offence of allowing a 'Barbarian Ship' to enter any Port other than those they are permitted to visit, is the loss of two degrees of official rank as a commutation for the corporal punishment of 80 blows of the bamboo. Without a reference to the Court or Emperor, no Mandarin could therefore undertake, on his own responsibility, to make the concessions we desire to obtain. The United States Commissioner and myself expect to arrange an early meeting with the High Officers, the result of which may determine our future proceedings in reference to the extension of our commercial relations in China, which are certainly not likely to be served by the progress of the rebellion, but rather to be endangered thereby. Your Lordship will no doubt come to the conclusion that neither to the *religious* element, nor to the *political* organization of the Insurgent power, can we look with hope or confidence.

I have the honor to be, with the highest respect,
Your Lordship's Most Obedient,
Humble Servant,
JOHN BOWRING.

Enclosure 1

Report by Messrs. Medhurst and Bowring of proceedings on mission up the Yangtzekiang.

Shanghai 14 July 1854

His Excellency,
Sir John Bowring,
H.B.M. Plenipotentiary etc. etc.

Sir,

With reference to our letter of the 7th. instant reporting our return from Chinkeangfoo and Nanking, whither we had proceeded in accordance with Your Excellency's instructions, we have now the honour to submit a more detailed report of our proceedings, already recounted in the letter above mentioned.

We left Shanghai on the 15th. ulto. and after some little detention owing to the difficulties of the navigation of the Yang-tsze-kiang, the channel of which has materially altered since the last survey, we reached Chinkeangfoo late on the evening of the 18th. idem. On arriving abreast of the fortified heights of that place a shot was fired across the bows of H.M. Steamer Rattler from a battery beneath, which obliged us to anchor and next morning we landed with Captains Mellersh and Woolcombe for the purpose of demanding an apology. We had interviews with the commander in chief of Chinkeang and Kwachow, and a subordinate General Officer, and although the reception we met with was at first by no means cordial, these officers eventually became very courteous and we parted on friendly terms. The apology tendered was most ample, and was brought off by the General Officer himself, who afterwards dined on board H.M. Steamer Rattler. We left the next morning taking with us one of the inferior chiefs and arrived off Nanking without further incident on 20th. June. No attempt was made to fire on us here, and we landed the chief forthwith on the understanding that he would visit us early the next day for the purpose of arranging an interview with the higher authorities.

As however he did not make his appearance and no persons seemed inclined to approach the ships, we requested Captain Mellersh to move the Rattler close in shore off the mouth of the suburb creek, and then landed at the nearest stockade, the officer in command of which (a General) we visited. He received us in no very complimentary manner, and having learnt our errand, advised us to 'petition' the Eastern King, whose full title and proper mode of address he wrote down for our guidance. Observing these to be of such an extravagant character as to make it inexpedient for us to employ them, we begged the General to allow us to address him as our equal, and to convey our letter to the Eastern King. To that he at once acceded, but on our expressing a wish to walk about the suburbs, he objected strongly to our so doing. We accordingly left and returned on board, observing among the soldiery around a marked disinclination to hold any communication with us. The following day we landed again, and while endeavouring to penetrate through a barrier, were politely but firmly stopped, and shown into the office of another General of higher rank than the former, who, to atone for the discourtesy of checking us, invited us to dinner.

On the 24th. June having seen or heard nothing of the chief whom we had accommodated with a passage from Chinkeangfoo, and having learnt through the General with whom we first communicated that the Eastern King was too much occupied with his multifarious duties to grant us an interview, we addressed to the General a letter of which we enclose a translation requesting him to procure for us definite replies to a series of questions put to the Eastern King, demanding at the same time a supply of coal and provisions, protesting against the impropriety of keeping us under such absurd and unfraternal restrictions, and informing him that we had found a coal store near which we proposed mooring the two ships. The following morning the Rattler was accordingly dropped down the creek and anchored alongside the coal shed, but finding a great unwillingness to supply us with its contents, and there being every indication of a hostile demonstration, shown in the bringing down guns from the suburb and training them in the direction of the ship, we returned to our first anchorage in the main stream. After receiving various communications, the tone of which was sufficiently conciliatory to warrant our waiting for the favourable result we anticipated, we received from the Eastern King on the 28th. June, the very remarkable document a translation of which we submitted to Your Excellency with our previous letter. The reference therein made to our application for coal appeared to us so unsatisfactory, that we deemed it useless to linger any longer. Accordingly after replying to the mandate, and queries of the Eastern King in a letter, of which we have likewise submitted a translation, we determined to quit Nanking. During the whole time we were there, namely from the 20th. to 30th. June, none of the people of the place visited the ships, in consequence, we were told, of rigid orders having been issued prohibiting them from holding any communication with us. This reception so different from what we had experienced at Chinkeang, caused us much surprise as did also the repellant demeanour assumed by the insurgents to whom no offence had been offered, and who were aware that in a friendly spirit we had just conveyed one of their officers from Chinkeang to Nanking. We were in doubt whether to attribute this to their having been affronted in some way by their American visitors on board the Susquehanna, or whether their conduct was merely part of a system of determined and growing aversion to contact with foreigners, and to this moment we are unable to account for it in any satisfactory manner. Our time being limited, we proceeded down the river, and on our arrival at Chinkeangfoo, discovered the same unwillingness to receive us that was manifested at Nanking, the General Officer who had previously visited us sending a trivial excuse as to his inability to come on board the Rattler.

On our way down we visited Eching, and other places held by the Imperialists, who received us with the greatest politeness, presenting a remarkable and pleasing contrast to the demeanour of the insurgents. We arrived at Shanghai on 7th. inst.

With reference to the present position and probable futurity of the T'ae ping wang movement and other matters which came under our observation, we beg to submit the following remarks.

Present position

The only places in the occupation of the insurgents between this and the furthest point we reached are Nanking, Kwachow and Chinkeangfoo. These are situated on the banks of the Yang-tsze-keang, as are also Woohoo and other towns higher up regarding which we could only procure hearsay information. Chinkeangfoo is a formidable stronghold, commanding the whole navigation of the river, here not a mile wide. The garrison consists of about 10,000 men, commanded by a 'Military Governor', to whom are subordinate several Tseang-Keun or Generals, and a proportunate number of inferior officers. The heights are crowned by batteries, and the river bord is defended by stockades rudely but stoutly constructed, and lined with a great number of guns of small calibre. The fortifications are rough but in efficient order, and there are strong bastions in the direction of the Imperialist encampment. There is also a small outpost on Golden Island in the vicinity. Chinkeangfoo is besieged by an Imperialist fleet lying off Silver Island four miles from the city, but with little prospect of success, the Mandarins in command being unwilling to come to close quarters. A large Imperialist force aggregating nearly 50,000 men is encamped on the hills about two miles from Chinkeang, with which skirmishes frequently take place, but no decisive actions have been fought. All foreign ships proceeding up the river will be fired at from this insurgent post, and it is probable that the first collision will occur here. Woo Jooheaou the Military

Governor is a young man of haughty and supercilious demeanour, and appears to possess influence over his followers, who are inspired with considerable enthusiasm and yield implicit obedience to their superiors, but are raw undisciplined vagabonds, badly armed and totally ignorant of European resources and power. The city was on its capture sacked and pillaged by the rebels and having been deserted by its former inhabitants presents a sad scene of desolation.

Kwachow, two or three miles up the river commands the entrance of the Grand Canal, and is therefore a place of considerable importance, giving the insurgents an untoward influence over the trade of the interior. The batteries command both the canal and the main stream. The town is invested by an Imperialist force which however has made no decisive effort to capture the place. This city has likewise been much injured by the rebels, and is in a great measure deserted.

Between Kwachow and Nanking a distance of 45 miles, the insurgents hold no territory.

Nanking, the headquarters of the insurgents, is the centre of their strength and is consequently well defended by a strong garrison, whose numbers can scarcely be less than 50,000. The great extent of the circuit of the walls must render it difficult to defend against an enterprising and sudden attack by land, but the inner city is quite unapproachable from the river, being far beyond the range of the largest gun. A hill on which some guns are planted intervenes between the inner city and the suburb and is girt by the strong and lofty outer wall. The suburb, which is small and insignificant, is manned by a considerable force, and the whole river side is covered with stockades, masked batteries, bamboo barriers, and floating rafts to prevent approach, and all admittance into or exit from the city is rigidly prohibited. Two batteries, of 7 or 8 guns each, defend the approach to the suburb creek leading past the Efung Gate by which the city is entered, while another creek which debouches close by is protected by two strong stockades, a third being placed on a tongue of land between the creek and the main stream. Generals are stationed at the outposts, and great activity is shown in the construction of stockades and batteries, while a careful look out is kept in raised wooden towers which command a good view of the country around. The city is besieged by an Imperialist encampment to the west, but the insurgents do not show any alarm as to the result. A smaller Imperialist force occupies P'ookow, a town on the opposite bank of the Yang-tsze-Keang, but is too far off to be serviceable. The suburb and its fortifications could easily be destroyed by large guns in foreign ships lying on the farther side of the river, but the

Imperialist vessels can make no impression. A considerable fleet of boats is in the hands of the insurgents, and is used for transporting troops in various directions, which they appeared to be busily occupied in doing during our stay. Communication with Kwachow and Chinkiang is difficult, owing to the intervening country being occupied by the Imperialists whose junks also scour the river constantly, and it is only effected by despatching armed boats or large bodies of men at a time.

Woohoo was not visited by us, but from all accounts it does not appear to be strongly garrisoned. We could not ascertain from the insurgents what other walled towns they occupy on the Yangtsze-Keang, but we do not believe that they possess any other cities of importance nor is the intermediate country occupied by them. In each case, of which we had cognizance, the insurgent post is invested by an Imperialist force, and the besieged, though confident as to the strength of their position, have not the power of collecting the land tax or levying imposts on the surrounding country. To the northward and westward, as far as we can judge from the imperfect information obtainable, their raid has not of late been attended with uniform success. On the contrary it would seem that recently they have met with a check, for during our stay at Nanking, a fleet of about 300 junks was despatched up the river with a reinforcement of 10,000 men for the purpose of retaking some place of importance wrested from them by the mandarins.

It is worthy of notice that they made no advance since last year in the immediate vicinity of the Yang-tsze-Keang, where they remain just as they were when visited by the 'Hermes' expedition.

Probability of ultimate success

The position of the insurgents north of the River Yangtsze-Keang appears to be unsettled, and their ultimate success and power of consolidating themselves are doubtful. Having for the most part been triumphant hitherto in the course of their aggressions upon the Imperial power, their victories having been many and their reverses few, they have been till lately flushed with success, and their zeal and fanaticism have carried them over all difficulties. It appears however, that their progress becomes more slow as they advance to the North and encounter in considerable bodies, and nearer his native country and climate, the more hardy Tartar, whom meeting in small numbers in the South they have found it easy to conquer and destroy. We believe that during the past year they have made little real progress in subjugating the country. They have occupied towns and proceeded onwards, it is true, but they have rarely retained what they have won, and consequently in case of defeat could have no stronghold north of the Yangtszekeang to retire upon. At first when they gave out that their object was to relieve the people from the oppression of the Mandarins, to remit taxes and to re-establish in its purity the ancient Chinese Rule, it is not improbable that popular sympathy may have been on their side. But the blessings and advantages held out by them have not been realised. Their progress has been marked by devastation and desolation. Houses have been plundered and burnt, lives ruthlessly sacrificed, property confiscated, women ill-used, and the peaceable inhabitants of towns driven out or forced to serve apart from their families as pressed soldiers. The towns of Kwachow and Chinkeang and the suburbs of Nanking present a lamentable scene of deserted homesteads and ruined trade. They have not been able moreover to reconstruct what they have destroyed. Instead of studiously courting the adherence of the literary classes, who constitute the bulwark of the whole Chinese social system and are the leaders of public opinion, round whom the people ever rally with delight and confidence, they have declared their honorary titles invalid and illegal, denounced their cherished ancient classics, burnt their public libraries, and made them enemies. Their proclamations, recently issued, inviting people to return to their homes have not been responded to. The wealthy, respectable, and educated citizens have betaken themselves elsewhere and the insurgent towns are mere military garrisons, stongholds without traffic, thinly populated and scantily supplied with the necessaries of life. Even the insurgents appear to feel the want of money, for although so long as the funds obtained by sack and pillage lasted, they were careless as to the future, now that their resources are considerably exhausted, it is by no means easy for them to procure a subsistence. Offers of service are held out to European adventurers, but the pay to be received is contingent on the ultimate success of the insurgents, so that it is not likely that this description of auxiliaries will ever join their standard. It seems evident that popular sympathy is not with them. They have done nothing to ameliorate the condition of the people, but on the contrary wherever they have been successful, they have been a curse and terror to the unfortunate, whose substance they have pillaged, whose gods they have insulted and destroyed, and whose houses they have burnt. In no instance are any of the towns they occupy, few though they be, in a flourishing condition. Trade is entirely extinct where their blighting influence has spread itself, and no measures have been taken to revive it, nor is it likely that the more wealthy merchants among the Chinese will voluntarily place themselves in the hands of people who have no resources but the ill gotten plunder obtained from peaceable and respectable members of society.

Appendix

Disposition towards strangers

As regards their disposition towards strangers, it is incumbent on us to state that it is repellant in the extreme, and even surpasses in insolent pretension the hauteur and pride of the Mandarins of the present regime. No desire is shewn to court the advances of foreigners, save on conditions too degrading to be entertained, they are looked upon with suspicion and distrust; and instead of being treated as equals by friends, they are considered to be inferiors and barbarians. It might be expected that a youthful power just struggling into existence would be only too anxious to receive aid and co-operation from Europeans, both from their power to assist and the fact of the insurgents having adopted the basis of their religious creed from the scriptures translated and distributed by foreigners. Such is not however the case, and the assumption of superiority religions, national, and social, which they at present affect will not be removed till a collision takes place which in its results shall demonstrate to them the superior power and resources of western nations. The greater part of the insurgents are natives of the inland Provinces of Hoonan and Hoopih and Kwangse whose inhabitants rarely if ever have come into contact with Europeans, while there is a large sprinkling of Cantonese among their prominent men, so that it is not at all extraordinary that they should feel a contempt and dislike for those whom they regard as 'outer barbarians'. The letter addressed to us by the Eastern King presents a curious mixture of insolence and fraternal feeling.

Means of extending commercial relations

It has been supposed that further intercourse with the insurgents might lead to an extension of our commercial relations with the interior; but it must be borne in mind that their position is not that of a consolidated power, anxious to foster commerce, and bent upon the development of its resources, but simply that of a military organization at war with the existing Government striving to gain the ascendancy by declaring as its ultimatum the extermination of the Manchoo Dynasty. Trade properly so to speak is utterly non-existent, and although we have reason to believe that coal, the great instrument for the navigation of the Yangtszekeang, is to be found in considerable quantities in the Province of Keangse in the vicinity of the country which has been overrun by the insurgents, they show no disposition to dispose of it to foreigners—and indeed prohibit vessels from coming to carry it away. The development of commercial intercourse with the populous valley of the Yangtszekeang is more likely to take place through a collision with the insurgents, than through any friendly relations we may enter into with them.

Civil organization

Not having been admitted to an interview with the higher authorities at Nanking it became somewhat difficult to ascertain to what extent the insurgents have established an organized system of Government. The replies given to our queries on the subject by the Eastern King are very vague and unsatisfactory, but it would appear that they have not hitherto promulgated any code of laws. They profess to make the ten commandments the foundation of their polity, and their high officers are said severally to lay down laws in accordance with the decalogue; but it is obvious that there is no definite system to Civil Government. We know that certain offences such as opium and tobacco smoking, drinking, debauchery, etc., are nominally prohibited on pain of decapitation, but it is doubtful whether the leaders of the movement implicitly follow these tenets. We were told that they inflict five penalties for misconduct, namely the bamboo, the cangue, imprisonment for a period not exceeding two months, decapitation and tearing asunder by means of horses, but we could discover no law by which these penalties are regulated in relation to crime. It would appear that they have not hitherto issued any new coinage one of the chief emblems of Govt. among orientals, a defect which they excuse on the plea of being unable to force such coins upon the inhabitants of the districts in the vicinity of their posts of occupation; neither have they established any record of their rise and progress or official history of their proceedings. Nor have they commenced publishing their decrees in the shape of public Gazettes, a custom in China inseparable from established supremacy, the instructions of the leaders to the common people being as yet couched in the form of proclamations posted on the walls of their towns.

Military capabilities

The organization we found appeared to be an authority partly military and partly religious, grounded on assumptions of a most extraordinary character by the leaders, believed in and upheld by the enthusiasm and fanaticism of their followers. The obedience paid by the soldiery to the orders of their superiors is most implicit and is not a little remarkable. Though without discipline and imperfectly armed, their weapons being chiefly halberds, short swords, spears and inferior matchlocks, they are certainly imbued with considerable military ardour, and their activity and alertness present a curious contrast to the inertness and imbecility of the Imperial soldiers who look upon their opponents with awe and confess themselves by no means able to cope with them on equal terms. It was difficult to judge of the number of the insurgents but it is probable that they aggregate in the towns held by them on the Yang-tsze-Keang at the very least 100,000 fighting men to say nothing of their pressed adherents. Of guns they have a very large number, but they are utterly ignorant how to employ them with effect, though unlike their Imperialist opponents they appear to be perfectly at home with the larger fire arms. We were unable to ascertain what leaders are in command of the forces at present in the North for the purpose of subjugating Peking, but it would seem that all the chief authorities are still at Nanking and have not themselves joined the expedition.

Religious creed

As regards the tenets adopted by the insurgents, which have excited so much interest in many quarters, we cannot do better than refer your Excellency to the extraordinary replies returned by the Eastern King to our queries, and to the no less eccentric questions put to us by him. It is a matter of grave doubt whether such a person as T'ae ping Wang alias Hung Seu Tseuen is in existence, for in all the correspondence we had with the Generals etc. the pleasure of the Eastern King, his power, his majesty, and his influence alone were brought prominently before us, while his reputed master received but a passing allusion, the Eastern King being evidently the prime mover in their political and spiritual system.

We cannot affirm that Taepingwang never did exist, but we cannot help conceiving it to be highly improbable that an individual possessed of the ability to organize and the energy to prosecute so remarkable a movement would permit a subordinate to appropriate so influential a post as the mouthpiece and oracle of God himself, the position which the Eastern King now most craftily arrogates to himself, and to make his master a mere puppet King, moved solely by *his* instigation. The reply given under this head to our enquiry was not such as in any way to resolve the doubt now prevalent as to the individual presence and identity of Taepingwang at Nanking. The assumption of Divinity by the Eastern King is so revolting and blasphemous as entirely to have shaken any belief we may have had as to the sincerity of the profession of Christianity made by the insurgents, nor can it be said that the title of the Holy Ghost taken by him was assumed in ignorance of its real meaning, for the questions of the Eastern King demonstrate that he has some acquaintance with the New Testament in reference to this very subject. The profanation is made worse by the assertion that the Father descends into the Person of the Eastern King, and makes known his Divine Will through him to the People, our Saviour going through the same process with the Western King. The officers and soldiery generally appeared to us ignorant of this particular mode of manifestation, but to the fact of manifestation they give implicit credence. To our minds the Eastern King has assumed the title of 'Holy Spirit' as an engine of political power, and that his principal object has been to veil his pretensions under the false covering of heavenly commands, to surround with a myth all that appertains to the existence of the 'Celestial King', T'aeping-Wang, and to strengthen his authority by the doctrine that the Father has himself vouchsafed to invest him with Divine attributes. There can be no doubt that he has succeeded to a marvellous degree in imbuing his followers with these tenets, which they receive with the utmost faith, and regard as revealed truth. His ability must be remarkable, as evinced by the absolute dominion held by him over the minds of the insurgents, and the more so as it does not appear that he is a man of even moderate literary attainments, the mandate addressed to us being the composition of one quite unacquainted with classical Chinese. And here we take leave to remark that we observed no respectable nor educated men among either chiefs or followers; with very few exceptions they appeared to us uncouth and ill conditioned fellows evidently gathered from the lowest classes of the people. The pretensions put forth by Yang, coupled with the fanaticism displayed by the rebels generally, hold forth little hope that missionary labours among them will meet with success. Indeed we are of opinion that the experiment would be attended with considerable danger, unless, as is not probable, they should show more readiness to meet the advances of foreign nations than they at present evince. We felt ourselves compelled by our peculiar position to reply, however imperfectly, to the questions asked by the Eastern King, considering it to be a duty which we were bound to perform although at the risk of being taxed with presumption. In our answer we judged it best to tell the Eastern King in plain terms the simple truth, and to endeavour to disabuse his mind of the vain and ridiculous pretensions he has so unwarrantably assumed.

Dress and food

The dress worn by the rebels is somewhat peculiar. The chiefs wear a yellow robe with a yellow cap drooping behind, over which the generals and other high functionaries wear a very peculiar gaudy head-dress, not unlike a fool's-cap, made of red cloth and covered with tinsel and embroidery. The soldiers wear a yellow uniform edged with red or vice versa, but in other respects there is nothing remarkable in their costume. They all seem very partial to gay shewy colours which circumstance gives them in general a very motley appearance. They all allow the hair formerly shaven to grow luxuriantly and twist the tail round the head, and they do not shave either beard or moustache so that they look unkempt and farouche and very forbidding at first sight. Not having been admitted into the city, and having seen no women in consequence of their being kept in a particular quarter separate from the men, we are unable to offer any remarks upon their style of dress.

There is nothing peculiar about the rebel diet. They seem to indulge in and to enjoy all the good things of this life relished by other Chinese, with the exception of opium, tobacco and wine, which are strictly prohibited. Grace is said before meat in the form of a doxology to God the Father, Jesus the Son and the Eastern King, the Holy Ghost, the supplicants alternatively standing and kneeling with a great shew of devotion; and in the houses of the officials the ceremony is accompanied by the beating of gongs and other music. They appear to be very careful not to neglect this duty.

Religious publications

Among the publications procured by us were three books of the Old Testament, namely Leviticus, Deuteronomy and Joshua, together with the following treatises not hitherto obtained.

1. 'Important Discourses on heavenly Principles.' A reprint of a Christian Tract on the attributes of God formerly written by Dr. Medhurst.

2. 'Discourses upon branding the impish dens (Province of Chihle) with the name of Tsuyle.' Substituting in fact 'Tsuy' crime, for 'chih' integrity—as a component part of the name.

3. 'Book of declarations of Divine Will' made during a late descent of the Father.

4. 'Discourses upon the expediency of affixing the Imperial seal to the Imperial Proclamations.'

5. 'Calendar of the Year 1854.'

6. 'Treatise on Land tenure &c.'

These contain much new and curious information corroborative of what is already in our possession. Like the works procured by Sir Geo. Bonham, they are written in a diffuse ungainly style.

Commercial capabilities of the Yang-tsze-keang

The Yang-tsze-keang is a magnificent stream, and presents peculiar facilities for the extension of our trade with China. Though its bed and banks constantly shift and change, yet with careful survey and continued attention, there is no doubt that its channel might be rendered perfectly secure for vessels of the largest burden, not only up to the point to which foreigners have already penetrated, namely Woo hoo, but doubtless for miles and miles beyond. Those parts of its banks which we passed are thickly inhabited by a thriving and industrious farming population, and no less than eight or nine large walled towns are washed by its waters and its immediate tributaries between this place and Nanking, to say nothing of the numerous well-known marts which it passes beyond the latter city, or of the numberless cities North and South of it, whose produce could be transported to its banks by easy and direct canal communication. At Keangyin, Fantoo, Chinkeang and Nanking, the water is so deep as to allow of vessels of any draft mooring alongside the wharves and taking in or discharging cargo. The existence of coal moreover in some of the districts upon its banks offers another inducement to the opening of this stream to foreign commerce, and this once effected, there can be little doubt that incalculable advantages will result both to China and Western nations.

In conclusion we beg to repeat our great obligations to Captains Mellersh and Woolcombe of H.M. steam sloops 'Rattler' and 'Styx' for the active and ready assistance invariably rendered by them in furthering the objects of the expedition.

> We have &c.
> (signed) W. H. MEDHURST
> ,,   L. BOWRING

True copy
W. H. Medhurst

Enclosure 2

Captain Mellersh R.N. commanding Her Majesty's Ships off Nanking, to the General in command of the suburb Stockade.

It was with much regret that I yesterday perused your reply informing me that the Eastern King is too busily engaged to grant me an interview. As it appears that I am to be denied any personal communication with your authorities, no alternative is left me but to place upon paper all that I had intended to say, and to hand you my statement for transmission to the Eastern King. I have accordingly drawn up the enclosed memorandum in which you will find set forth in order all the points on which I require information, and I beg that a definite reply may be accorded to each several query, or, failing that, that some intelligent person may be sent on board to answer my questions verbally. I especially beg that none of them may be passed over, or evaded, as it is for the express purpose of obtaining this information that I have come here, and if I get no reply to my letter, I shall be unable to account properly for the mission on which I am sent, and my superiors will possibly find it necessary to depute a second naval armament on the same errand, and thus again give you trouble as well as ourselves.

The Eastern King's reply, which you communicate, contains I observe, no allusion to our purchase of coals. As, however, in your former letter on the subject, you assured me it was but reasonable that our request should be complied with, and a supply be provided, I infer that you will not grudge me this favor. I find you have several sheds on the River bank at Heakwan, containing not less than 1,000 tons, and I propose moving my vessels into the creek and anchoring them opposite the gate of the coal sheds, where it will be easy for me to take a cargo on board, much more so indeed than by transhipping it through your boats. To this end I intend to move day after tomorrow at daylight when I beg you will have coolies ready on the spot to assist my men in lading the vessel and thus evince that brotherly feeling which you so strongly advocate.

As regards provisions for the ships' crews, it may be that you are yourselves scantily supplied, in which case pray oblige me with only a small quantity, which will no doubt prove sufficient, and at the same time give abundant proof of your friendly feeling.

For the Books which I have received I return by best thanks. But you have sent me far too few to enable me to distribute them among my countrymen and you have omitted, no doubt through inadvertence, to furnish a copy of your new edition of the Four Books. Pray allow me to request that the deficiency may be supplied.

It having proved impossible to grant me the interview I desired, it is needless for me to press that point. But as friendly relations have been established between us, it is meet that our respective countrymen should have the liberty of access to each other. Why is it then that though I have been in this anchorage now some days, your people have been altogether prohibited from gratifying their curiosity by visiting our vessels, while myself and officers have never approached the shore without being obstructed on all sides and prevented from moving a step, a treatment not at all justified by the laws of courtesy, and altogether contrary to that experienced by the British Man of War that visited you last year, or by the other vessels that have since come up the river. It may be that the Eastern King is ignorant of the conduct of the subordinate authorities in this matter, and I therefore venture to call his notice to it. This course of policy against foreigners will certainly militate against your remaining on friendly terms with them for any length of time. My officers and myself are extremely desirous of visiting the far famed Porcelain Tower, and I trust the Eastern King will be able to send us a guide with a few horses to take us to see the Tower day after tomorrow or next day, and thus still further evince that fraternal affection so highly commended in your letter.

I have a word more to say and I must beg you will excuse prolixity. Your letter contains a few expressions on which I find it necessary to remark, such as 'doing homage at your Court', 'looking upon the lustre of the Imperial countenance', &c. and in various proclamations which I have seen in your streets, I have found a frequent repetition of the sentence, 'the myriad nations will come to do homage', and others of a similar import. When moreover I have had the pleasure of seeing you and others of your officers, both here and at Chinkeang, they have always received me seated *alone* in state, and without attempting to rise either to welcome me in or escort me to the door. From all which facts I presume that you consider our country a dependency of yours. Allow me to observe that if this be your idea you are grievously mistaken, and you show great ignorance of the real position of foreign states. In the Western Hemisphere there are many great nations, who possess extensive territories and immense resources both of wealth and power. Not one of them acknowledges a superior. Is it likely then that they will do homage to your Sovereign. As regards England I may say that she pays tribute to no nation. She gladly enters into treaty relations with such countries as desire to trade with her, and she proves a faithful and powerful ally. But those who have the hardihood to offend or insult her, she has the will and the ability severely to punish. There is no spot on the known globe where she does not find means to afford protection to the meanest of her subjects. I would therefore advise you for the future to be more courteous in your behaviour towards any of my countrymen that may hereafter visit you; so only you will evince true friendly feeling.

While at anchor off Chinkeangfoo it came to my ears that 3 black men were in custody of the Authorities of that city, they having been taken in the act of offering you their services. According to our laws British Subjects are not permitted under heavy penalties, to hire themselves into the Military Service of a foreign Power; and I must request the Eastern King to direct the Generalissimo at Chinkeangfoo to hand over these 3 men to me that I may carry them back for trial to Shanghae.

I write this reply wishing you every felicity.

24th June 1854

True copy
    W. H. Medhurst.

Appendix

Enclosure 3

Extract from the 'Regulations of the Six Boards'—edition of 1843.
'Limits assigned to the Trade of Barbarian vessels. There are certain places which the merchant vessels of Barbarian Foreigners are allowed to visit for the purposes of Trade. If, on any occasion, they should attempt to visit other than those to which they are limited, and request permission to land their cargoes at any port in the interior—and the Governor-General, Governor, and Superintendent of Customs do not at once turn them back within their proper limits, but suffer them to enter at the Custom House and discharge their cargoes, and after this allow them to return to their country— these officers will be guilty of a public offence, and, although retained in their situations, shall be severely punished according to the law of impropriety, nominally with eighty blows of the Bamboo, commuted to a degradation in rank of two degrees.'

Signed. H. N. LAY

Official interpreter.

True copy
  W. H. Medhurst.

Appendix

3. DESPATCH No. 133 OF THE EARL OF CLARENDON TO SIR JOHN BOWRING

London, September 25, 1854

Sir,

I have to acquaint you in reply to your despatches No. 78 and 85 of the 7th. and 14th. July that Her Majesty's Government approve the instructions which you gave to Mr. Medhurst and Mr. Bowring on sending them to communicate with the insurgents at Nankin and other places on the Yang-tse-kiang, and they also approve the manner in which, so far as circumstances permitted, your instructions were executed by those gentlemen, whose able and interesting reports do them great credit.

Her Majesty's Government observe with regret that the mission appears to have only been successful in establishing the fact that the person styled the Eastern King is an impudent imposter, and that the Imperial Authorities are more friendly to Great Britain than the rebels.

I am with great truth and regard, Sir,

Your most obedient, humble servant.

CLARENDON.

Notes

Introduction

1. F. Michael, *The Taiping Rebellion*, p. 199. For further accounts and analysis of the movement in English see G. E. Taylor, 'The Taiping Rebellion' in the *Chinese Social and Political Science Review*, vol. 16, No. 4 (Jan. 1933), pp. 545–614; Teng Ssu-yu, *New Light on the Taiping Rebellion* and the biographies of Taiping leaders in (ed.) A. W. Hummel, *Eminent Chinese of the Ch'ing Dynasty*.

2. On this aspect of the Taiping revolution see especially J. Levenson, *Confucian China and its Modern Fate*, vol. ii, ch. 8.

3. See Chien (Jen) Yu-wen, 'The Marxian Interpretation of Taiping Tienkuo', in *Procs. of the International Association of Historians of Asia*, Oct. 1962, pp. 766–73, and F. Michael, op. cit., pp. 192–94.

Chapter 1

1. For examples see E. P. Boardman, *Christian Influence Upon the Ideology of the Taiping Rebellion*, p. 20; C. B. Maybon and J. Fredet, *Histoire de la Concession Francaise de Changhai*, pp. 51–2; H. B. Morse, *International Relations of the Chinese Empire*, vol. i, p. 453; T. Dennett, *Americans in East Asia*, pp. 216–20; K. Latourette *History of Christian Missions in China*, pp. 291–2.

2. Cit. W. G. Costin, *Great Britain and China*, pp. 149–50. On the breakdown of the first treaty system see also J. K. Fairbank, *Trade and Diplomacy on the China Coast*, chs. 15–19, and H. B. Morse, op. cit., vol. i, ch. 14.

3. Cit. Costin, op. cit., p. 78.

4. FO 17/181 Bonham to Hammond, Dec. 29, 1851.

5. A+P 1857 (2173) p. 12, Malmesbury to Bowring, July 21, 1852; cf. also ibid., p. 3, Granville to Bowring, Jan. 19, 1852.

6. FO 17/207 Bowring to Granville, Nov. 24, 1852.

7. FO 17/210 Clarendon to Bowring, Feb. 13, 1854; also in Morse, op. cit., vol. i, Appendix Q.

8. FO 17/169 Bonham to Palmerston, Sept. 28, 1850.

9. ibid., Bonham to Palmerston Aug. 23, 1850, enclosing Meadows' report of Aug. 16.

10. FO 17/170 Bonham to Palmerston, Oct. 29, 1856.

11. FO 17/188 Bowring to Granville, April 23 and May 5, 1852.

12. FO 17/178 enc. in Bonham to Palmerston, June 21, 1851.

13. FO 17/180 enc. in Bonham to Palmerston, Sept. 29, 1851. The *Chinese Repository* for 1851, pp. 497–8, also reported that there was 'a very general impression in Canton and its vicinity that they are somehow connected with foreigners and with Christianity . . .'.

14. FO 17/189 Bowring to Granville, May 5, 1852.

15. FO 17/187 Bonham to Palmerston, Jan. 29, 1852, and FO 17/188 Bowring to Granville, April 19, 1852.

Chapter 2

1. FO 228/148 Alcock to Bowring, Nov. 1, 1852.

2. FO 228/161 Alcock to Bowring, Jan. 24, 1853.

3. ibid. Alcock to Bonham, Feb. 26, 1853.

4. ibid. Alcock to Bonham, March 3, 1853.

5. FO 17/200 Bonham to Malmesbury, March 10, 1853.

6 ibid. Bonham to Malmesbury, March 11, 1853.

7. FO 17/200 Bonham to Russell, March 28, 1853.

8. Lo Erh-kang, *T'ai-ping t'ien-kuo shih-kao*, pp. 161–2; Mou An-shih, *T'ai-p'ing t'ien-kuo*, p. 181.

9. FO 228/161 Bonham to Alcock, Feb. 22, 1853.

10. FO 17/200 Bonham to Russell, March 28, 1853; see also ibid., Bonham to Malmesbury, March 11, 1853, enc. 2.

11. A+P 1852–3 (1667) p. 5, Meadows to Alcock, March 26, 1853.

12. On Bonham's general inclination to let things take their course, note also Costin, op. cit., p. 161. Alcock also abandoned this line of policy as thoroughly as he had once pursued it: 'I do not think there can have been two opinions since Nanking fell into the hands of the insurgents as to the impossibility of any judicious intervention on the part of the Foreign Powers, and the existence of an imperative obligation to observe an absolute and unequivocal neutrality. My opinion individually on such a matter of national polity is of course, very unimportant . . .' (FO 228/161 Alcock to Bonham, Aug. 6, 1853).

13. FO 17/198 Clarendon to Bonham, May 7, 1853.

14. FO 27/957 Clarendon to Cowley (Paris), May 17, 1853;

FO 5/561 Clarendon to Crampton (Washington), May 20, 1853; and FO 65/421 Clarendon to Seymour (St. Petersburg), May 17, 1853.

15. See FO 27/968 Cowley to Clarendon, May 26, 1853, where Cowley reports briefly that the French Foreign Minister 'mentioned to me this morning' that instructions had been sent to the French representative in China in accordance with Clarendon's suggestion; cf. FO 5/565 Crampton to Clarendon, June 13, 1853, and FO 65/427 Seymour to Clarendon, June 17, 1853.

16. cf. J. F. Cady, *The Roots of French Imperialism in East Asia*, pp. 108–11.

17. A+P 1852–3 (1667) p. 16, Bonham to Clarendon, April 22, 1853.

18. For Bonham's account of this voyage see A+P 1852–3 (1667) pp. 21–35; cf. also T. T. Meadows, *The Chinese and Their Rebellions*, ch. 17, and E. G. Fishbourne, *Impressions of China and the Present Revolution*, ch. 4.

19. Meadows, op. cit., p. 280.

20. FO 17/201 Bonham to Clarendon, May 28, 1853.

21. FO 17/202 Bonham to Clarendon, June 7, 1853.

22. FO 17/203 enc. in Bonham to Clarendon, July 22, 1853; see also *China Mail*, July 14, 1853.

23. For Bonham's query dated Sept. 21, 1853, see FO 17/204 and for Clarendon's reply dated Nov. 24 see FO 228/153.

24. Morse, op. cit., vol. i, ch. 18, and vol. ii, ch. 6; also Hsia Ching-lin, *Studies in Chinese Diplomatic History*, pp. 49–50.

25. On the peculiar legal status of these areas, especially at Shanghai, see L. Oppenheim, *International Law* (7th edn., H. Lauterpacht), vol. i, pp. 456–7, note 8; Hsia Ching-lin, op. cit., ch. 2, and F. C. Jones, *Shanghai and Tientsin*, ch. 2.

26. 'Since neutrality is an attitude of impartiality, it excludes such assistance and succour to one of the belligerents as is detrimental to the other, and, further, such injuries to the one as benefit the other. . . . [It] is not incompatible with sympathy with one belligerent and disapproval of the other, so long as these feelings do not find expression in actions violating impartiality. . . . Again [it]. . . . does not compel [neutrals] to remain inactive when a belligerent in carrying on hostilities violates the rules of International Law' (L. Oppenheim, op. cit., vol. II, pp. 654–5; see also G. H. Hackworth, *Digest of International Law*, vol. vii, pp. 348, 352, 434).

27. FO 228/161 Bonham to Alcock, May 30, 1853.

28. FO 17/204 Bonham to Clarendon, Aug. 4, 1853.

29. ibid. and FO 17/198 Clarendon to Bonham, Oct. 3, 1853.

Chapter 3

1. For examples of this kind of argument see Lo Erh-kang, op. cit., p. 168; Mou An-shih, op. cit., pp. 181–2; Shih Li-ch'eng, 'Ts'ung tui wai kuan-shih k'an t'ai-ping t'ien-kuo ti fei-chu' (The tragedy of the Taiping state seen from the standpoint of its foreign relations) in *Li-shih yen-chiu* (Historical Research), 1961, p. 14; Hu Sheng, *Imperialism and Chinese Politics*, p. 42; G. Karamurza, *The Taipings*, pp. 74–5, 82–3.

2. FO 17/205 Bonham to Alcock, enc. in Bonham to Clarendon, Oct. 10, 1853.

3. J. Scarth, *Twelve Years in China*, pp. 261–3.

4. The account of the customs issue which follows is based upon J. K. Fairbank, op. cit., chs. 21–3; see also S. F. Wright, *Hart and the Chinese Customs*, ch. 4.

5. FO 228/153 Clarendon to Bonham, Nov. 24, 1853.

6. Note Bowring to his son Edgar, June 6 and 9, 1854: 'The state of things here is lamentable—trade destroyed and if I cannot come to some understanding on the payment of duties I know not what is to restore it, for it is certain that the Mandarins will not allow Tea and Silk to come to a place where the merchants have managed to run goods in, and ship goods in, in utter disregard of Treaty obligations. I have indeed a difficult task, but I hope I shall preserve if not extend the trade. Yet the anarchy and disorder exceed all belief' (Bowring Papers 1228/2, f. 91, p. 3).

7. The U.S. Commissioner explicitly claimed in his report of July 27, 1854, that the measures taken for the efficient administration of the customs at Shanghai had been achieved 'without infringing upon the belligerent rights of those within the walls of the City' (U.S. Congressional Papers, McLane Correspondence, pp. 122–3).

8. Lo Erh-kang, op. cit., pp. 168, 308; Fan Wen-lan, *Chung-kuo chin-tai shih*, pp. 122–3; cf. Chien Yu-wen, *T'ai-p'ing t'ien-kuo tien-chih t'ung-kao*, vol. ii, pp. 856–61, who clearly distinguishes between the British and French roles in the recapture of Shanghai and sees the British as maintaining an essentially neutral stand, despite the pro-Imperial attitude of certain officials.

9. On this incident see A+P 1854 (1792); *North China Herald*, April 5 and 8, 1854; C. B. Maybon and J. Fredet, op. cit., pp. 92–7; M. T. Yates, *The Taiping Rebellion*, pp.16–19. On the Western side the *North China Herald* listed casualties as 2 killed and 15 wounded (10 seriously); the Chinese reported 9 barbarians killed with similar losses on their own side (IWSM-HF.7, 22a).

10. IWSM-HF.7, 22 a–b. The reports of Chinese officials about

this time frequently complained that the English were the most troublesome and least co-operative of the barbarians: egs. HF.7, 2b, 4b, 28a, and HF.8, 31b–32a.

11. A+P 1854 (1792) p. 9, Alcock to Bonham, April 13, 1854; cf. also *North China Herald*, April 15, 1854: 'During the affair some of the skirmishers from both sides occasionally crossed the boundary within our lines when, either from the Americans or a small party of the Marines conveniently posted, they were most impartially warned off by a few shots.'

12. FO 228/176 Alcock to Bonham, May 1, 1854, enclosing joint notification of April 24; cf. also FO 17/227 Bowring to Clarendon, Jan. 25, 1855, complaining of the difficulty of dealing with 'a host of filibustering cut-throats and deserters (subjects of the Queen) who, under the pretence of joining the patriots, are committing every species of robbery and outrage. . . . Our neutrality, as it now exists, has brought into full activity every element of disorder.'

13. See E. Swisher, *China's Management of the American Barbarians*, pp. 287–90; J. K. Fairbank, op. cit., pp. 430–1; Chien Yu-wen, op. cit., p. 854.

14. FO 228/177 Alcock to Capt. Callaghan, enc. in Alcock to Bowring, Dec. 29, 1854.

15. FO 17/224 Clarendon to Bowring, Jan. 4, 1855. For other correspondence on the wall question see esp. FO 17/218 Bowring to Clarendon, Dec. 6 and 31, 1854; FO 17/219 Alcock to Hammond, Oct. 21 and Nov. 1, 1854; FO 17/226–7 Bowring to Clarendon, Jan. 5 and 29, 1855; FO 228/177 Alcock to Bowring, Nov. 23 and Dec. 22, 1854. Both Alcock and Bowring were irked by the stand taken by the British naval authorities in China. At Shanghai, Alcock complained of Admiral Stirling that 'what we won with peril of life in April he has since with great industry and success played away to our own cost and loss' (Alcock to Bowring, Jan. 23, 1855, enc. in Bowring to Edgar, Jan. 28, f. 115 in Bowring Papers 1228/2).

16. FO 228/195 Alcock to Bowring, Jan. 11, 1855.

17. FO 17/224 memo attached to draft of Clarendon to Bowring, Jan. 4, 1855.

18. FO 17/211 Clarendon to Bowring, Sept. 25, 1854.

19. Fairbank, op. cit., pp. 410–13, and S. Wright, op. cit., p. 91.

20. FO 17/213 enc. in Bowring to Clarendon, April 28, 1854.

21. Lo Erh-kang, op. cit., p. 168.

22. Swisher, op. cit., p. 303.

23. A+P 1864 (525) p. 18.

24. On the Drinker affair see FO 17/218 Bowring to Clarendon, Dec. 9, 1854.

25. See FO 17/218 Bowring to Clarendon, Dec. 11 and 25, 1854; also Bowring Papers 1228/2, f. 111, Bowring to Edgar, Dec. 25, 1854.

26. FO 17/230 Bowring to Clarendon, May 14, 1855. On the problem of piracy on the China coast at this time see Grace Fox, *British Admirals and Chinese Pirates*.

27. FO 17/218 Bowring to Clarendon, Dec. 23, 1854, and FO 17/228 Bowring to Clarendon, Feb. 28, 1855.

28. FO 17/224 Memo attached to draft of Clarendon to Bowring, Jan. 4, 1855.

29. FO 17/233 enc. in Bowring to Clarendon, Sept. 10, 1855.

30. FO 228/162 enc. in Alcock to Bonham, Nov. 1, 1853.

31. FO 17/214 Bowring to Clarendon, June 27, 1854.

32. FO 17/213 Bowring to Clarendon, April 28, 1854; cf. also ibid., May 21.

33. Bonham merely commented on this trip that the French appeared to have been received in the same manner as he had been (FO 17/212 to Clarendon, Jan. 10, 1854). The *North China Herald*, Dec. 24, 1853, interpreted the visit as bearing out its then very favourable view of the rebellion, whereas the always hostile *China Mail* argued on Jan. 12, 1854, that it had served to show how deluded enthusiasts such as the *Herald* were. On the views of these and other China coast papers about the rebellion at this time see Ch. 4.

34. U.S. Congressional Papers, McLane Correspondence, p. 50: 'Whatever may have been the hope of the enlightened and civilized nations of the earth in regard to this movement, it is now apparent that they neither profess nor apprehend Christianity, and whatever may be the true judgment to form of their political power, it can no longer be doubted that intercourse cannot be established or maintained on terms of equality.'

35. FO 17/214 Bowring to Clarendon, June 10, 1854.

36. For the reports in full see Appendix. The *North China Herald* of July 29, Aug. 5, 12, 19, and Sept. 23, 1854, carried translations of some of the pamphlets brought back from Nanking by the expedition, but no detailed reports or accounts of it.

37. FO 17/214 Medhurst to Bowring, July 7, enc. in Bowring to Clarendon of same date.

38. ibid., Medhurst to Bowring, July 14, enc. in Bowring to Clarendon of same date.

39. FO 17/211 Clarendon to Bowring, Sept. 25, 1854.

40. J. F. Cady, op. cit., p. 128.

41. FO 228/164 Bowring to Medhurst, May 11, 1854, enc. in Bowring to Clarendon, May 15, 1854.

42. Clarendon Deposit C. 19, f. 443(b), Bowring to Clarendon, May 31, 1854.

43. For Medhurst's report, dated Nov. 9, see FO 17/217 enc. 3 in Bowring to Clarendon, Nov. 10, 1854. The two extracts quoted come at pp. 23–4 and 42–3 of the unnumbered report. For the report of the U.S. interpreter, Dr. Parker, see U.S. Congressional Papers, McLane Correspondence, pp. 305–22, and esp. p. 321 for the threat of turning to the rebels. For the Chinese reports see E. Swisher, op. cit., pp. 234–6, 241–2, 252–4, 261–2.

44. See FO 17/217 enc. 6–11 in Bowring to Clarendon, Nov. 10, 1854, for reports of the conversations between the plenipotentiaries themselves and the Imperial Commissioner. Chung-lun's reports are in Swisher, op. cit., pp. 262–6, and Elgin to Malmesbury, May 9, 1858, enc. translations by Wade, in FO 17/288. That a general offer of assistance was not made during these or earlier negotiations is indicated plainly by McLane's report dated Nov. 19, 1854 (in U.S. Congressional Papers, McLane Correspondence, p. 292), in which he stated that although he thought the Imperial authorities had hoped for an offer of aid this was an idea he had 'never entertained and which I do not suppose could command the favour of the government of the U.S.' The same was certainly true for the British government at this time.

45. Clarendon Deposit C. 19, f. 498(b), Bowring to Clarendon, Sept. 5, 1854; also FO 17/216 Bowring to Clarendon, Oct. 4, 1854; and in Morse, op. cit., vol. i, App. S, esp. p. 683. Others also thought the Peiho expedition 'very doubtful in its results'. Hammond, who had no regard at all for Bowring, told Clarendon, 'If I did not feel that he has no chance of doing anything at the Peiho I should be more anxious for the result of his mission there than I am for that of the siege of Sevastapol' (Clarendon Deposit C. 19, f. 517(b), Hammond to Clarendon, Nov. 19, 1854), while Alcock wrote to Hammond on Oct. 20 from Shanghai saying, 'The Ministers Plenipotentiary may possibly succeed in obtaining a promise of an Imperial Commissioner being sent here to confer with them (and grant them nothing), but unless they are prepared to hold out some tangible and material benefit to the Chinese Imperial cause as the reward for a better treaty and enlarged facilities on our side I confess I am at a loss to conceive upon what principle they can expect the Emperor . . . of his own free grace to give us anything? If they are prepared to join him in a fair quid pro quo (which I doubt) then there may be some hope. However we shall see in time!' (Hammond Papers, FO 391/1). The whole expedition seems evidence more of energy and

ambition on Bowring's part than of any really practical policy of negotiation.

46. FO 17/217 Bowring to Clarendon, Nov. 10, 1854.

47. Bowring Papers 1228/2, f. 106, Bowring to Edgar, Nov. 9, 1854.

48. FO 17/224 Clarendon to Bowring, Feb. 24, 1855.

49. FO 17/214 Bowring to Clarendon, June 5, 1854; note also FO 228/165 Alcock to Bowring, July 21, 1854, where Alcock felt that the state of affairs generally in China was becoming 'disastrous beyond all remedy'.

Chapter 4

1. See below, ch. 8.

2. For example, A Michie, *China and Christianity*, p. 43, wrote: 'The Protestant missionaries then in China were elated by the outbreak of the Great Rebellion. . . . For eight years and perhaps longer [they] continued to be partisans of the Rebels. . . . The tide eventually turned and in view of the decidedly polygamous proclivities of the Wang himself, and some rather serious aberrations in doctrine, the missionaries gradually withdrew their sympathy, washed their hands of the new Christians . . . and passed by on the other side.'

3. *Church Missionary Record* (1848), p. 292.

4. Cit. D. McGillivray, *A Century of Protestant Missions in China*, p. 175.

5. *Missionary Magazine* (1853), p. 29.

6. ibid., 1852, p. 170.

7. A+P 1852–3 (1667), p. 43.

8. London Missionary Society, China Letters, Box I, 4, No. 25, Milne to Tidman, May 6, 1853; also *Missionary Magazine* (1853), pp. 205–6.

9. Church Missionary Society, China Letters, Hobson to Venn, May 31, 1853; cf. also the Bishop of Victoria to the Archbishop of Canterbury, May 23, 1853, in *Church Missionary Intelligencer* (1853) pp. 193–4: 'There is, of course, much in these imperfectly enlightened men which may lead into fanatical excesses; and we must use great caution lest we crudely identify Protestant Missions with a movement of which the whole character has not as yet been fully developed. . . . Yet some sympathy may surely be felt with the population of a vast continent now awaking from the long slumber of ages, and at last, it is to be hoped, about to enter into the great fraternity of civilized and Christian nations.'

10. *Proceedings of the Church Missionary Society* (1853–4), p. 140.

11. *Missionary Magazine* (1853), pp. 204, 246–51; also Tidman to Legge, Oct. 24, 1853, in London Missionary Society, Outgoing Letters, China, Box IV.

12. J. B. Littell, 'Missionaries and Politics in China—the Taiping Rebellion', in *Political Science Quarterly*, vol. xliii (1928), pp. 566–99, dealt with the early reactions of American missionaries and emphasized 'The great divergences in American opinion. . . . Contrary to the almost universal ideas of historians, missionary opinion even at the glorious beginning of the Taiping rebellion was anything but unanimous' (pp. 570–1). J. M. McCutcheon, in his thesis, *The American and British Missionary Concept of Chinese Civilization in the 19th Century* (Wisconsin, 1959), pp. 41–6, has argued similarly, again mainly from American records. British missionaries appear to have been nearly unanimous in welcoming the rebellion in its first years, but they certainly varied in the strength of their hopes about its 'good' as against their doubts about its 'bad' features.

13. *Wesleyan Missionary Notices* (1853), p. 158.

14. London Missionary Society, Central China Letters, Box I, 4, Muirhead to Tidman, Oct. 20, 1853.

15. Church Missionary Society, Bishop of Victoria's Letters, to Archbishop of Canterbury, April 7, 1854, and London Missionary Society, Central China Letters, Box I, 4, Medhurst to Tidman, Dec. 29, 1853.

16. Church Missionary Society, China Mission Book (1851–9), p. 433, Dec. 7, 1853; see also his article 'Recent Events in China' in the *Calcutta Review*, March 1854.

17. W. Gillespie, *The Land of Sinum* (1854), pp. 210–38, and the *Chinese Missionary Gleaner*, April 1854, pp. 73–4.

18. For this scheme see W. Canton, *A History of the British and Foreign Bible Society*, vol. ii, pp. 447–52, and vol. iii, pp. 434–6. On its working, note Rev. J. S. Burdon in *Church Missionary Intelligencer*, 1860, p. 283: 'The million scheme is still being carried into effect; but experience is showing that it was at least a premature step. The Bibles were to have been printed for the benefit of imperfectly enlightened Christians. . . . [But] the military occupation of great parts of the country has neutralized all efforts at Missionary work among the insurgents; and the Bible hitherto have had to be distributed among those who know nothing of, and care less for, the subjects of which the Bible treats, and thus the rebels having disappointed us, it has been found difficult judiciously to dispose of such an immense number of Bibles in the limited districts of the heathen to which we have been confined.'

19. *Christian Times*, May 20, July 22, Aug. 5, 1853.

20. W. H. Rule, *The Religious Aspect of the Civil War in China* (1853), pp. 38–9, 63.

21. Minute of the Committee of the Church Missionary Society on the Present State and Future Prospects of China, in *Church Missionary Society Circulars and Other Papers*, vol., i. No. 75, p. 7; also W. Gillespie, op. cit., pp. 228–9, *Wesleyan Missionary Notices* (Sept. 1853), p. 137.

22. See J. B. Littell, op. cit., pp. 578–86, on the visits and attempted visits of American missionaries to the rebels at this time. Among British missionaries the Presbyterian W. C. Burns attempted to get to Nanking in 1855 (*Reports of the China Mission at Amoy*, Nov. 1855, p. 6), but he appears to have been the only exception.

23. *Missionary Magazine* (1854), p. 56. According to the *Anglo-Chinese Calendar 1854* there were 29 British in a total Protestant missionary force of 79 in China in December 1853; a *List of Protestant Missionaries sent to the Chinese*, compiled by S. W. Williams on July 1, 1855, gives the figures as 30 and 90 respectively, while William Dean's *The China Mission* (1859), pp. 160–64, gives them as 33 in a total of 107. Appeals were launched and funds raised, but it was difficult to get suitable candidates (see Tidman to Medhurst, Sept. 2, 1854, in London Missionary Society, Outgoing Letters, China, Box V).

24. London Missionary Society, Central China Letters, Box I, 4, Wylie to Tidman, June 26, 1854.

25. London Missionary Society, Outgoing Letters, China, Box V, Tidman to Muirhead, Oct. 22, 1854.

26. London Missionary Society, Central China Letters, Box II, 1, Medhurst to Tidman, Sept. 6, 1855.

27. *Church Missionary Record* (1857), pp. 334–5.

28. *Chinese Missionary Gleaner* (Jan. 1857), p. 16.

29. *China Mail*, May 26 and July 7, 1853.

30. *Overland Register and Prices Current*, May 24, July 23, Oct. 27 and Dec. 27, 1853.

31. *North China Herald*, Nov. 26, 1853.

32. ibid., Jan. 7, 1854.

33. ibid., July 8, 1854.

34. *Overland Friend of China*, Aug. 5, 1854, cit. P. Clarke, *The Development of the English Language Press on the China Coast 1827–81*, p. 181.

35. F. H. King and P. Clarke, *A Research Guide to China Coast Newspapers 1822–1911*, pp. 9, 22.

36. Jardine, Matheson Papers, Private Letter Book (1852–54), p. 115, April 21, 1853, to J. R. Hadow.

37. ibid., p. 125, May 21, 1853, to C. B. Skinner.

38. ibid., Private Letters from Shanghai, Dallas to Jardine, April 12, 1853.

39. ibid., Private Letter Book (1852–54), p. 132, June 26, 1853, to J. R. Hadow.

40. ibid., Local Correspondence Shanghai, July 31, 1853.

41. ibid., Europe Letter Books, vols. 30–31, Circular Letters of Aug. 21, 1854, March 14 and July 9, 1855.

42. The views expressed by this large firm were, however, not necessarily those of the majority of British merchants on the coast. At Shanghai in particular many merchants were undoubtedly sympathetic to the Triad occupation of the city, though much more from considerations of quick profit than anything else. Bowring and Alcock both complained of the wide support given the rebels there from 'the smuggling Merchants [and] the meddling Missionaries' (Bowring Papers 1228/2, f. 107, Bowring to Edgar, Nov. 22, 1854)

43. *Economist*, May 21, 1853, where the circular is printed.

44. Lawson's *Merchant Magazine*, June 1853, pp. 429–37.

45. ibid., Sept. 1853, pp. 652–57; cf. *North China Herald*, March 11, 1854.

46. *British Banner*, May 18, 1853.

47. This is further illustrated by the publication of a pamphlet, *The Religious Precepts of the Taeping Dynasty*, by the import firm of Hewett & Co., which it 'presented gratuitously' to its customers. Besides advertising their own wares, this provided translations of some of the religious documents of the rebels, introduced by a letter from the firm expressing strong support for the movement and suggesting that any attempt to stop its progress would be fruitless. This may have been in answer to the circular of Moffat & Co.

48. (H. Vizetelly) *The Chinese Revolution* (1853). Vizetelly was probably the author or compiler as well as the publisher. The last part of the pamphlet is composed largely of extracts from newspaper editorials on the subject.

49. *Daily News*, Sept. 19, 1853, and *The Times*, July 18, 1853.

50. *Morning Post*, Aug. 10, 1853.

51. *Chambers' Edinburgh Journal*, Sept. 10, 1853, p. 165.

52. *Blackwood's Magazine*, Jan. 1854, p. 72.

53. (Anon.) *The History of the Christian Missions and of the Present Insurrection*, pp. v–vi. Like *The Chinese Revolution* (n. 48, above), this was partly put together from newspaper editorials.

54. *Standard*, July 30, 1853.

55. *British Journal*, Oct. 1853, pp. 290–1.

56. *Eastern Star*, July 30, 1853.

57. *The Times*, Aug. 2, 1853.

58. J. M. Callery and M. Yvan, *History of the Insurrection in China* (tr. with a supplementary chapter by J. Oxenford), p. 312.

59. *Spectator*, Aug. 13, 1853, and *Daily News*, Sept. 19, 1853; note also *Fraser's Magazine*, Nov. 1853, p. 606: 'While we gladly welcome their awakening from idolatry, we cannot but fear that the Chinese reformers are still far from Christian', though 'of the ultimate success of the insurrection there seems little doubt'.

60. *Quarterly Review*, Dec. 1853, p. 193.

61. J. Kesson, *The Cross and the Dragon* (1854), Preface and pp. 238–41.

62. *The Times*, Aug. 15, 1853; also May 20, 1853.

63. C. MacFarlane, *The Chinese Revolution* (1853), pp. 35, 208.

64. *Spectator*, Oct. 22, 1853.

65. *Fraser's Magazine*, Nov. 1853, p. 605, and *Quarterly Review*, Dec. 1853, p. 193.

66. *The Times*, Jan. 14, 1854.

67. *Athenaeum*, 1853, pp. 1,059–60, and 1854, p. 715.

68. *Daily News*, July 28, 1854.

69. *The Times*, Sept. 20, 1854; cf. also *Christian Times*, Sept. 29, 1855. E. G. Fishbourne, op. cit., ch. 6, was at some pains to answer the objections raised after the visit of the *Rattler* and the *Styx*.

70. *Spectator*, Dec. 2, 1854, and *Blackwood's Magazine*, May 1856, p. 502.

71. *Edinburgh Review*, April 1855, p. 441.

72. Fishbourne, op. cit., pp. 180–4. Fishbourne was on the General Committee of the Chinese Evangelization Society (*Chinese Missionary Gleaner*, May 1855, p. 192, and June 1858, p. 73) and was the author of a number of devotional works.

73. *British Quarterly Review*, July 1855; *Athenaeum*, 1855, pp. 971–2, and *Spectator*, March 31, 1855.

74. *Bombay Quarterly Review*, Oct. 1855, pp. 234–5.

75. *Manchester Examiner and Times*, Oct. 7, 1856; cf. also *Scottish Guardian*, Sept. 23, 1856.

76. *Daily News*, Oct. 6, 1856.

77. *The Times*, Dec. 29, 1856, p. 10.

78. *Eclectic Review*, Dec. 1856, pp. 550–60.

79. *Athenaeum*, 1856, pp. 771–2.

80. In its obituary article on Meadows of Nov. 28, 1868, the *North China Herald* commented that many copies of the book still burdened the shelves of Cornhilll

81. *The Times*, Jan. 19, 1858.

Chapter 5

1. Hu Sheng, op. cit., p. 44; Ueda Toshio, 'The International Relations of the Taiping Rebellion' in the *Japan Annual of Law and Politics* (1953, No. 2,) p. 139; Mou An-shih, op. cit., pp. 301, 437. Hu Sheng goes on to argue that one of the reasons why the British launched the war was to pave the way for co-operation against the rebels, but I have seen no evidence to support this assertion.

2. FO 17/230 and FO 17/233 Bowring to Clarendon, May 26 and Aug. 10, 1855.

3. FO 228/195 Robertson to Bowring, Dec. 22, 1855.

4. FO 17/244 enc. in Bowring to Clarendon, Jan. 14, 1856.

5. FO 17/246 Bowring to Clarendon, April 12, 1856, enclosing report by Wade.

6. ibid., see also *North China Herald*, April 26, 1856, for this report.

7. FO 17/255 Clarendon to Bowring, Dec. 8, 1855, in reply to Bowring of Sept. 13 (in FO 17/233) in which Bowring argued that 'the state of China will press itself with growing urgency upon Your Lordship's notice, and delay in deciding on a future policy will, I fear, only augment present difficulties and bring new complications'.

8. FO 17/246 Robertson to Bowring, April 3, enc. in Bowring to Clarendon, April 13, 1856.

9. FO 228/220 Robertson to Bowring (69), April 15, 1856.

10. ibid., enc. in Robertson to Bowring (72), April 15 and July 12, 1856.

11. ibid., Robertson to Bowring, June 28, 1856.

12. FO 17/248 Bowring to Clarendon, July 5, 1856.

13. FO 228/208 Clarendon to Bowring, Sept. 9, 1856; enc. is Clarendon to Admiralty asking that more ships be directed to Shanghai and their commanders instructed to repel any attack on the city, for 'a bona fide observance of neutrality' did not require that British property at Shanghai 'be exposed to plunder in a conflict between the rebels and the Imperialists brought on by an attack made by the Rebels upon that City'. There was no suggestion of waiting to see how the rebels would behave if they captured the city.

14. See A+P 1861 (2754) pp. 60, 65, 70–1. Bruce was widely criticized at the time for this decision, but he never justified it in his despatches on the ground that it was in conformity with the instructions given in 1856. The person one would have expected to point this out was Edmund Hammond, the Permanent Under-Secretary of State for Foreign Affairs and the man chiefly responsible for drafting despatches to China. The draft of Clarendon's

despatch of Sept. 9, 1856, in FO 17/243 is in Hammond's handwriting, and judging from the table of absences in Appendix 3 of Mary Anderson's thesis on him he was not absent from the Foreign Office when Bruce's reports of August 1860 were received. Presumably he simply forgot what had been authorized in 1856.

15. FO 17/248–9 Bowring to Clarendon, July 1 and Aug. 21, 1856, enclosing his correspondence with Parker; also Morse, op. cit., vol. i, Appendices U and V, esp. p. 690. For the failure of Parker's attempt see Morse, pp. 416–18; T. Dennett, op. cit., pp. 279–91 and Tong Te-kong, *U.S. Diplomacy in China 1844–60*, pp. 173–84.

16. FO 228/209 Clarendon to Bowring, Nov. 4, 1856.

17. ibid., Clarendon to Cowley, Sept. 24, 1856, enc. in Clarendon to Bowring, Nov. 8, 1856.

18. FO 17/261 Clarendon to Bowring, Feb. 9, 1854, enclosing printed copy dated Dec. 31, 1856, of the correspondence with the French Government.

19. A+P 1857 (2163) pp. 50–1 and A+P 1859 Session 2 (2571) p. 454.

20. A+P 1859 Session 2 (2571) pp. 1–6, Clarendon to Elgin, April 20, 1857.

21. FO 17/329 Russell to Elgin, April 17, 1860; the French also instructed their Minister, Baron Gros, that 'il ne saurait, en effet, entrer dans nos vues de renverser le souverain de la Chine . . .' (H. Cordier, *L'Expedition de la Chine de 1860*, p. 136).

22. FO 17/263 Bowring to Clarendon Jan. 12, 1857, enclosing Robertson to Bowring, Jan. 2, and FO 17/261 Clarendon to Bowring, March 4, 1857.

23. FO 228/257 Robertson to Bowring, Jan. 6, 1858; for Wade's reports during 1857 see FO 17/265 March 14, FO 17/269 May 9 and 25, FO 17/272 Oct. 14, and FO 17/273 Nov. 29.

24. *Treaties, Conventions, etc., between China and Foreign States*, vol. i, p. 408.

25. IWSM–HF.33, 18b–19a; for other expressions of concern by the Emperor see ibid., HF.32, 18a–19a, and HF.35, 1b–2a; note also Swisher, op. cit., pp. 539ff.

26. Lo Erh-kang, op. cit., pp. 214–15; Mou An-shih, op. cit., pp. 301–2; Shih Li-ch'eng, op. cit., p. 16.

27. For Elgin's report see A+P 1859 Session 2 (2571) pp. 440–5.

28. T. F. Wade, *Account of the Expedition to Han K'au*, a copy of which is in FO 17/371 enc. in Bruce to Russell, April 10, 1862.

29. FO 17/312 Bruce to Malmesbury, Feb. 5, 1859.

30. FO 17/311 Malmesbury to Bruce (5), March 1, 1859.

31. Baron Gros suspected Elgin of having secret instructions and

reported on Oct. 19, 1860, 'il agit comme s'il cherchait a rénverser la Dynastie pour tendre la main aux rebelles de Nanking' (see H. Cordier, op. cit., pp. 200, 397–400). As already shown, Elgin's instructions explicitly enjoined upon him not to overthrow the dynasty, but for his more sympathetic view of the rebellion by the end of 1860 see Ch. 6.

32. FO 17/331 Elgin to Bruce, Oct. 12, 1860, enc. in Elgin to Russell of same date. Elgin wrote: 'There are also circumstances connected with the general condition of affairs in China at present and the prospects of the existing dynasty which cannot be overlooked in dealing with this subject. It is advisable to take a step which will identify Great Britain more closely with this dynasty at a time when it seems tottering to its fall?'

33. For reports on the situation at Shanghai in mid-1860 see A+P 1861 (2754) pp. 60–2, 68–70, 101, 129–36, etc.

34. Bruce in fact later defended it as a means of keeping clear of involvement in the struggle (Russell Papers, PRO 30/22/49, f. 290, Bruce to Russell, July 24, 1861). Ueda Toshio, op. cit., p. 144, and Chien Yu-wen, op. cit., pp. 901–6, 939, both argue that this action did not represent an abandonment of the existing policy of neutrality; cf. A. F. Lindley, *Ti-ping Tien-kwoh*, vol. i, p. 271, and F. Anderson, *The Rebel Emperor*, p. 271.

Chapter 6

1. H. Cahill, *A Yankee Adventurer*, p. 286, who says, 'The troops used in that war and which were being held in China until the indemnities should be paid were available for use against the Taipings'; also Lo Erh-kang, op. cit., p. 181, and Mou An-shih, op. cit., p. 437. The figures which follow are drawn mainly from the Monthly Returns of British Troops in China 1860–64 (WO 17/1723–7 in the Public Record Office, London).

2. FO 17/363 War Office to FO, April 20, 1861.

3. FO 17/366 Correspondence between War Office and FO of Sept. 26, 30, Oct. 9 and 10, 1861; note also Russell to Bruce, April 10, 1861: 'The Government will be very glad, and the War and Finance Departments especially so, to have the troops sent away from Tientsin as soon as it can prudently be done. You will have therefore, to have very good reasons if you keep them there longer' (Russell Papers, PRO 30/22/101).

4. FO 17/367 and FO 17/380 War Office to FO, Dec. 27, 1861 (enclosing Michel Report), and Jan. 9, 20 (for Elgin), 31, Feb. 5 and 18, 1862.

5. FO 17/357 enc. in Bruce to Russell, Dec. 31, 1861.

6. Grace Fox, *British Admirals and Chinese Pirates*, p. 195.

7. FO 17/363 War Office to FO, April 20, 1861, quoting Elgin's views. So far was he from thinking of using Shanghai as a British base from which to attack the rebels that a few weeks before he left China he wrote to Rear-Admiral Hope: 'If I was going to stay here to watch events I should be disposed to ask the general to take away all his troops and look to you for any protection which the settlement might from time to time require. I am not sure that I may not do this, even as it is, but with my brother at so great a distance I hesitate about taking a step so decided' (Elgin to Hope, Dec. 11, 1860, in Elgin–Bruce Papers at Broomhall). At that time there were about 1,200 British troops at Shanghai; twelve months later there were about 650. Elgin was very suspicious of possible French action against the rebels at Shanghai (see Elgin to Russell, Dec. 22, 1860, in Russell Papers, PRO 30/22/49, f. 231).

8. Elgin–Bruce Papers at Broomhall, Elgin to Bruce, Dec. 11, 1860.

9. ibid., Elgin to Bruce, Feb. 28, 1861.

10. For Bruce's hostile reports on the rebellion during 1860 see A+P 1861 (2754) pp. 91, 101, 129–33; note also Bruce to Elgin, Dec. 29, 1860, in FO 228/281.

11. For example, see FO 17/350, Bruce to Wade, Feb. 9, 1861, enc. 6 in Bruce to Russell, March 12, 1861: 'If the Emperor will only return and show that he really accepts the treaty and the principle of International equality and of friendly intercourse which he has consented to on paper, I should hope to get rid of the occupation soon. But while he holds aloof from his capital . . . I cannot state to my Government that everything is settled, that there is no fear of reaction, and that the troops may be therefore withdrawn. . . . The events of 1858 and 1859, the rupture of negotiations last year, the circumstances attending the capture of the prisoners and their subsequent treatment will produce a profound feeling of distrust in Europe of the intentions of the Chinese Government, and nothing will overcome it short of some decided step on the Emperor's part which will show both China and Europe that his attitude towards foreign nations is changed.'

12. FO 17/350 Bruce to Wade, Jan. 26, 1861, enc. 5 in Bruce to Russell, March 12, 1861.

13. ibid.; the 'hundred names' is a Chinese term for the population at large.

14. ibid., enclosures 7 and 8, Wade to Bruce, Jan. 11 and 20, 1861.

15. M. Banno, *China and the West 1858–61*, pp. 207–10, suggests that both the Russian and a French offer of aid about this time were

in response to overtures from the Chinese side, but notes that the British avoided making any kind of offer.

16. IWSM–HF.71, 1a–3b.

17. IWSM–HF.71, 9b–12a; also Swisher, op. cit., pp. 689–92.

18. IWSM–HF.70, 18b–20 and 71, 34b–37.

19. IWSM–HF.71, 12a–13b; also Swisher, op. cit., pp. 692–3.

20. IWSM–HF.72, 3a–8b, esp. 4b–5a; also Swisher, op. cit., pp. 693–8.

21. IWSM–HF.72, 9b–11a, esp. 10a.

22. The importance attached to this warning is indicated by the fact that when the question was reopened in January 1862 it was again referred to in an Imperial Edict—see IWSM–TC.3, 49b.

23. A+P 1862 (2976) p. 2.

24. ibid., pp. 60, 111, Russell to Bruce, Sept. 7, 1861, and to Admiralty, March 11, 1862.

25. FO 17/361 Meadows to Russell, Feb. 19, 1861, and FO 17/348 Russell to Bruce, April 22, 1861.

26. FO 17/349 Russell to Bruce, July 5, 1861. Further on this question of payment see A+P 1861 (2754) p. 250, Bruce to Russell, Oct. 20, 1860; FO 17/363 War Office to FO, April 20, enc. report by Maj.-Gen. Grant; FO 17/354 Bruce to Russell, Oct. 28, 1860.

27. A+P 1861 (2777) pp. 1–4.

28. See Wade's reports to Bruce, as above, Note 14.

29. IWSM–HF.70, 4b–5a.

30. See A+P 1861 (2840), pp. 1–3, Elgin to Hope, Jan. 20, and Elgin to Parkes, Jan. 19, 1861; also Elgin to Hope (private), Dec. 11, 1860, and Jan. 3, 1861, in Elgin–Bruce papers at Broomhall.

31. A+P 1861 (2840) p. 5. Hsuch Huan expressed some fears about possible Anglo-rebel co-operation resulting from this expedition, but an Imperial Edict in reply stated that 'The English have just exchanged treaties with China, and although they will not help to eradicate the rebels they are not likely to connive with them and start hostilities again' (IWSM–HF.73, 29a and 31a–b).

32. A+P 1861 (2840) p. 7, Hope to Admiralty, March 8, 1861; for reports on the negotiations with the rebels see ibid., pp. 7–9, 32–3, and A+P 1862 (2976) pp. 10–15.

33. For these regulations see A+P 1861 (2840) pp. 18–21. There was nothing in them forbidding trade with rebel centres and the notification of Parkes attached to them seems to imply that such trade was expected to develop, as Elgin had certainly expected it to develop.

34. A+P 1862 (2976) pp. 23–35, Parkes to Bruce, May 10, 1861.

35. ibid., pp. 3–6, Meadows to Russell, Feb. 19, 1861. A few

months after writing this despatch Meadows was transferred from his post at Shanghai to the remote port of Newchwang, in Manchuria. Some writers (e.g. Chien Yu-wen, op. cit., p. 954) have seen a close causal connection between these events. It is certainly true that Meadows' well-known sympathy for the rebels was an important reason, though not the only one, why Bruce was anxious to move him from Shanghai, but it is an oversimplification of the situation to see Meadows as the unfortunate victim of the intolerance of his superiors in this matter of transfer. His position was never more than that of Acting-Consul at Shanghai; Newchwang had been his gazetted appointment since 1859 and for reasons of health he was quite happy, even anxious, to go there. See my article in *Historical Studies: Australia and New Zealand*, vol. 12, no. 47, Oct. 1966, pp. 435–39. For later private comments on British policy by Meadows, and a remarkable attempt to explain it in terms of the self-interest and self-seeking of leading British officials in China, excepting only himself, see extract of a letter to an unnamed correspondent dated July 17, 1863, appended to Meadows to Stanley, Jan. 30, 1867, in FO 17/482.

36. A+P 1861 (2840) pp. 27–30, Forrest's Report of a Journey from Shanghai to Nanking, March 28, 1861. For his more tolerant view of the rebellion than that of most consular officials see also his article in the *Journal of the North China Branch of the Royal Asiatic Society*, Dec. 1867, pp. 187–8, and J. W. Blakiston, *Five Months on the Yangtze*, chs. 2, 3.

37. A+P 1862 (2976) pp. 52–3, Bruce to Russell, June 23, 1861.

38. Elgin–Bruce Papers at Broomhall, Bruce to Elgin, Aug. 24, 1861.

39. A+P 1862 (2976) pp. 56–9, Bruce to Hope, June 16, 1861; for Hope's reply see ibid., p. 60. On Bruce's anxiety to avoid collisions with the rebels note also his private letter to Russell, Jan. 18, 1862, in Russell Papers, PRO 30/22/49, ff. 388–9: 'You will see that I have steadily set my face against collision with the Insurgents under any pretext whatever. I consider that merchants who trade in a country overrun with contending robber bands, for so Chinese armies are most aptly described, do so at their own risk, and I do not admit that if they are occasionally plundered they are entitled to demand ships of war and soldiers to exact redress. If plundering foreigners becomes a system of action the case must be laid before H.M. Govt., which will consider of a remedy. To protect our interests, as far as possible, without recourse to actual force is our policy. . . .'

40. A+P 1862 (2976) p. 60, Hope to Bruce, July 11, 1861. On

Hope's views see also A Michie, *The Englishman in China*, vol. i, pp. 375–80.

41. A+P 1862 (2976) p. 70, Bruce to Russell, Aug. 23, 1861; see ibid., pp. 62–3, and *North China Herald*, June 22 and 29, 1861, for examples of the kind of incident which occasionally occurred.

42. A+P 1861 (2840) p. 10, Hope to Admiralty, April 6, 1861.

43. A+P 1862 (2976) p. 22, Russell to Bruce, July 24, 1861.

44. See ibid., p. 51, Bruce to Russell, June 22, 1861.

45. FO 17/354 Bruce to Russell, Aug. 7, 1861, enc. Medhurst to Bruce, July 28, 1861. For other similar proposals and reactions by Bruce see FO 228/281 Bruce to Elgin, Aug. 31, 1860; FO 228/327 Medhurst to Bruce, Jan. 20, 1862, and A+P (3104) pp. 87, 92.

46. Bruce in fact told Russell that perfect neutrality was an impossible stand to maintain in this situation: 'There is no course open to us but to protect important places like Shanghae from a regard to our own interests. To protect them and leave them in the hands of the Imperialists certainly is not neutrality, for they derive revenue from them even if they don't make them bases of operations. But it is the only practicable course consistently with the rights of self-preservation and we are driven to adopt it by the conduct of the rebels themselves. If they wish for perfect neutrality let them change their mode of warfare. Let them cease to be brigands and land pirates and become recognizable as a political body, from which condition they are as distant as ever' (Russell Papers, PRO 30/22/49, f. 360, Bruce to Russell, Dec. 2, 1861).

47. A+P 1862 (2976) p. 46, Hope to Admiralty, June 27, 1861. On the aid given in organizing Ningpo's defences see ibid., pp. 16, 46–50, 143.

48. See *Hansard*, vol. 168 (1862), col. 62, and FO 17/380 memo, of Feb. 22, 1862. The government claim that the Taipings had failed to observe agreements made was challenged by Earl Grey, ibid., cols. 883, 899, and even so steady a supporter of government policy as the *North China Herald* observed (Oct. 10, 1863) that 'It is a matter of sincere regret to every Englishman to reflect on one startling fact—that with regard to the carrying out of the provisions of Admiral Hope's agreement with the Rebels, the conduct of the latter contrasts very favourably with our own. We are unaware of any instance in which the Taepings as a body violated the engagements made at Nanking, whereas we have in many instances neglected both the letter and spirit of these engagements. . . . The English nation will appear to have been lamentably backward in fulfilling the obligations entered into by its accedited representative.'

49. A+P 1862 (2976) pp. 60–1, Bruce to Russell, July 3, 1861.

50. FO 17/349 Russell to Bruce, Aug. 8, 1861.

51. FO 17/355 Bruce to Russell, Oct. 1, 1861; see also *North China Herald*, June 8, 1861.

52. Elgin–Bruce Papers at Broomhall, Elgin to Hope, Jan. 3, 1861.

53. IWSM–HF.80, 14a–15b.

54. A+P 1862 (2976) pp. 70–77.

55. A+P 1863 (3104) p. 80, Bruce to Russell, Aug. 24, 1862; also ibid., pp. 121–2 and 156–8, for merchant objections and FO support.

56. See Banno, op. cit., pp. 214–18.

57. FO 17/356 Bruce to Russell, Nov. 12, 1861, and Russell Papers, PRO 30/22/49, ff. 349–50.

58. *North China Herald*, Nov. 30 and Dec. 7, 1861.

59. A+P 1862 (2976) p. 143, Bruce to Russell, Jan. 18, 1862.

60. FO 17/370 Bruce to Russell, Feb. 23, 1862, and *Hansard*, vol. 165, (1862), col. 1812.

61. A+P 1862 (2976) p. 82, Hope to Admiralty, Dec. 7, 1861, and ibid, p. 143, Bruce to Russell, Jan. 18, 1862; also PRO 30/22/49, f. 360, Bruce to Russell, Dec. 2, 1861: 'According to the latest accounts Ningpo was in danger. If it falls we shall see what is its fate. If our influence avails to save the town from plunder and destruction and the Imperialists still continue helpless at Shanghae it may be a question whether we should not come to terms. Hitherto all experience shows that rebel occupation and destruction are synonymous.'

62. FO 17/370 Bruce to Harvey, Jan. 18, 1862, enc. in Bruce to Russell of same date.

63. For Harvey's strong predisposition against the rebels see A+P 1862 (2976) pp. 82, 107, 112. When presented with conflicting reports of rebel behaviour at their capture of Hangchow on Dec. 29, 1861, Chinese informants reporting wholesale massacres, Europeans reporting none, Harvey himself had no doubt that 'Hangchow suffered most dreadfully' (FO 228/326 Harvey to Bruce, March 18, 1862; cf. Hummel, op. cit., vol. I, p. 461, and Forrest in *Journal of the North China Branch of the Royal Asiatic Society*, Dec. 1867, p. 188); he first reported no customs administration whatever being set up by the rebels at Ningpo, but when challenged on this admitted that 'a pseudo-Customs establishment' had existed (A+P 1863 (3104) pp. 76–7; cf. *Wesleyan Missionary Notices*, May 1862, p. 72, where a Wesleyan missionary reports visiting the Taiping Customs house in January 1862); and he judged the 'tone' of rebel replies to British communications at Ningpo to be much more offensive and challenging than did other interpreters (A+P 1862 (3058) pp. 38, 46–7).

64. A+P 1862 (2992) pp. 12–16, Harvey to Bruce, March 20, 1862.

65. For hostile contemporary comments on Harvey's report see *Hansard*, vol. 167 (1862), col. 1617; vol. 170 (1863), col. 1786; vol. 172 (1863), col. 318; and Lindley, op. cit., pp. 521–5. For Bruce's commendation see A+P 1862 (3058) p. 18.

66. FO 17/360 Parkes to Hammond, Nov. 23, 1861.

67. There appears always to have been some confusion about the duration of the agreement made in March 1861. A Taiping edict dated March 1861 instructed rebel commanders not to attack the ports 'for the present year', but in June Bruce referred to it as being 'for a twelvemonth' (cf. A+P 1861 (2840) pp. 32–3, and A+P 1862 (2976) pp. 56, 103.

68. For Hope's report on this visit see A+P 1862 (2976) pp. 97–104.

69. A+P 1862 (2976) pp. 157–8, and A+P (3058) p. 10.

70. A+P 1862 (3058) pp. 6–7, Bruce to Russell, March 4, 1862, and FO 17/382, FO to War Office and Admiralty, May 6, 1862.

71. For the presence of a British consular official at Nanking during 1862 see FO 17/375 Bruce to Russell, Nov. 22, 1862, enclosing a letter of resignation from W. T. Lay after his 'miserable existence' in a boat 'scarcely fit for a Chinese to live in' and with little correspondence to carry on with the Taiping authorities. The suggestion of a possible renewal of negotiations with the rebels after they had been 'chastised' at Shanghai came from Bruce, but was not favoured by Hope (see A+P 1862 (3058) p. 20, and 1863 (3104), p. 9).

Chapter 7

1. Lo, op. cit., p. 175. Morse, vol. ii, p. 111, says that foreign aid was 'given grudgingly in 1860, but with no sparing hand in the years 1862 and 1863'.

2. FO 17/339 Bruce to Alston, Dec. 31, 1860. Bruce continued: 'I have set my heart on effecting this change, and I am persuaded that the interests of our trade and of China herself require that it should be made without delay.'

3. His official despatches and private correspondence contain many further statements of this approach. For example, he wrote to Russell on Jan. 15, 1863: 'I proposed that we should make the Chinese Government feel that the result of our presence here, if they act fairly by us, will be to put an end to irregular and violent proceedings, to introduce a peaceful mode of settling our differences, to strengthen the hold of the Imperial Government on its provincial

authorities, and to maintain its prestige in the eyes of the people. To achieve this end it is necessary that our policy in China should be materially changed. . . . We should act as if we assumed that the Chinese Government is desirous to observe the Treaty, and to afford redress when appealed to, and as if we were sincere in our language when we urged upon China the acceptance of diplomatic relations at Peking as indispensable to peace and goodwill, and as sufficient to ensure those advantages. I do not admit that China is a moral monster, and that her Government is insensible to those considerations, partly moral and partly selfish, which induce nations as well as individuals to observe generally good faith in their dealings with each other. Should such unfortunately be the character of her people and Government then no Treaty will be binding, and no peace permanent' (Russell Papers, PRO 30/22/50, ff. 6–6a). On the general application of this moderate, 'co-operative' policy towards China during the eighteen-sixties see Mary C. Wright, *The Last Stand of Chinese Conservatism*.

4. A+P 1862 (3058) p. 9, Bruce to Russell, March 26, 1862. Some British officials were doubtful of the wisdom of strengthening the Manchu government, at least until it was certain that the treaties would be observed in good faith and that other reforms would be initiated, but Bruce was confident that there was no danger to long-term British interests. He wrote to Russell in December 1861: 'As to the ultimate use the Chinese might make of an improved military system, it is to be recollected that the more insight they have into the mystery, the more palpable their deficiencies will become to themselves. They are not likely to be encouraged to try the fortunes of war against ourselves, but a very moderate improvement would enable them to quell anarchy and save important cities from pillage and destruction' (Russell Papers, PRO 30/22/49, f. 377).

5. Bruce himself would not have denied this. He frequently insisted that any aid given the Manchu Government was from interest, not sentiment.

6. For Bruce's efforts to encourage a more moderate approach among consuls see his circular to them dated September 2, 1862, in A+P 1863 (3104) pp. 85–6. On merchant criticism of his policies see below, ch. 8, and N. Pelcovits, *Old China Hands and the Foreign Office*, pp. 21–5.

7. On November 6, 1863, after the defeat of his attempts to have Burgevine confirmed as commander of the Ever Victorious Army, he wrote to Russell: 'The provincial influences have made themselves more and more felt at Peking, and the hopes of centralizing authority and responsibility at headquarters are becoming more and more

faint. This tendency increases our difficulties, but we must work on as best we can' (Russell Papers, PRO 30/22/50, f. 134).

8. An excise tax on internal trade, imposed and collected by provincial authorities—see E. G. Beal, *The Origin of Likin* (Harvard, 1958).

9. Russell Papers, PRO 30/22/50 f. 128, Bruce to Elgin, Nov. 6, 1863, enc. in Bruce to Russell, Nov. 9. This was written in criticism of Lay's plans for the Lay-Osborn flotilla. Wade also argued in this way and wrote to Gordon, July 21, 1863: 'I shan't be sorry if you take no more places or if the rebels proceed to worry the government seriously. It will only then be that it, the Government, will see the necessity of falling to *systematically* as it has done in the Customs. What it ought to want is not our force but our wisdom, and I should rejoice to see you charged with formation and instruction *only*' (Gordon Papers, MS. 52386 f. 57; also ibid, f. 89, Bruce to Gordon, Oct. 7, 1863.)

10. FO 17/370 Bruce to Russell, Feb. 23, 1862.

11. A+P 1862 (3058) p. 25, Bruce to Staveley, April 23, 1862.

12. For example, he wrote to Russell on May 14, 1862: 'I confess to feeling worn out and dispirited with buffetting among a sea of troubles, and I cannot expect to go on summer after summer without breaking down. The constant pressure of serious responsibility without anyone to share it, and the absence of social relaxations which are so valuable as a relief and a refresher to the intellect and spirits, renders the post a very trying one. Body and soul want patching up' (Russell Papers, PRO 30/22/49, f. 428).

13. FO 17/349 Russell to Bruce, Dec. 9, 1861: 'Her Majesty's Government entirely approve of the spirit of forbearance and conciliation in which your intercourse with the Chinese is conducted.'

14. A+P 1862 (3058) p. 26, Russell to Bruce, July 7, 1862.

15. *Hansard*, vol. 168 (1862), col. 897.

16. Russell wrote privately to Bruce: 'I suppose you could not do otherwise than keep some troops, as well as some Marines, at Shanghae. The trade of the district is too important for us to give it up quietly. But you must limit the expense as much as possible' (Russell Papers, PRO 30/22/101, June 26, 1862).

17. IWSM–TC.4, 28a, where Tseng states that he has received letters from P'an and others, and 1WSM–TC.6, 13b, where Kung refers to P'an coming to the capital. On gentry pressure for the protection of Shanghai, note also S. Spector, *Li Hung-chang and the Huai Army*, pp. 29–37, 47–50.

18. IWSM–TC.4, 28a–29a; also Spector, op. cit., p. 94, n. 125.

19. IWSM–TC.6, 13a–16a.

20. IWSM–TC.4, 26b–27a.

21. IWSM–TC.8, 42a–43b, where Tseng quotes the views of Tso. See also W. J. Hail, op. cit., pp. 256–8, and W. L. Bales, *Tso Tsung t'ang*, pp. 150–1. Li Hung-chang also complained, in October 1863, 'Why should the British and French pour their forces into Shanghai, come here and hope to become masters of the situation' (J. C. Cheng, *Chinese Sources for the Taiping Rebellion*, p. 121). Ueda Toshio, op. cit., pp. 145–47, further illustrates the uncertainties of the Manchu Government about foreign aid, and says that it 'reflected, feared and doubted again and again'. Marxist accounts, however, generally suggest that the aid was sought and accepted without any qualms.

22. IWSM–TC.5, 55a.

23. For illustration of Chinese difficulties with the Ever Victorious Army see Cheng, op. cit., ch. 6.

24. The Monthly Returns of British Troops in China for the years 1862–64 (WO 17/1725–27 in PRO) show a Total Effective Strength of 5,395 in January 1862, of 4,849 in January 1863, and of 4,440 in January 1864. The details for Shanghai are taken from the Distribution Sheets in these returns and include, after August 1862, the garrisons stationed in small towns such as 'Fahwah' and 'Naujaw' near Shanghai. The Rev. W. Muirhead reported from Shanghai on Jan. 23, 1862, to the London Missionary Society: 'Our foreign force here is by no means large. It consists of 700 English and Sikhs, 4 or 500 French, 250 volunteers and a number of blue jackets' (London Missionary Society, Central China Letters, Box III). The naval force under the East India and China Command, which was responsible for more than just China waters, increased from 38 ships with a complement of 4,017 men in March 1862 to 50 ships with 6,230 men in March 1863 (see table in Grace Fox, *British Admiral and Chinese Pirates*, p. 195).

25. Adm. 1/5790, Rear-Admiral Hope to Admiralty, June 17, 1862; cf. also Hope to Elgin, June 18, 1862, in Elgin Papers (India Office Library) Letters from Miscellaneous 1861–63, pp. 845–58.

26. FO 17/399 enc. in WO to FO, Feb. 16, 1863.

27. A+P 1864 (3295) p. 68, Bruce to Staveley, March 12, 1863.

28. FO 17/380 Memo by Hammond, Feb. 22, 1862.

29. For these instructions see A+P 1862 (2976) p. 111. They were sent to Bruce by telegraph via Russia on March 12 (FO 228/318). The War Office was informed of them but not requested to send comparable instructions to the military commander in China (FO 17/381, FO to WO, March 11, 1862). In May Bruce told Prince Kung that the British Government was 'inclined' to use its naval

forces to protect the treaty ports but not its land forces. He added that unless the Manchu government improved its own forces at these ports he would recommend that only the foreign settlement areas be defended (FO 17/373 Bruce to Kung, enc. in Bruce to Russell, July 8, 1862).

30. A+P 1862 (2976) pp. 140–41, Medhurst to Bruce, February 3, 1862; also ibid., pp. 151–3.

31. For Hope's first action against the rebels beyond the walls of Shanghai itself see A+P 1862 (2992) pp. 1–6; for his recommendation of more extensive action and his confidence that the home government would approve see A+P 1862 (3058) pp. 10, 38; for Bruce's qualified agreement see ibid., pp. 10–11, 20, 24–5. Bruce told Russell in a private letter dated May 8, 1862, that he concurred in the expediency of Hope's proceedings provided that a firm defensive line was established, since this 'may enable us to keep out of a war' (Russell Papers, PRO 30/22/49, f. 419b).

32. A+P 1863 (3104) p. 44, Staveley to War Office, July 17, 1862.

33. For reports of these two campaigns see A+P 1862 (3058) pp. 17, 28–9, 33–5, 41–2, and A+P 1863 (3104) pp. 11, 14–15, 24–5, 38–40, 102–4 etc. See also D. C. Boulger, *The Life of Sir Halliday Macartney*, pp. 47ff.

34. FO 17/375 Bruce to Russell (private letter) Dec. 11, 1862: 'You are aware that the 30 mile radius around Shanghae was not my scheme. Admiral Hope had embarked on it before I was consulted and I consented to it on certain conditions which were not observed.' Bruce went on to object that it was a misuse of limited forces, concentrating on short-term objectives (protecting Shanghai, which Bruce argued could not be starved out while the river remained open) rather than long-term ones (attacking major rebel bases, although Bruce did not suggest that the British forces under Hope should have been used for this purpose, only the Chinese auxiliaries). For later criticism of the scheme by Bruce see A+P 1864 (3295) p. 162.

35. FO 17/382 FO to War Office and Admiralty, May 6, 1862, and FO 228/319 Russell to Bruce, July 10, 1862.

36. FO 17/373 Bruce to Russell, July 8, 1862, and FO 228/319 Russell to Bruce, Oct. 17, 1862.

37. A+P 1862 (3058) p. 26.

38. ibid., p. 51.

39. For details of the situation at Ningpo see A+P 1862 (3058) pp. 29–31, 36–40, 44–52, and FO 228/326. For FO approval see A+P 1863 (3104), p. 35. Adm. 1/5790 Hope to Admiralty, May 11, 1862, includes a map of the action. See also L. Brine, *The Taeping*

Rebellion in China, pp. 312–36, and A. E. Wilson, *The Ever Victorious Army*, ch. 7.

40. On the training of Chinese troops see FO 17/370 Bruce to Russell, Feb. 23, 1862, A+P 1863 (3104) pp. 16, 24, 42–3, and A+P 1864 (3295) p. 68.

41. On the transport of Chinese forces in British vessels see A+P 1862 (2992) pp. 9–10, and FO 228/329 Medhurst to Bruce, Dec. 19, 1862; note also Spector, op. cit., p. 33.

42. FO 17/376 India Office to FO and reply, Nov. 21 and 22, 1862.

43. FO 17/375 enc. in Bruce to Russell, Nov. 25, 1862.

44. A+P 1863 (3104) pp. 25, 42, 102–3.

45. A+P 1863 (3104) pp. 58–9, 74–5. For further correspondence on this question between the FO and the Colonial Office see FO 17/386, 402–3, 417.

46. A+P 1863 (3104) pp. 153–4, and A+P 1864 (3295) p. 141. Note also *North China Herald*, July 4, 1863, for further regulations, dated June 17, prohibiting the import of arms in British vessels except under special licence and with a guarantee that they will not be used 'against Her Majesty's Ally, the Emperor of China'.

47. On the Lay-Osborn flotilla see A+P 1862 (3057) and A+P 1864 (3271). Accounts of it are to be found in S. F. Wright, *Hart and the Chinese Customs*, ch. 9, and J. L. Rawlinson, 'The Lay-Osborn Flotilla; its Development and Significance' in *Harvard Papers on China* No. 4 (1950). The most thorough study of its origin, character and fate is by J. Gerson, *H. N. Lay: His Role in British Relations with China 1849–65* (Ph.D. thesis, London, 1966). On the mixed objectives of the scheme see esp. Gerson, pp. 345–59.

48. H. N. Lay, *Our Interests in China*, p. 25.

49. FO 17/395 Bruce to Russell, Nov. 19, 1863: 'The Chinese Government has latterly shown its inability or indisposition to carry out the various suggestions I have made for strengthening the Central power, of which the flotilla is only one, and it was evident that there was no disposition on the part of the Chinese to incorporate it into their system so as to subscribe the general purposes of police and revenue but that, if forced to accept it they would have directed it against Nankin and would have left it to be disorganised by the ill will and intrigues of the provincial authorities.'

50. FO 17/374 Bruce to Russell, Oct. 13 and 14, 1862, and FO 228/329 Medhurst to Bruce, Sept. 25, Oct. 2, 6 and 9, 1862.

51. For FO approval of the Medhurst-Staveley proposal see FO 228/319 Russell to Bruce, Dec. 29, 1862. For the Orders in Council see A+P 1863 (341) or *London Gazette*, Sept. 2, 1862 and Jan. 13, 1863. The main legal obstacle they were intended to sur-

mount was the Foreign Enlistment Act of 1819 (59 Geo. III, c. 69), although Bowring's Neutrality Ordinance of 1855 was an additional complication.

52. A+P 1864 (3295) pp. 21–2.

53. A+P 1864 (3295) pp. 59–62.

54. FO 228/338 Russell to Bruce, May 22, 1863. Staveley further suggested raising a force of 10,000 Chinese to be trained and officered by Europeans, but Bruce thought this 'neither practicable nor expedient' (FO 17/394 Bruce to Russell, Oct. 29, 1863).

55. FO 17/392 enc. in Bruce to Russell, June 25, 1863. Note also Bruce to Russell, Aug. 22, 1863, in Russell Papers 50, ff. 83–4: 'Your Lordship is aware that I have steadily but unsuccessfully resisted the course that has been pursued at Shanghae and Ningpo. It is in spite of me that British officers have gone beyond their legitimate province of defending those cities. My object was to have proper garrisons organized for those places and have given instructions to the Chinese if they wished to organize a disciplined force, but not to have given them our officers to lead their men in the field against the Tae-pings. But neither naval nor military authorities could be brought to confine their action to these legitimate and safe objects. . . . I do not wish to pronounce any opinion as to the propriety of the courses they have followed—on the contrary I supported them as far as lay in my power, as soon as they had committed themselves, because although I doubted its expediency it was too late to change it—but I certainly must decline any responsibility for its failure or success.'

56. On the composition of the Ever Victorious Army see A+P 1864 (3295) pp. 26–29, and A. E. Wilson, op. cit., pp. 126–35, which closely follows a 'Memo on the Composition of the Disciplined Chinese Force' in the Gordon Papers, MS. 52393, ff. 26–67.

57. See Bruce letters to Gordon in Gordon Papers MS. 52386, ff. 88–9, and MS. 52387, ff. 13–14 and ff. 43–9, etc.

58. A+P 1864 (3295) p. 156, Bruce to Russell, Sept. 9, 1863; see also ibid., p. 96.

59. FO 17/394 Bruce to Russell, Oct. 29, 1863.

60. A+P 1864 (3295) p. 69, Russell to Bruce, May 23, 1863; also FO 228/339 Russell to Bruce, Sept. 7, 1863.

61. These would appear to have been very few if any in number. Originally Gordon had hoped to replace many of the original officers of the corps with British officers, but his retrospective account of the composition of the force after its dissolution makes it plain that this did not happen (Gordon Papers, MS. 52386, ff. 2b–4, and MS 52393, ff. 26–7). See also *Hansard*, vol. 173 (1864), col. 1473;

A+P 1864 (3295) pp. 198–9, and C. Beatty, *His Country was the World*, pp. 50–1.

62. See A+P 1864 (3295) pp. 153–4, 157, and FO 228/339 Russell to Bruce, Nov. 10, 1863: 'Under present circumstances British officers on field pay should be allowed to join force under Major Gordon's command and to serve beyond the 30 mile radius.' Bruce complained to Elgin that he was 'labouring against my instructions to preserve the country being drifted into fresh Chinese complications. But admirals and generals have gone Taeping mad. I try to prevent British officers serving beyond the radius around the ports, and I am overborne by orders from home' (Bruce to Elgin, Nov. 8, 1863, in Elgin–Bruce Papers at Broomhall).

63. FO 17/407 enc. in Bruce to Russell, Feb. 12, 1864; see also A+P 1864 (3408).

64. A+P 1864 (3295) pp. 192–3.

65. FO 228/318 Russell to Bruce, May 6, 1862. For enquiries about atrocities see A+P 1863 (3104) pp. 70–1, 78, 112–19, and A+P 1864 (3295) pp. 108–10, 116–22, 126.

66. Hansard, vol. 173 (1864) col. 1473; also A+P 1864 (3295) pp. 198–9.

67. FO 17/408 Bruce to Russell, June 8, 1864.

68. cf. C. P. Fitzgerald, op. cit., pp. 573, 576, 585.

Chapter 8

1. *Missionary Magazine* (1859) p. 43; cf. also *Church Missionary Record* (1858) p. 349.

2. *Church Missionary Record* (1859) pp. 2–3; also in *Missionary Magazine* (1859) pp. 25–7, and *China Mail*, Oct. 18, 1858.

3. But compare G. Wingrove Cooke, *China in 1857–8*, pp. 106–8. Cooke was *The Times'* special correspondent in China during these years, and reported that 'the missionaries still hang their hopes upon this rebel cause'. The reports and other records of British missionaries about this time do not support this claim, however. Alexander Wylie of the London Missionary Society travelled up the Yangtze with the Elgin mission at the end of 1858 and reported that such Christian element as there had been in the movement was 'overborne by other interests', and he saw little chance of the rebels being led to 'abandon their errors' (see *Missionary Magazine* (1859) pp. 179–81 and also FO 17/322 Admiralty to FO, March 2, 1859). W. C. Milne also discounted the religious worth of the movement in his *Life in China* (1857) pp. 513–14. James Legge, in a sermon published in 1859 as *The Land of Sinim*, reviewed the favourable pros-

pects for the evangelization of China but did not include the rebel movement among them, as he surely would have done a few years earlier, and J. Edkins, in the concluding chapter of his book, *The Religious Condition of the Chinese* (1859), anticipated the eventual defeat of the rebellion without suggesting that this would seriously set back missionary prospects.

4. *Missionary Magazine* (1860) pp. 273–4.

5. London Missionary Society circular, 'Chinese Insurgents', dated Aug. 28, 1860, in vol. ii of Newspaper Cuttings in LMS Library.

6. FO 17/347 Rev. J. Hamilton to FO, Nov. 22, 1860.

7. For accounts of these visits see *Missionary Magazine* (1860) pp. 296–302 and (1861) pp. 54–8; also *Baptist Missionary Herald*, July 1861, pp. 105–11. Bruce was much opposed to these 'indiscreet visits', and did his best to dissuade Edkins and Johns from making them (A+P 1861 (2754) pp. 77, 92).

8. Griffith John, *The Chinese Rebellion* (1861), p. 13 etc.

9. *Missionary Magazine* (1861) pp. 54–8. The Edict of Toleration is printed there and also in *North China Herald*, Dec. 29, 1860.

10. Church Missionary Society, China Mission Book (1859–62) p. 80, Hobson to Venn, Sept. 3, 1860. Hobson added: 'Some of them seem determined to write up the Rebels with an amount of faith, hope and charity sufficient to whitewash the blackest character who ever lived', and he also warned Venn against the pro-rebel sympathies of the Bishop of Victoria.

11. London Missionary Society, South China Letters, Box VII, 2, Legge to Tidman, July 25, 1860. For a time Legge did have some hopes for the reform of the movement through Hung Jen-kan, who had spent several years in L.M.S. employ at Hong Kong, but 'Hung Jin' proved a great disappointment. Legge wrote to Tidman on Oct. 27, 1860 (ibid.), 'At first when I heard of his being among them and read his Essays and Memorials, I was willing to hope that he would be able to remedy the crying evils which disfigured their movement. But then came the melancholy fact of his own adoption of the practice of polygamy. It was wrong to fight against them as the French and English did at Shanghae, but the salvation of China does not seem likely to come through them.'

12. A+P 1862 (2976) pp. 18–22.

13. Church Missionary Society, China Letters, Hobson to Venn, May 18, 1861. Hobson also denied that there was any real popular support for the movement: 'Call the Rebels "the national party"! . . . Why, the people loathe them, the very land abhors them.' A more judicious assessment of the degree of popular support for the move-

ment by this stage was that of the Presbyterian W. C. Burns, one of the most enterprising and impressive of the British missionaries on the China coast at this time. He wrote in March 1861: 'In regard to whether the population are generally favourable to this rebel movement, I would remark that it can hardly be supposed possible that they should be favourable to this or any other movement in which they are the chief sufferers. . . . At first, indeed, when the Nankin party seemed to be going to victory, there was evidently a Chinese national feeling in favour of their success; but that feeling has, I fear, long since given place to a sad despondency at the prospect of an indefinitely prolonged civil war. Of late years the ranks of the rebel party have been recruited partly by the banditti, who abound everywhere, and partly by forcibly carrying off the flower of the youth from the various places which they visit. When these new followers have been a few months among them, and have passed into regions where, in language as well as in other respects, they are strangers, it is almost impossible for them to make their escape, and so, from necessity, they become adherents of the party.'

14. London Missionary Society, Central China Letters, Box II, 3, Edkins to Tidman, May 12, 1861; also J. Edkins, 'Narrative of a Visit to Nankin', printed as an appendix to Jane Edkins, *China's Scenes and Peoples*, pp. 241–307.

15. J. Edkins, *China's Scenes and Peoples*, p. 281.

16. *Missionary Magazine* (1862) p. 212.

17. *Wesleyan Missionary Notices* (May 1862) pp. 64–6. The only Western missionary to stay any time in Nanking was Hung's quondam teacher at Canton, the American Baptist I. J. Roberts, but he departed in disgust in January 1862. On Hung's relations with Roberts see Yuan Chung-teng, 'Rev. I. J. Roberts and the Taiping Rebellion' in *Journal of Asian Studies*, vol. 23 (1963–4), pp. 55–68.

18. Cit. *Evangelical Christendom*, April 1862, p. 207. For Church Missionary Society reports on Ningpo see China Mission Book (1859–62), pp. 182–94; *C.M.S. Record*, 1862, pp. 34–5, 66–7; *Proceedings of the Church Missionary Society 1861–2*, pp. 192–9, and A. E. Moule, *Personal Recollections of the T'aip'ing Rebellion 1861–3*.

19. Eugene Stock, *History of the Church Missionary Society*, vol. ii, p. 312; also J. Foster, 'The Christian Origins of the Taiping Rebellion' in *International Review of Missions*, vol. XI (April 1951) pp. 156, 167, and C. P. Fitzgerald, *Revolution in China*, pp. 123–4, 141–2. I have argued against this view more fully in an article in the *Journal of Religious History*, vol. ii, No. 3 (June 1963) pp. 204–18.

20. For these views see respectively *Missionary Magazine* (1862) p. 212; Church Missionary Society, China Mission Book (1859–62)

p. 188, Russell to Venn, Jan. 15, 1862; J. Hudson Taylor, *China: its Spiritual Needs and Claims* (1865) p. 43; *Baptist Missionary Herald*, Aug. 1862, p. 122.

21. *Missionary Magazine* (1862) p. 286.

22. FO 17/385 Tidman to FO, Oct. 30, 1862.

23. Jardine, Matheson Papers, Europe Letter Book, vol. 40 (1861–2) p. 122, to Matheson & Co., May 1, 1861.

24. ibid., Private Letter Book (1860–63), to C. H. Brown, June 12, 1862; cf. also ibid. to J. Baumbach, Sept. 10, 1862: 'The allies as usual have occasional brushes with the Rebels around Shanghae, which must be looked for until we either take active measures to put down the movement or endeavour to make terms with them. The latter in my opinion would be our best and wisest course to adopt.'

25. ibid., Europe Letter Book, vol. 41 (1861–2) pp. 293–5, to S. Mendel and others; also Correspondence In—Great Britain 1862–3, Sept. 25, 1862 (Mendel), and Dec. 27, 1862 (Calvert).

26. ibid., Europe Letter Book, vol. 41 (1861–2) pp. 256, 283, to Matheson & Co., June 27 and July 12, 1862.

27. ibid., Europe Letter Book, vol. 41 (1861–2) pp. 209, 336, 471, and vol. 42 (1863–4) p. 496.

28. A+P 1864 (3240) pp. 20–21. Paragraph 32 of this letter as printed reads 'It may *not* be too late. . .' but this is a misprint for 'now' (see original in FO 17/404; also *China Mail*, Jan. 4 and 14, 1864).

29. A+P 1861 (2840) p. 12; also A+P 1862 (2976) pp. 7–9.

30. Cit. *Hansard*, vol. 174 (1864) cols. 1536–9. Layard also quoted Michie's views in July 1862—*Hansard*, vol. 168 (1862) cols. 61–2. *The London and China Express*, May 10, 1864, p. 378, said of Michie that his experience and judgment 'eminently mark him as the representative of British merchants in communicating with the Government', but it is certain that many merchants would not have chosen him as their spokesman on policy towards the rebellion.

31. *China Overland Trade Report*, Feb. 28, 1862, etc. For views of the *Friend of China* see Prescott Clarke, op. cit., pp. 277, 351, and the (anon.) pamphlet, *The Position of Affairs in China* (1863).

32. See *North China Herald*, March 8, 1862, and March 21, 1863, and *China Mail*, Oct. 8 and 15, 1863.

33. *Hansard*, vol. 172 (1863) cols. 296, 329.

34. *The Times*, July 13, 1863, p. 6, July 20, p. 12, and July 22, p. 6.

35. *Hansard*, vol. 168 (1862) cols. 29–81.

36. These details were obtained by checking the names given in House of Commons Division List for July 8, 1862, against the information on members in *Dod's Parliamentary Companion* and in

Walfort's *Shilling House of Commons*. The information given in these handbooks is very brief, so that the figures should be taken as approximate only.

37. For this debate see *Hansard*, vol. 175 (1864) cols. 527–45. Thos. H. Horsfall, M.P. for Liverpool and a former President of the Liverpool Chamber of Commerce, told the Chamber in August 1864 that 'With regard to the war in China, Lord Palmerston stated, I think to some extent erroneously, that that war was carried on for the protection of the commercial interests of the country. That war was to a certain extent carried on for the protection of the commercial interests so far as this, that notice had been given that British interests would be protected for 30 miles around the various treaty ports. Had the war been confined to these 30 miles, I am satisfied it would have been a comparatively unimportant war; but it was because Major Gordon, acting I believe with the concurrence of the Government, went beyond that circle that the great difficulty arose' (Liverpool Chamber of Commerce Reports, Aug. 1864, p. 35).

38. Palmerston's second Cabinet in which Russell was Foreign Secretary included 'three dukes and the brother of a fourth, five peers and sons of peers, three baronets of ancient standing and landed property, and only three men without titles' (E. L. Woodward, *The Age of Reform* (1938), pp. 155, 166, 641).

39. For contemporary criticism of the opium-traders as the chief instigators of intervention see A. F. Lindley, op. cit., pp. 55–6, 209–10, 561, and W. H. Sykes, *The Taeping Rebellion in China*, pp. ii-iii and 30; for the gun-runners as its chief opponents A+P 1862 (2976) p. 154 and 1863 (3104) pp. 76–7 and Bruce to Russell (private), March 20, 1864, in Russell Papers 50, ff. 190–1, where Bruce also suggested that land speculators had 'no wish to see the insurrection effectually driven beyond the limits of the province, as they see that it will be followed by a large exodus to Soochow of the Chinese accumulated in the foreign settlement of Shanghae, and by a corresponding fall in the enormous rents they at present derive from their property situated at that Port and tenanted by Chinese'.

40. Such as that of M. Baranovsky in *Voprosy Historii*, Jan. 1952, 'The Anglo-American Capitalists throttle the Taiping Uprising'. Chien Yu-wen, op. cit., p. 1179, is one of the few writers on the subject to indicate any division of opinion among the merchants.

41. For example, an editorial of *The Times* of Aug. 13, 1860, argued strongly against intervention against the rebellion, since it would be 'a scandal to humanity . . . to sustain a despotism so faithless, so feeble and so dreadful in its effects as this'. On Jan. 16, 1861, it stated that 'Whether Tartar or Ming (i.e. Taiping) shall sit

upon the throne of China is no business of ours; and, so far as one can judge from the known facts, is not of great consequence to the people themselves.'

42. *Spectator,* April 13, 1861.

43. See, for example, *British Quarterly Review,* April 1861, *London Quarterly Review,* April 1861, and *Dublin University Magazine,* May 1861.

44. *Hansard,* vol. 165 (1862) col. 1806. See also Sykes' pamphlet *The Taeping Rebellion in China* (1863) and A+P 1863 (3104) pp. 18–19, 143–5.

45. *Hansard,* vol. 172 (1863) cols. 270–301.

46. *Hansard,* vols. 168 (1862) cols. 63–7, and 175 (1864) cols. 914–23 and 974–9.

47. *Hansard,* vol. 168 (1862) col. 71–78, and *Spectator,* July 12, 1862, p. 762.

48. For these debates see *Hansard,* vol. 165 (1862) cols. 1802–19; vol. 168 (1862) cols. 29–81 and 882–901; vol. 170 (1863) cols. 1783–1803; vol. 172 (1863) 270–329; vol. 173 (1864) cols. 441–52; vol. 174 (1864) cols. 1505–23, and vol. 175 (1864) cols. 527–45 and 916–80.

49. Russell Papers 101, Russell to Bruce, June 10, 1863.

50. *The Times,* Dec. 12, 1861.

51. See *The Times* editorials on Feb. 26, March 11, May 16, July 22 and 29, Aug. 9 and 15, Dec. 12, 1862; Jan. 30, Apr. 4, July 7 and 9, Nov. 24, 1863; Jan. 5 and 11, Feb. 16, Apr. 23 and Sept. 28, 1864.

52. *Morning Post,* July 9 and 17, 1862; also July 8, 1863, and *Manchester Guardian,* July 9, 1863.

53. For these memorials see FO 17/383–5 and 402. There are about ten altogether, some with up to fifty signatures, others with one only on behalf of a group.

54. *Daily News,* June 1, 1864; also July 7, 1863.

55. For these press comments see the regular 'Spirit of the Press' column in the *London and China Express,* 1862–64.

56. *Spectator,* July 12 (pp. 672–3) and July 19 (pp. 785, 792–3), 1862; also Aug. 2, 1862, May 23 and July 11, 1863.

57. *Athenaeum* (1862), vol. ii, pp. 658–60.

58. *London Quarterly Review* (1863), pp. 326–7.

59. *London and China Express,* Oct. 10, 1864, p. 817; also the *Standard,* Sept. 30, 1864. The legend has long survived among Gordon's many biographers, but the most recent of them, A. Nutting, *Gordon: Martyr and Misfit* (1966) makes a more balanced assessment of his role than most of his predecessors.

60. *Standard,* Sept. 30, 1864.

61. *The Times*, Dec. 30 and 31, 1864.

Chapter 9

1. For examples of this kind of argument see Lo, op. cit., p. 160; Fan Wen-lan (ed.), *T'ai-p'ing t'ien-kuo ko-ming yun-tung lun-wen chi* (Collected Essays on the Taiping Revolutionary Movement), p. 150; Chen Po-ta, *Criticism of Chiang Kai-shek's 'China's Destiny'* (in S. Gelder, *The Chinese Communists*, pp. 264–5); C. P. Fitzgerald, op. cit., p. 573: 'The Manchus were preserved because they were weak and defenceless, the Taipings opposed because their victory would have made China strong and independent.'

2. A+P 1863 (3104) pp. 8–9, Bruce to Russell, May 8, 1862.

3. A+P 1862 (3058) p. 16, Russell to Bruce, June 18, 1862.

4. FO 17/370 Bruce to Russell, Feb. 23, 1862; see also A+P 1862 (2976) p. 56.

5. On this point generally see C. A. Bodelsen, *Studies in Mid-Victorian Imperialism* (London 1960 edn.), pp. 41, 81–2; A. P. Thornton, *The Imperial Idea and its Enemies* (1959), ch. 1, and R. Koebner and H. D. Schmidt, *Imperialism* (1964), pp. 41–4. Koebner quotes an article in the *Edinburgh Review* of 1859 which argued against the prevailing 'theory of nationality', then successfully asserting itself in Italy, as liable to lead to the dissolution not only of European empires but of the British also, but his comment is that 'seen in retrospect this demand for co-ordination between European and British imperial causes . . . assumes the appearance of a warning cry of a lone Cassandra'. Sympathy for nationalist movements abroad remained general in Britain, including Palmerston and Russell (see H. Temperley and L. Penson, *Foundations of British Foreign Policy, 1792–1902*, 1966 edn., pp. 281–6).

At the same time, it cannot be assumed that what was held to be desirable and inevitable for European peoples was necessarily held to be so for Asians also. A colonial separatist such as Dilke still argued in favour of continued British rule in India but, significantly, on the ground that a sense of national identity had still to be created in India and that the British presence was necessary for this. Once it came, British withdrawal should follow (see C. Dilke, *Greater Britain* (1868), Part IV, ch. 20; also J. Seeley, *Expansion of England* (1883), Lecture 4 of the Second Course). It is misleading to project back into the mid-nineteenth century the kind of antagonism between nationalist aspirations and imperialist interests which was to develop by the twentieth century. The 'theory of nationality' was hardly thought of as relevant to the Asian scene at that time, and nationalism in general was not seen as something likely to be hostile to an empire of commerce.

6. Lo, op. cit., p. 174.

7. *The Times*, Sept. 16, 17, and Oct. 23, 1859. On Aug. 15, 1853, *The Times* also speculated whether the overthrow of the Manchus by the Taipings, which it then regarded as a virtual *fait accompli*, might not affect India's security by creating a power vacuum in central Asia and so encouraging Russian ambitions there, but it did not suggest it might do so by stimulating an independence movement within India itself.

8. W. Eberhard, *A History of China*, p. 311; Hsieh Hsing-yao, *Taiping t'ienkuo shih-shih lun-tsung*, p. 244.

9. FO 228/164 Bowring to Clarendon, June 11, 1854, and *Bombay Quarterly Review*, April 1856, p. 297.

10. FO 17/263 Robertson to Bowring, Jan. 2, 1857, enc. in Bowring to Clarendon, Jan. 12, 1857, and A+P 1861 (2840) p. 29.

11. See A+P 1862 (2976) pp. 52–3 and A+P 1861 (2754) p. 131, where Bruce refers to Hung's proposals as 'a crafty device' to deceive the missionaries.

12. W. J. Hail, op. cit., pp. 228–9; also H. Cahill, *A Yankee Adventurer*, pp. 285–6.

13. FO 17/372 Bruce to Russell, July 2, 1862; also FO 17/370 Bruce to Russell, April 13, 1862.

14. FO 17/373 Bruce to Russell, July 8, 1862.

15. For Foreign Office reports (via the embassy in St. Petersburg) on Russian interest see FO 228/318 Russell to Bruce, March 25 and April 8, 1862; FO 228/337 Russell to Bruce, Feb. 23, 1863, and A+P 1863 (3104) pp. 121, 155.

16. Bruce told Russell in August 1860 that 'the profession of novel doctrines resting on the testimony of a modern and obscure individual must tend not only to deprive the revolt of its character as a national rising against the Tartar yoke, but must actually transfer to the Tartars and their adherents the prestige of upholding national tradition and principles against the assaults of a numerically insignificant sect' (A+P 1861 (2574) p. 91).

17. A+P 1863 (3104) p. 33, Bruce to Russell, June 1, 1862; ibid., p. 43, for Russell's agreement.

18. On the importance of religious considerations in French policy see Cady, op. cit., *passim*, and P. Giquel, *La Politique Francaise en Chine*, pp. 44–6.

19. For examples of this argument see Fan Wen-lan, *Chung-kuo chin-tai shih* (Chinese Modern History), vol. i, p. 124; Hsieh Hsing-yao, op. cit., p. 243; Ueda Toshio, op. cit., pp. 140–1; A. F. Lindley,

op. cit., vol. ii, p. 555; C. Spielmann, *Die Taiping Revolution in China*, pp. 95, 102, etc.

20. FO 228/164 Bowring to Clarendon, June 5, 1854; see also A+P 1857 Sess. 2 (2221) p. 38, Bowring to Clarendon, Jan. 8, 1856: 'The prohibition [of opium] is made one of the Commandments in the rebel decalogue; but . . . the information I have obtained from various localities to which the rebellion has extended, leads me to believe that the supporters of the insurrection are no more free from the contamination of opium than the rest of their countrymen.'

21. Jardine, Matheson Papers, Private Letter Book (1854–6) p. 186, David Jardine (?) to R. S. Cowie.

22. ibid., Local Correspondence (Shanghai), Jan. 9, 1857.

23. Cit. R. Wardlaw Thompson, *Griffith John*, p. 137.

24. A+P 1859 Sess. 2 (2571) p. 451.

25. A+P 1862 (2976) pp. 26, 56–7, and S. Lane-Poole, *The Life of Sir Harry Parkes*, vol. i, pp. 421–2; G. J. Wolseley, *Narrative of the War in China in 1860*, pp. 347–8; cf. A. F. Lindley, op. cit., pp. 555–61, who says that all offenders were decapitated. Lindley's experience of the Taipings was mainly with the Loyal King's forces where discipline was possibly tighter than elsewhere.

26. Wood Collection, F. 78/88/2 Bartle-Frere to Wood, Oct. 7, 1861.

27. ibid., F. 78/58/2 Laing to Wood, April 9, 1862; cf. also R. Temple, *Men and Events of My Time in India*, p. 220, and D. E. Owen, *British Opium Policy in China and India*, p. 285.

28. Political and Secret Records: Confidential Abstract of Letters from India (Printed Series) 1863, p. 386—Financial Statement by Sir Charles Trevelyan, April 30, 1863.

29. Letters to India on Finances 1861 (No. 773) p. 66, Wood to Indian Finance Department, April 8, 1861; see also Wood Collection, Letter Book 7 (Wood to Canning, March 20, 1861) and Letter Book 13 (Wood to Trevelyan Aug. 20, 1863)—'I never can be happy with too large a proportion of your income depending upon opium. If I mistake not it went down £1,000,000 in one year about three years ago, and though I have no apprehension that we shall not always have a good opium revenue, it has now attained such a height that I cannot help fearing a fall.' On the problem of stabilizing revenue from the opium trade see Owen, op. cit., ch. 10.

30. S. Laing, *England's Mission in the Far East*, pp. 49–55.

31. See D. E. Owen, op. cit., pp. 229–34, and A+P 1857 Sess. 2 (2221).

32. T. R. Banister, A *History of the External Trade of China 1843–81*, p. 28.

33. ibid.
34. A+P 1862 (2976) p. 68. In 1858 about 73,000 bales were exported from Shanghai.
35. A+P 1863 (3104) p. 43.
36. The value of silk exports from China to Britain fell from £3,034,442 in 1862 to £1,627,223 in 1863 and to £472,636 by 1864. British exports to China (excluding opium) slumped from £5,308,036 in 1860 to £3,137,342 in 1862, but this probably reflected the effects of post-treaty speculation more than of the rebellion. They had recovered to £4,711,478 by 1864. Imports into Britain from China grew from £9,323,764 in 1860 to £12,137,095 in 1862 and £14,186,310 by 1864 (see A+P 1871, vol. L. (347), *Return for Each Year since 1858 of the Value of Exports and Imports from and to the U.K. and India, China and Hong Kong . . .* pp. 2, 4).
37. *Hansard*, vol. 175 (1864) col. 973.
38. A+P 1862 (3058) p. 19. Bruce to Russell, April 10, 1862. Bruce further argued in this despatch that British trading prospects faced 'practical annihilation' as a result of the 'process of demolition' that the rebellion represented.
39. Chien Yu-wen, op. cit., p. 1165; Lo Erh-kang, op. cit., p. 173
40. On the British attitude to the anti-Tokugawa movement in Japan see W. G. Beasley, *Select Documents on Japanese Foreign Policy*, pp. 77–84.
41. H. B. Morse, op. cit., vol. ii, p. 65.
42. This 'anarchical' view seems to be endorsed, at least for the last years of the Taiping movement, in the final evaluation of F. Michael, op. cit., pp. 192–97.
43. *Hansard*, vol. 175 (1864) col. 937, statement by Layard, Parliamentary Under-Secretary for Foreign Affairs.

Bibliography

The material used has been arranged as follows:

I   *Official Papers*   1. British   (a) Manuscript
                                               (b) Printed

                            2. Other

II   *Private Papers*

III   *Missionary Records*

IV   *Merchant Records*

V   *Contemporary Newspapers and Weeklies*

VI   *Contemporary Journals*

VII   *Contemporary Books and Pamphlets*

VIII *Later Books and Articles*

IX   *Unpublished Theses*

I
OFFICIAL PAPERS

1. (a) British Papers in Manuscript

In the Public Record Office, London

Foreign Office   General Correspondence, China 1850–64 FO 17/165–417.
Consular and Embassy Archives, China 1850–**64**, FO 228/113–360.

(Note: A considerable part of the FO correspondence on the Taipings, especially for the years 1860–64, was printed in various Parliamentary Papers, listed below. In general, where possible I have given the printed rather than the less accessible manuscript reference.)

Admiralty   In letters from the East India and China Station 1861–3, Adm. 1/5762, 5790 and 5824.

War Office   Monthly Returns of Troops Stationed in **China** 1860–64, WO 17/1723–27.

(Note: Correspondence and reports from the War Office and the Admiralty, as well as from other government departments, relating to affairs in China are generally to be found either in original or copied form in the 'Domestic Various' volumes in the Foreign Office General Correspondence Series.)

In the India Office Library, London
Political and Secret Records (Printed Series): Abstract of Letters from India 1861, 1862.
Confidential Abstract of Letters from India 1863.
Letters to India on Finances 1860–64.
Financial Letters From India 1860–63.

(b) Printed British Papers

Hansard's Parliamentary Debates (3rd Series) 1853–64 (cited as *Hansard*, vol., year and column).

House of Commons Division Lists, 1862.

Bibliography

Accounts and Papers. The bound series of British Parliamentary Papers. Cited A & P, year, number of the paper and the page. The chief papers used were:

Year	Volume	Number	Title
1847	V	654	Report of Select Committee on Commercial Relations with China.
1852–3	LXIX	1667	Papers Respecting the Civil War in China.
1854	LXXII	1792	Correspondence Respecting the Attack on the Foreign Settlement at Shanghae.
1857	XII	2163	Papers Relating to the Proceedings of Her Majesty's Naval Forces at Canton.
1857	XII	2173	Correspondence Relative to Entrance into Canton, 1850–5.
1857	XII	2175	Correspondence Respecting Insults in China.
1857 (2)	XLIII	2221	Papers Relating to the Opium Trade in China, 1842–56.
1859 (2)	XXXIII	2571	Correspondence Relative to the Earl of Elgin's Special Mission to China and Japan, 1857–9.
1860	LXIX	2587	Correspondence with Mr. Bruce.
1860	LXIX	2606, 2641, 2677	Further Correspondence with Mr. Bruce.
1861	LXVI	1754	Correspondence Respecting Affairs in China, 1859–60.
1861	LXVI	2777	Further Correspondence Respecting Affairs in China.
1861	LXVI	2840	Correspondence Respecting the Opening of the Yangtzekiang River to Foreign Trade.
1862	XXXII	138	Return of the Number and Description of Troops of All Arms at the Different Stations in China.
1862	LXIII	2976	Papers Relating to the Rebellion in China and Trade in the Yangtze Keang River.
1862	LXIII	2992	Further Papers Relating to the Rebellion in China.
1862	LXIII	3057	Correspondence on the Employment of British Officers by the Government of China.
1862	LXIII	3058	Further Papers Relating to the Rebellion in China.

Year	Volume	Number	Title
1863	LXXIII	3104	Further Papers Relating to the Rebellion in China.
1863	XXXV	341	Order in Council Authorizing the Enlistment of Officers and Men and the Equipment and Fitting out of Vessels of War for the Service of the Emperor of China.
1864	XLII	525	Copy of all Orders in Council at Present in Force (May 30, 1864) for the Punishment of Breaches of Neutrality by British Subjects in the Civil War Raging in China.
1864	LXIII	3240	Correspondence Respecting Statements in Mr. Lay's Memorandum dated January 11, 1862.
1864	LXIII	3271	Correspondence Respecting . . . the Anglo-Chinese Fleet.
1864	LXIII	3295	Papers Relating to the Affairs of China.
1864	LXIII	3345	Extract of a Despatch from Sir F. Bruce Respecting the Maintenance of Treaty Rights in China.
1864	LXIII	3408	Correspondence Relative to Lieut.-Col. Gordon's Position in the Chinese Service after the Fall of Soochow.

2. Other Official Papers

U.S. Congressional Papers

Congress 33.1 House Executive Documents, No. 123 (Marshall Correspondence).

Congress 35.2 Senate Executive Documents No. 22 (vol. 8 McLane Correspondence; vol. 9 Parker Correspondence).

Congress 36.1 Senate Executive Documents, No. 30 (Reed and Ward Correspondence).

Ch'ing Tai Ch'ou Pan I Wu Shih Mo (Details of the Management of Barbarian Affairs in the Ch'ing Dynasty (Peking 1930). Cited as IWSM, followed by initials of the reign period, chuan and page numbers.

Treaties, Conventions, etc., between China and Foreign States. (Printed by the Imperial Maritime Customs, Shanghai 1907–8.)

II

PRIVATE PAPERS

Bowring Papers   In the John Rylands Library, Manchester. A collection of letters and papers, described in the *Bulletin of the John Rylands Library*, vol. 41.2 (March 1959), 269–71, and also in the articles by G. F. Bartle listed below (Section VIII). I have used only the collection of letters from Bowring to his son Edgar, listed as Eng. Mss. 1228.

Clarendon Deposit   In the Bodleian Library, Oxford. Contains correspondence to Lord Clarendon respecting affairs in China, especially from Sir John Bowring. I have used the volumes for 1853, 1854 and 1855, listed as C.8, 19 and 37 respectively.

Elgin-Bruce Papers   At the residence of Lord Bruce, Broomhall, Dunfermline, Scotland. A large collection of papers, including much correspondence to and from both Lord Elgin and Sir Frederick Bruce during their years in China.

Elgin Papers   In the India Office Library. A selection from the above collection covering Lord Elgin's years in India but including some correspondence relating to affairs in China.

Gordon Papers   In the British Museum. A collection of correspondence and other papers, described in the *British Museum Quarterly*, vol. XXVIII (1964), pp. 75–85. I have used the collection of correspondence covering Gordon's years in China (Add. Mss. 52386–7) and the papers concerning the Ever Victorious Army (Add. Mss. 52393–4).

Hammond Papers   In the Public Record Office, listed as FO 391, and consisting of several volumes of correspondence to the Permanent Under-Secretary of State for Foreign Affairs, some of which refers to events in China.

253

Russell Papers	In the Public Record Office, listed as PRO 30/22. The correspondence between Lord Russell and Sir Frederick Bruce between 1860 and 1864 is contained in vols. 49, 50 and 101 of the collection.
Wood Collection	In the India Office Library, listed as MS. Eur. F.78. Includes some correspondence to and from the Secretary of State for India relating to the prospects of the opium trade with China.

III

MISSIONARY RECORDS

Society Records and Publications

London Missionary Society

Manuscript   Central China Letters, Boxes I–III (1843–66). South China and Ultra-Ganges Letters, Boxes V–VI (1845–68).
North China Letters Box I (1860–6).
Outgoing Letters—China Boxes IV–V (1853–63).

Printed   Missionary Magazine and Chronicle (1843–65).

Church Missionary Society

Manuscript   Letter Books—China 1851–9 and 1859–62 (vol. for 1863–7 missing).
China Letters (3 boxes, arranged alphabetically by writers).
Bishop of Victoria's letters (1844–64).

Printed   Church Missionary Record (1844–65).
Church Missionary Intelligencer (1849–65).
Proceedings of the C.M.S. for Africa and the East (1852–65).
Circulars and Other Papers (vols. I–II).

Presbyterian Missionary Society

Manuscript   Letters Relating to the China Mission, Box II (1855–62).

Printed   Reports of the China Mission at Amoy (1855–65).
The English Presbyterian Messenger (1853–64).

Methodist Missionary Society
Printed   Reports of the Wesleyan Missionary Society (1853–64).
                Wesleyan Missionary Notices (1853–64).

Baptist Missionary Society
Printed   Reports of the Baptist Missionary Society (1853–64).
                The Missionary Herald (1853–64).

Chinese Evangelization Society
Printed   The Chinese Missionary Gleaner (1851–9).

Religious Press

The Christian Times 1853–4.
Evangelical Christendom 1853–4, 1860–4.

Contemporary Publications Relating Especially to Missionary Work in China

(Anon.)   *The History of Christian Missions and of the Present Insurrection* (London, 1853).

Dean, W.   *The China Mission* (N.Y. 1859).
Edkins, J.   *The Religious Condition of the Chinese* (London, 1859).
Edkins, Jane   *Chinese Scenes and Peoples* (with 'Narrative of a Visit to Nanking' by Joseph Edkins) (London, 1863).
Gillespie, W.   *The Land of Sinim, or China and the Chinese Missions* (Edinburgh, 1854).
James, J. A.   *God's Voice from China to the British Churches* (London, 1858).
John, G.   *The Chinese Rebellion* (Canton, 1861).
Kesson, J.   *The Cross and the Dragon, or the Fortunes of Christianity in China* (London, 1854).
Legge, J. D.   *The Land of Sinim* (London, 1859).
Matheson, D.   *Our Mission in China* (London, 1866).
Medhurst, W. H.   *The Connection between Foreign Missionaries and the Kwang-se Insurrection* (Shanghai, 1853).
Milne, W. C.   *Life in China* (London, 1857).
Moule, A. E.   *Personal Recollections of the T'ai-p'ing Rebellion, 1861–3* (Shanghai, 1884)

255

Rule, W. H.	*The Religious Aspect of the Civil War in China* (London, 1853).
Smith, G.	*Narrative of an Exploratory Visit to each of the Consular Cities of China* (London, 1847).
Taylor, J. H.	*China: Its Spiritual Needs and Claims* (London, 1865).
Wylie, A.	*Memorials of Protestant Missionaries to the Chinese* (Shanghai, 1867).
"	*Extract from a Journal of a Cruise up the Yangtze Keang* (n.p. 1859).

Later Publications Relating to the Missionaries in China

Band, E.	*Working His Purpose Out: The History of the English Presbyterian Mission* (London, 1948).
Boardman, E. P.	*Christian Influence Upon the Ideology of the Taiping Rebellion* (Wisconsin, 1952).
Canton, W.	*A History of the British and Foreign Bible Society* (London 1910).
Findlay, G. G., and Holdsworth, W.	*A History of the Wesleyan Methodist Missionary Society* (vol. V) (London, 1924).
Foster, J.	'The Christian Origins of the Taiping Rebellion' (in *International Review of Missions*, xl, No. 158 (April 1951), 156–67).
Gregory, J.	'British Missionary Reaction to the Taiping Movement in China' (in *Journal of Religious History*, ii, 3 (1963), 204–18).
Latourette, K. S.	*A History of Christian Missions in China* (New York, 1929).
Littell, J. B.	'Missionaries and Politics in China—The Taiping Rebellion' (in *Political Science Quarterly*, xliii, 4 (Dec. 1928), 566–99).
Lovett, R.	*The History of the London Missionary Society* (vol. II) (London, 1899).
Macgillivray, D. (ed.)	*A Century of Protestant Missions in China (1807–1907)* (Shanghai, 1907).
Michie, A.	*China and Christianity* (Tientsin, 1892). *The Political Obstacles to Missionary Success in China* (London, 1901).
Parker, E. H.	*China and Religion* (London, 1905).

Stock, E.   *History of the Church Missionary Society*,
           vol. II (London, 1899).
Thompson, R. W.   *Griffith John* (London, 1907).

IV

MERCHANT RECORDS

There is little consolidated material which can be definitely labelled 'merchant', as there is for the official and the missionary view of the rebellion. For other sources of merchant opinion see references to Chapters 4 and 8.

Jardine, Matheson & Co. Correspondence, in the University Library, Cambridge. A great mass of essentially business correspondence. Comments on political matters are most readily found in the Europe Letter Books.

Proceedings of the Manchester Chamber of Commerce, 1839–67, in the Public Library, Manchester.

Report of the Liverpool Chamber of Commerce, in the Offices of the Chamber of Commerce, Liverpool.

Lawson's Merchant Magazine, Statist and Commercial Review (London 1853–55), in the British Museum Library.

V

CONTEMPORARY NEWSPAPERS AND WEEKLIES

Great Britain   Daily News 1853–54, 1860–64.
               Economist 1853–64.
               London and China Express 1858–64 (contains regular column of extracts of press opinion on China affairs).
               Manchester Guardian 1863.
               Morning Post 1853–54, 1860–63.
               Standard 1853, 1864.
               The Times 1850–64.

Bibliography

Newspaper Cuttings on China 1847–59 (two vols. originally compiled by The Chinese Evangelization Society, now in the Library of the London Missionary Society).

China   China Mail 1845–58, 1863–4.
China Overland Trade Report 1860–64.
North China Herald 1850–65.
Overland China Mail 1858–61.
Overland Register and Prices Current 1853–4, 1860–1.

India   Friend of India 1853–4, 1859.
Times of India 1862–3.

VI

CONTEMPORARY JOURNALS

See also Poole's Index to Periodical Literature, 1802–81. Known or possible authors are put in brackets after the title of the article.

Athenaeum 1853–64 (various book reviews).

Blackwood's Edinburgh Magazine
July 1852   The Celestials at Home and Abroad.
Jan. 1854   The Past and Future of China.
April 1860   Our Position in China (S. Osborn).
Jan. 1863   Progress in China (S. Osborn).
Feb. 1863   The Taepings and their Remedy (S. Osborn).
Dec. 1866   Foreign Interference with the Taipings (A. E. Wilson).

Bombay Quarterly Review
Oct. 1855   The Chinese Empire and its Destinies (R. Alcock).
April 1856   The Chinese Empire in its Foreign Relations (R. Alcock).

British Journal
Oct. 1853   The War in China.

British Quarterly Review
July 1855   The Insurgent Power in China.
April 1861   Review article based on Meadows, Huc, Fortune, Oliphant, etc.

Bibliography

Calcutta Review
March 1854   Recent Events in China (G. Smith, Bishop of Victoria).

Chambers' Edinburgh Journal
Sept. 1853   The Rebellion in China.

Cornhill Magazine
Jan. 1860   The Chinese and the 'Outer Barbarians' (Sir John Bowring?).
Nov. 1864   Colonel Gordon's Exploits in China.

Dublin University Magazine
May 1861   China.

Edinburgh Review
April 1855   M. Huc's Travels in China.
April 1857   British Relations with China.
Jan. 1860   Lord Elgin's Mission to China and Japan.

Eclectic Review
Dec. 1856   Review of Meadows, *The Chinese and Their Rebellions*.

Fraser's Magazine
Nov. 1853   The Insurrection in China.
1865   Rebellion, Diplomacy and Progress in China.

Journal of the North China Branch, Royal Asiatic Society
Dec. 1867   The Christianity of Hung Tsue-tsuen (R. J. Forrest).

London Quarterly Review
April 1861   The Chinese Insurgents and Our Policy Towards Them.
July 1863   The Taiping Rebellion in China.

New Monthly Magazine (Colburn's)
Sept.-Dec.
1853   The Chinese Revolution.
Dec. 1859   China.

Quarterly Review
Dec. 1853   Religion of the Chinese Rebels.
Jan. 1860   China and the War.
Oct. 1862   The Taeping Rebellion.

Revue des Deux Mondes
July 1861 L'Insurrection Chinoise (R. de Courcy).
April 1863 La Chine depuis le traité de Pekin—Les Anglo-Français, les Imperiaux et les Taipings (M. des Varannes).

Tait's Edinburgh Magazine
Oct. 1860 The Chirstian Revolution in China (J. Scarth?).

Westminster Review
April 1858 China: Past and Present.

VII

CONTEMPORARY BOOKS AND PAMPHLETS

(Anon.) *A History of China to the Present Time, Including an Account of the Rise and Progress of the Present Religious Insurrection in that Country* (in Bentley's Parlour Bookcase Series) (London, 1854).

Alcock, R. *The Capital of the Tycoon* (vol. 1) (London, 1863).

Blakiston, J. W. *Five Months on the Yangtze . . . and Notices of the Present Rebellion in China* (London, 1862).

Bowring, J. *Autobiographical Recollections* (London, 1877)

Brine, L. *The Taeping Rebellion in China* (London, 1862).

Callery, J. M.,
and Yvan, M. *History of the Insurrection in China* (London,
(trans. J. Oxenford) 1853).

Cooke, G. W. *China in 1857–8* (London, 1858).

Davis, J. F. *China* (London, 1857).

Fishbourne, E. G. *Impressions of China and the Present Revolution* (London, 1855).

Fisher, A. A. C. *Personal Narrative of Three Years Service in China* (London, 1863).

Fortune, R. *A Residence among the Chinese* (1853–6) (London, 1857).

Giquel, P. *La Politique Francaise en Chine depuis les traites de 1858 et de 1860* (Paris, 1872).

Laing, S.	*England's Mission in the Far East* (London, 1863).
Lay, H. N.	*Our Interests in China* (London, 1864).
Lindley, A. F.	*Ti-ping Tien-kwoh* (London, 1866).
Macfarlane, C.	*The Chinese Revolution* (London, 1853).
Mackie, J. M.	*The Life of Tai Ping Wang* (New York, 1857).
Meadows, T. T.	*Desultory Notes on the Government and People of China* (London, 1847).
,,	*The Chinese and their Rebellions* (London, 1856).
Oliphant, L.	*Narrative of the Earl of Elgin's Mission to China and Japan in 1857–8* (Edinburgh & London, 1858).
Osborn, S.	*The Past and Future of Our Relations with China* (London, 1860).
Rennie, D. F.	*British Arms in North China and Japan 1860–62* (London, 1864).
Scarth, J.	*Twelve Years in China* (Edinburgh, 1860).
,,	*British Policy in China* (Edinburgh, 1861).
Sykes, W. H.	*The Taeping Rebellion in China* (London, 1863).
(Vizetelly, H.)	*The Chinese Revolution* (London, 1853).
Wilson, A. E.	*England's Policy in China* (Hong Kong, 1860).
,,	*The Ever Victorious Army* (London, 1868).
Wolseley, G.	*Narrative of the War in China in 1860* (London, 1862).
Yates, M. T.	*The T'aiping Rebellion* (Shanghai, 1876).

VIII

LATER BOOKS AND ARTICLES

Allen, B. M.	*Gordon in China* (London, 1933).
Anderson, Flavia	*The Rebel Emperor* (London, 1958).
Bain, C. A.	'Commodore Perry, Humphrey Marshall and the Taiping Rebellion' (in *Far Eastern Quarterly*, X, 3 (May 1951,) 258–70).
Bales, W. L.	*Tso Tsung t'ang* (Shanghai, 1937).
Banister, T. R.	*A History of the External Trade of China, 1834–81* (Shanghai, 1931).
Banno, M.	*China and the West 1858–61* (Harvard, 1964).

Baranovsky, M. I.   'The Anglo-American Capitalists Throttle the Taiping Rebellion' (in *Voprosy Istorii* No. 1, 1952, Eng. translation in *Soviet Press Translations* No. 7 (May 1, 1952), 227–37).

Bartle, G. F.   'Sir John Bowring and the *Arrow* War in China' (in *Bulletin of the John Rylands Library*, 43.2 (March 1961), 293–316).

,,   'Sir John Bowring and the Chinese and Siamese Commercial Treaties' (ibid, 44.2 (March 1962), 186–308).

Beatty, C.   *His Country was the World* (London, 1954).

Boulger, D. C.   *A Short History of China* (London, 1893).

,,   *The Life of Gordon* (London, 1896).

,,   *The Life of Sir Halliday Macartney* (London, 1908).

Cady, J. F.   *The Roots of French Imperialism in Eastern Asia* (New York, 1954).

Cahill, H.   *A Yankee Adventurer* (New York, 1930).

Chesneaux, J.   'La Revolution Taiping d'apres quelque travaux recents' (in *Revue Historique*, t. 209 (1953), 33–57).

Chien Yu-wen   *T'ai-ping t'ien-kuo t'ien-chih t'ung-kao* (Studies on the Institutions of the Taiping Heavenly Kingdom) (Hong Kong, 1958).

,,   'The Marxian Interpretation of Taiping Tienkuo' (in *Procs. of International Association of Historians of Asia*, 2nd Biennial Conference, Oct. 1962, pp. 745–76) (Taipei, 1963).

Ch'en Po-ta   Criticism of Chiang Kai-shek's 'China's Destiny' (in S. Gelder, *The Chinese Communists*, London, 1946).

Cordier, H.   *Expedition de Chine* (Paris, 1905–6). *Histoire des relations de la Chine avec les Puissances Occidentales, 1860–1900* (Paris, 1901).

Costin, W. C.   *Great Britain and China, 1833–60* (Oxford, 1937).

Dennett, T.   *Americans in East Asia* (New York, 1922).

Eberhard, W.   *A History of China* (London, 1950).

Elton, Lord   *General Gordon* (London, 1954).

Fairbank, J. K.   'The Manchu Appeasement Policy' (in *Journal of the American Oriental Society*, 59 (1939), 169–84).

Fairbank, J. K.	*Trade and Diplomacy on the China Coast* (Harvard, 1953).
,,	'Meadows on China' (in *Far Eastern Quarterly*, xiv, 3 (May 1955), 365–71).
Fan Wen-lan	*T'ai-p'ing t'ien-kuo yun-tung lun-wen chi* (Collected essays on the Taiping revolutionary movement) (Peking, 1951).
Feuerwerker, A,. and Cheng 5.	*Chinese Communist Studies of Modern Chinese History* (Harvard, 1961).
Fitzgerald, C. P.	*China: a Short Cultural History* (London, 1961).
,,	*Revolution in China* (London, 1952).
Fox, Grace	*British Admirals and Chinese Pirates* (London, 1940).
Granston, E.	'Shanghai in the Taiping Period' (in *Pacific Historical Review*, 5 (1936), 147–60).
Gregory, J. S.	'British Intervention Against the Taiping Rebellion' (in *Journal of Asian Studies*, xix, 1 (Nov. 1959)).
,,	'The Transfer of T. T. Meadows from Shanghai to Newchwang' (in *Historical Studies Australia and New Zealand* 12 (Oct. 1966), 435–39).
Hail, W. J.	*Tseng Kuo-fan and the Taiping Rebellion* (Yale-Oxford, 1927).
Hake, E.	*The Story of Chinese Gordon* (London, 1884).
Hertslet, E.	*Recollections of the Old Foreign Office* (London, 1901).
Ho Ping-ti	*Studies on the Population of China* (Harvard, 1959).
Hsia Ching-lin	*Studies in Chinese Diplomatic History* (Shanghai, 1926).
Hsieh Hsing-yao	*T'ai-p'ing t'ien-kuo shih-shih lun-tsung* (Miscellaneous essays on Taiping History) (Shanghai, 1935).
,,	*T'ai-p'ing t'ien-kuo ts'ung-shu shih-san chung.* (Thirteen collected documents on the Taipings) (Shanghai, 1938).
Huang Ta-shou	*Chung-kuo chin-tai shih* (A modern history of China) (Taipei, 1953).
Hummel, A. W. (ed.)	*Eminent Chinese of the Ch'ing Dynasty* (Washington, 1943).

Hu Sheng *Imperialism and Chinese Politics* (Peking, 1955).

Hughes, E. R. *The Invasion of China by the Western World* (London, 1937).

Jung Meng-yuan *Chung-kuo chin pai nien ko-ming shih-lueh* (A Short History of Revolutions in the last Hundred Years in China) (Peking, 1954).

Karamurza, G. S. *The Taipings* (in an English translation by J. Gershevitch, part of an M.A. thesis for the University of Melbourne, 1964. Page references are to the Russian text) (Moscow, 1957).

King, F. H., and Clarke, P. *A Research Guide to China Coast Newspapers* (Harvard, 1965).

Laai Yi-faai 'River Strategy: a Phase of the Taipings Military Development' (in *Oriens*, 5 (1952), 302–29).

Lane-Poole, S. *Life of Sir Henry Parkes* (London, 1894).

Leger, F. *Les influences Occidentales dans la Revolution de l'Orient* (Paris, 1955).

Levenson, J. *Confucian China and its Modern Fate* (London, 1958–64).

Li Chien-nung *A Political History of China, 1840–1928* (Princeton, 1956).

Lo Erh-kang *T'ai-p'ing t'ien-kuo shih-kang* (An Outline History of the Taipings) (Shanghai, 1948).

,, *T'ai-p'ing t'ien-kuo shih-kao* (Peking, 1955).

Martin, W. A. P. *A Cycle of Cathay* (Edinburgh & London, 1896).

Mason, Mary *Western Concepts of China and the Chinese* (New York, 1939).

Maybon, C. B., and Fredet, J. *Histoire de la Concession Francaise de Chang-hai* (Paris, 1929).

Michael, F. *The Taipings* (Seattle & London, 1966).

,, 'Military Organisation and the Power Structure of China during the Taiping Rebellion' (in *Pacific Historical Review*, 18 (1949), 469–83).

Michie, A. *The Englishman in China* (Edinburgh & London, 1900).

Monalto de Jesus *Historic Shanghai* (Shanghai, 1909).

Morse, H. B. *The International Relations of the Chinese Empire* (London, 1910–18).

264

Morse, H. B., and McNair, H. F.	*Far Eastern International Relations* (Cambridge (Mass.), 1931).
Mou An-shih	*T'ai-p'ing t'ien-kuo* (The Taiping Heavenly Kingdom) (Shanghai, 1962).
Nutting, A.	*Gordon: Martyr and Misfit* (London, 1966).
Owen, D. E.	*British Opium Policy in China and India* (Yale, 1934).
Pannikar, K. M.	*Asia and Western Dominance* (London, 1953).
Pelcovits, N.	*Old China Hands and the Foreign Office* (New York, 1948)
Rawlinson, J. L.	'The Lay-Osborn Flotilla: its Development and Significance' (in *Papers on China*, 4 (1950), 59–93 (Harvard)).
Redford, A.	*Manchester Merchants and Foreign Trade, 1794–1858* (Manchester, 1934).
Renouvin, P.	*La Question d'Extreme Orient* (Paris, 1946).
Rowe, D. N.	*Index to Ch'ing Tai Chou Pan I Wu Shih Mo* (Connecticut, 1960).
Roy, M. N.	*Revolution and Counter-Revolution in China* (Calcutta, 1946).
Rumbold, H.	*Recollections of a Diplomatist* (London, 1902).
Sargent, A. J.	*Anglo-Chinese Commerce and Diplomacy* (Oxford, 1907).
Shen Lien-chih	*Role des General C. G. Gordon dans la repression de l'Insurrection des Thai Phing* (Paris, 1933).
Shih, V. Y. C.	'The Ideology of the Taiping Tienkuo' (in *Sinologica*, 3 (1953), 1–15).
Shih Li-ch'eng	'Tsung tui wai kuan-shih k'an T'ai-p'ing T'ien-kuo ti fei-chu' (The Tragedy of the Taiping State viewed from the standpoint of its Foreign Relations) (in *Li-shih Yen-chiu* (Historical Research) 1961, 1, 13–20).
Smedley, Agnes	*The Great Road* (London, 1958).
Spector, S.	*Li Hung-chang and the Huai Army* (Seattle, 1964).
Spielmann, C.	*Die Taiping Revolution* (Halle a.s. 1900).
Stelle, C. C.	'Ideologies of the Taiping Insurrection' (in *Chinese Social and Political Science Review*, 20, 1 (1936), 40–49).
Swisher, E.	*China's Management of the American Barbarians* (Yale, 1951).

265

Taylor, G. E. 'The Taiping Rebellion' (in *Chinese Social and Political Science Review*, 16, 4 (1933), 545–614).

Teng Ssu-yu *New Light on the Taiping Rebellion* (Harvard, 1950). *Historiography of the Taiping Rebellion* (Harvard, 1962).

Temple, R. *Men and Events of my Time in India* (London, 1882).

Tong Te-kong *United States Diplomacy in China, 1844–60* (Seattle, 1964).

Ueda Toshio 'The International Relations of the Taiping Rebellion' (in *The Japan Annual of Law and Politics* No. 2, 1953, 119–48).

Woodward, E. L. *The Age of Reform* (Oxford, 1938).

Williams, S. Wells *A History of China* (London, 1897).

Wright, Mary *The Last Stand of Chinese Conservatism* (Stanford, 1957).

Wright, S. F. *Hart and the Chinese Customs* (Belfast, 1950).

Wu J. T. K. 'The Impact of the Taiping Rebellion upon the Manchu Fiscal System' (in *Pacific Hist. Review*, 19 (1950), 265–75).

Yap, P. M. 'The Mental Illness of Hung Hsiu-ch'üan' (in *Far Eastern Quarterly*, xiii, 3 (1954), 287–304).

Yuan Chung-teng 'Rev. I. J. Roberts and the Taiping Rebellion' (in *Journal of Asian Studies*, xxiii, 1 (1963–4), 55–68).

VIII

UNPUBLISHED THESES

Anderson, Mary A. Edmund Hammond: Permanent Under-Secretary of State for Foreign Affairs 1854–73 (Ph.D., London, 1956).

Chao Tang-li *Anglo-Chinese Diplomatic Relations 1858–70* (Ph.D., London, 1956).

Chiang Pei-huan *Anglo-Chinese Diplomatic Relations 1856–60* (Ph.D., London, 1939).

Clarke, P. *The Development of the English Language Press on the China Coast 1827–81* (M.A., London, 1961).

Davies, W.	*British Diplomatic Relations with China 1854–69* (M.A., Swansea, 1939).
Gerson, J.	*Horatio Nelson Lay: His Role in British Relations with China 1849–65* (Ph.D., London, 1966).
McCutcheon, J. M.	*The American and British Missionary Concept of Chinese Civilisation in the 19th Century* (Ph.D., Wisconsin, 1959).
Tong Ling-tch'ouang	*La Politique Francaise en Chine Pendant les Guerres des Taipings* (Doctorat, Paris, 1950).

Index

Index

Index

Index

DATE DUE

DE 8 '80			
AP 8 '82			
GAYLORD			PRINTED IN U S A.